Supporting Learning and Teaching

Second Edition

Edited by Christine Bold

 Routledge
Taylor & Francis Group

LONDON AND NEW YORK

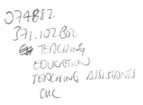

074882
371.102 BOL
☒ TEACHING
EDUCATION
TEACHING ASSISTANTS
CUC

First edition published 2005
by David Fulton Publishers

This edition published 2011
by Routledge
2 Park Square, Milton Park, Abingdon, Oxon, OX14 4RN

Simultaneously published in the USA and Canada
by Routledge
711 Third Avenue, New York, NY 10017

Routledge is an imprint of the Taylor & Francis Group, an informa business

British Library Cataloguing in Publication Data
A catalogue record for this book is available from the British Library

Library of Congress Cataloging-in-Publication Data
Supporting learning and teaching / [edited by] Christine Bold. – 2nd ed.
  p. cm.
  Includes bibliographical references and index.
  1. Reflective teaching. 2. Action research in education. I. Bold, Christine.
  LB1025.3.S87 2011
  371.102–dc22   2010050463

ISBN: 978–0–415–58355–8 (hbk)
ISBN: 978–0–415–58356–5 (pbk)
ISBN: 978–0–203–81836–7 (ebk)

Typeset in Aldine 401 BT
by Florence Production Ltd, Stoodleigh, Devon

MIX
Paper from
responsible sources
FSC
www.fsc.org
FSC® C004839

Printed and bound in Great Britain by
CPI Antony Rowe, Chippenham, Wiltshire

Contents

Illustrations

Extracts

About the authors

Roshan Ahmed was employed and trained by EMAS (Ethnic Minority and Achievement Service), and she worked in two primary schools as a teaching assistant promoting the learning and language development of children from nursery to Year 2. She completed a BA in Inclusive Education at Liverpool Hope University, where she developed an interest in teaching bilingual children. Having undergone teacher training, Roshan currently teaches Year 1 (ages 5–6) in a primary school with a high proportion of children from minority ethnic groups.

Anthony Barnett worked as a primary school teacher in a range of schools in London and the south of England and was a science and ICT coordinator. For the last ten years he has been a senior lecturer at the University of Worcester, where he has taught Primary ICT, D&T and Science on a range of undergraduate, postgraduate, educational studies and returning to teaching modules. He has an MA in Primary Education from the Open University and is currently working on a Ph.D. thesis, developing a creative analytic research paradigm in relation to the Early Years learning environment.

Alan Barrow is a retired primary head teacher. He was head of two very different schools and had the advantage of being able to experience headship before the advent of the National Curriculum and afterwards. He continued to work for local universities after retiring in 2002, working with Foundation degree students and with postgraduates. He has continued his involvement in education as a consultant for a local primary school, being particularly interested in creativity.

Christine Bold has experience in teaching at all levels, from nursery through to higher education. Her main academic and research interest is in reflective practice and research processes that enable professional development. She has published two books, chapters in various texts and papers in refereed journals, and she is on the editorial panel for an academic journal, *Reflective Practice*. Christine currently works full-time on postgraduate courses for teachers.

Jean Clarkson is a senior lecturer. She has worked as a teacher for 16 years and has been at Liverpool Hope University for 21 years. During that time, she has worked with the English curriculum team and has coordinated international exchange for 14 years. She is presently coordinating the MA in Education. Her research interests are student retention rates and international education.

Sue Cronin is a Senior Lecturer in Mathematics and has experience in leading many undergraduate and postgraduate modules. She has published web-based materials for gifted and talented pupils for John Moores Astronomy Department, and Excellence in Liverpool. Sue is an active member of the Association of Mathematics Education Teachers (AMET). She is an active researcher engaged in presenting at conferences and academic publication.

Gareth Crossley is a graduate of Liverpool Hope University with an Honours degree in Inclusive Education. He began his educational career in a support role in the state sector working with children with special educational needs. He then moved to a teaching role in an independent primary school, where he became Key Stage 2 Special Educational Needs Coordinator. Having completed his degree programme, Gareth continues to teach in Key Stage 2 in the independent sector. He is also involved in researching independent education and is a member of the Christian Schools Trust's National Education Team.

Joe Gazdula is a senior lecturer at Liverpool Hope University, where he has recently led a number of initiatives that involved Education Studies students in out-of-hours learning activities in schools and other settings. He is also an Enterprise Fellow and has recently had a digital activity game for children brought to market.

Pat Hughes is a senior lecturer at Liverpool Hope University. She has published widely with Fulton, Scholastic, Oxford University Press, Heinemann, Nelson, Hopscotch, Folens, Multilingual Matters and Paul Chapman.

Lois Kelly is a senior lecturer in Primary Science at Liverpool Hope University. She taught in primary schools for 20 years, during which time she was a science coordinator and a science advisory teacher. She is an active member of the Association for Science Education and is on the Primary Committee. She has also worked with teachers from Tibetan Children's Villages and SOS Children's Villages, providing continuous professional development (CPD) in Primary Science.

Elaine McBlain is a recent graduate in BA Inclusive Education at Liverpool Hope University. She has experienced working as a teaching assistant and learning mentor throughout the implementation of the Workforce Remodelling reforms. She is a trained A1 Assessor for teaching assistants with Salford Council and a trained practice teacher for social worker placements. She is on the Senior Leadership Team in school.

Shirley Potts is programme leader for Disability Studies at Liverpool Hope University. She also teaches a module on Early Childhood Studies that enables graduates to have an understanding of grief and loss issues in young children's lives. Professionally and academically trained and employed as a counsellor prior to academic life, she utilises past experiences in her current research, writing and teaching.

Abbreviations

ADD	attention deficit disorder
ADHD	attention deficit hyperactivity disorder
AfL	Assessment for Learning
APP	Assessing Pupil Progress
APR	annual percentage rate
ARG	Assessment Reform Group
ASD	autistic spectrum disorder
ATM	Association of Teachers of Mathematics
AWPU	age-weighted pupil unit
BERA	British Educational Research Association
BESD	behavioural, emotional and social difficulties
BEST	Behaviour and Education Support Team
BICS	basic interpersonal communication skills
BSF	Building Schools for the Future
CAF	Common Assessment Framework
CALP	cognitive academic language proficiency
CAMHS	Child and Adolescent Mental Health Services
CEDP	Career Entry and Development Profile
CPD	continuous professional development
CRB	Criminal Records Bureau
CWDC	Children's Workforce Development Council
D&T	Design and Technology
DCD	developmental coordination disorder
DCSF	Department for Children, Schools and Families
DES	Department of Education and Science
DfE	Department for Education
DfEE	Department for Education and Employment
DfES	Department for Education and Skills
DH	Department of Health
DS	Down's syndrome
EAL	English as an additional language
EAZ	Education Action Zone
EBD	emotional and behavioural difficulties
EiC	Excellence in Cities

EMAS	Ethnic Minority Achievement Service
ERA	Education Reform Act
EYFS	Early Years Foundation Stage
FAM	Family Action
FAS	foetal alcohol syndrome
FASD	foetal alcohol spectrum disorder
GCSE	General Certificate of Secondary Education
GTCE	General Teaching Council for England
HI	hearing impairment
HLTA	Higher Level Teaching Assistant
IBP	individual behaviour programme
ICT	information and communications technology
IEP	individual education plan
ITT	Initial Teacher Training
LAC	looked-after children
LEA	local education authority
LMS	Local Management of Schools
LP	lead professional
MLD	moderate learning difficulties
MTL	Masters in Teaching and Learning
NALDIC	National Association for Language Development in the Curriculum
NC	National Curriculum
NFER	National Foundation for Educational Research
NHSP	National Healthy Schools Programme
NINDS	National Institute of Neurological Disorders and Stroke
NNEB	National Nursery Examination Board
NSPCC	National Society for the Prevention of Cruelty to Children
Ofsted	Office for Standards in Education
PC	personal computer
PE	physical education
PPA	preparation, planning and assessment
PSHE	Physical, Social and Health Education
QCA	Qualifications and Curriculum Authority
QTS	Qualified Teacher Status
RBA	'Raising Boys' Achievement'
RE	religious education
SATs	Standard Assessment Tasks
SEAL	Social and Emotional Aspects of Learning
SEBP	social, emotional and behavioural difficulties
SEN	special educational needs
SENCO	Special Educational Needs Coordinator
SIP	School Improvement Partner
SLCN	speech, language and communication needs
SLD	severe learning difficulties
SSD	single-sided deafness
TDA	Training and Development Agency for Schools

TGAT	Task Group on Assessment and Testing
VAK	visual, auditory and kinaesthetic
VI	visual impairment
ZPD	zone of proximal development

Introduction

Christine Bold

An overview

This second edition is written in the same spirit as the first edition, but it is intended for a wider audience of students on a range of education-related degree courses. It is devoted to providing you with understanding of practical workplace issues in relation to relevant academic knowledge. Its purpose is to encourage you to reflect upon your own experiences, from your own schooling, placements and workplace activity, to analyse situations more critically and to apply knowledge from beyond your immediate sphere of practical experience. Each chapter provides some information and raises some issues worthy of further discussion. The authors do not have the space to discuss all these issues in depth, but will direct thoughts and provoke interest. Each author writes in a personal style but there are some special features common to each chapter.

Special features

Values and beliefs

Each author will provide a statement of their values and beliefs, since these are fundamental to the way they write their chapters and the discussion of issues within the chapters. Readers will note that this text does not focus strongly on current English national legislation and guidance, since the authors believe that students should explore ideas beyond legislative boundaries and that they should value their freedom to challenge and question the political and educational thinking of the day. Most importantly, a newly elected British government in May 2010 has stated that it has its own plans for curriculum development and we must 'watch this space' as developments unfold.

Discussion starters

The 'discussion starters' are a pedagogical feature for tutors of education-based degree programmes to use with their students, or for students to develop their own supportive discussion groups. The purpose of these is to encourage students to develop and debate their own ideas based on their own experiences and be confident in expressing their own views supported by experiential evidence from their schooling, placements or workplace activity. Each chapter raises different issues to discuss that can transcend age range, setting and the varying nature of student experiences, thus enabling participants on courses to gain a broader picture of the educational scene. In my own experience, students often find common ground, even though one might work with three-year-old children and another with sixteen year olds.

Reflecting on practice

In this section, each author suggests at least two activities for students to experience in an educational setting, with their peers, with children in school, or within an out-of-school learning situation. The aim is to stimulate reflection. The development of reflective practice is essential for effective professional development. I also invite you to disagree and challenge ideas presented in the text, but do so in the knowledge that authors have formulated their ideas over many years, drawing on their own and others' experiences, together with engagement in various academic pursuits. Hopefully, you will glean from this text that, in the study of educational settings, we should reflect on practice in relation to academic thinking about that practice, with the *intention* to build both professional and academic knowledge and possibly change practice in some way in the future.

Useful resources

Many of the useful resources provided by the authors are website addresses, sometimes with brief notes of their content with the aim of supporting students in finding information that will further support their studies. In these days of electronic media, more and more information is becoming freely available worldwide, which releases us from always having to rely on finding a particular book in under-resourced academic libraries. Having said that, we must have a word of warning about the use of electronic sources, as we ourselves found that the content of some sites might be rather dubious in relation to educational theory and referencing sites can become rather intrusive when written in text because of their length. In terms of content, you must ensure that you are clear about the nature of the content. You might ask questions such as these:

- Who 'owns' the site?
- Is the site related to an educational organisation, or other type of organisation?
- Does it consist of the writer's own opinion?
- Or does it contain some evidence to support the writer's ideas?
- Is the information in it based on research or other evidence?
- Who is the author of a particular page or article?
- What date was the webpage or article created?

Such questions (I am sure you can think of many more) help to ensure clarity about where information is coming from, and that when we relate these ideas to someone else we represent them accurately. When looking at a website you ought to consider what the values and beliefs are of the author of the materials on the site. Because of the overlong nature of some specific web-page addresses, the website references in the text, in the reference lists and in the Website sections are all reduced to an accessible size, so that you can find either the home page or similar and explore further links from there. As you will know, website addresses are continually changing and, although the home addresses remain relatively stable, some others do not. If a website fails, we invite you to explore the words within the website address by performing a search and this will usually bring up the required reference; for example, in www.nfer.ac.uk is the abbreviation 'nfer' – a search for 'nfer' will find the desired website. By their very nature, some websites are easier to navigate than others.

References

Each chapter has its own reference list, some long and some short. Each, in addition to providing support for some of our assertions, provides a useful source of further reading should readers wish to pursue a particular line of interest. Too many students look for lots of references in order to impress their tutors in assignments and, indeed, some tutors perpetuate the myth that more references mean a better depth of understanding. The two do not necessarily go hand in hand and my advice to you is to aim for quality understanding of two or three core texts rather than a weak understanding of many. Some of our chapters do have many references, to illustrate the range of relevant texts and websites available for further investigation, but not in order to impress the reader.

Common strands

On reading through the chapters, some ideas repeat themselves in relation to different areas of learning. For example, Vygotsky's (1978) 'zone of proximal development' (ZPD) appears several times where the authors relate the ZPD to children's learning. This is an interesting unplanned phenomenon, but it demonstrates the strength of ideas that developed because of research by someone who died in 1934. Vygotsky was not an educationalist, but a Soviet psychologist from a very different culture from that in the UK today. His interests lay in the processes of learning, language acquisition and the relationship between language and thought. On translation in the 1960s and 1970s, his research began to influence education in England and other English speaking countries. Since then almost everyone in education knows about and thinks there is strength in the idea of the ZPD.

A recurring phrase is that of the 'teaching team', with teachers and teaching assistants working in a collaborative partnership for the benefit of children. The term 'teaching assistant' is used throughout as an overarching term for anyone who is not a qualified teacher but who supports learning in a variety of ways, while the authors recognise that there are many titles given and several different levels of responsibility. Where appropriate, we mention other roles, such as the learning mentor. Not only are collaborative partnerships encouraged within the classroom, but the development of larger teams within educational settings are necessary, for example when setting up and organising an out-of-school club. All adults who support learning and teaching in educational settings are usually part of several teams or groupings and hold several positions within those teams. This sounds rather complicated, but most educational organisations are, because we have to work in teams that cut across one another's responsibilities for different purposes. Here are a few examples of teams to which one teaching assistant might belong:

- a collaborative partnership – with the teacher or other assistants;
- a team leader – when working with children, or taking responsibility for a project in school;
- a team member of the overall hierarchical staff team within the school;
- a team member in the Special Educational Needs Coordinator's (SENCO's) team;
- a Key Stage 1 (ages 5–7) team member.

More and more teaching assistants are taking on responsibilities for various aspects of school life and areas of the curriculum, as discussed in Chapter 1.

Conclusion

Editing this second edition has been an interesting but challenging experience. It has required endless checks of websites and book references, of consistency in factual content, of pedagogical features and of opportunities for retaining individuality in approach in order to make it interesting to the reader. I hope that in the role of editor any changes I have made for the sake of accuracy or clarity have not altered the message that each author wished to make as an expert in his or her own field. Most of all I hope that readers find the book stimulating and useful in their studies when trying to make sense of different academic ideas about everyday practice.

1

Professional Partnerships: Changing Roles

Christine Bold and Elaine McBlain

Our backgrounds, values and beliefs

One of us was programme leader of a Foundation degree for people who support learning in schools, and its associated top-up Honours degree, and the other a graduate of that degree programme, currently studying for a Masters degree. We both value the various support roles that have developed in school over the past few years; they are essential to the smooth running of the organisation and, most important, to the education and care of children in school and beyond the school day. We believe that the many roles currently filled by people with various qualifications, from teaching assistants certificates through to MA degrees in specialist areas such as mentoring, are now an essential part of the twenty-first-century school workforce. As such, teachers and other professionals in children's services must work in partnership with them and acknowledge the qualities they bring to their roles.

Introduction

The chapter is organised into three sections. The first reflects back upon the teaching assistants' situation in 2004. It illustrates changes to their situation since then. In the second section, Elaine describes her role as Inclusion Manager, providing some of the history of her professional development over the past eleven years. It serves to demonstrate the importance of such roles, the level of responsibility and the ways in which schools have changed to meet the needs of a changing society. It also highlights the necessity for various partnerships and collaborations with other agencies and parents in supporting the education of children in a school in 2010 and beyond. The final section summarises the chapter.

Changing roles and relationships 2004–10

The media dubbed the new additions to the teaching workforce the 'Mum's Army' when the government first announced the increased use of teaching assistants (*The Times*, 1999). The unions, in particular one teachers' union, thought it was an unacceptable use of unqualified people, who would be taking the roles of currently employed qualified teaching staff. Many thought that unqualified staff could not meet the needs of an increasingly diverse school community. However, this was precisely one of the reasons for introducing staff who would take on roles that teachers could not, and therefore provided children with much-needed individual attention. Unfortunately, some schools employed teaching assistants to do things they were not trained or qualified to do. In some schools, this may still be the situation, but it is less likely since there are now various qualifications that teaching assistants have to achieve to work at different levels of responsibility. In fact, many people are now viewing employment as a teaching assistant as a second career, having previously been in a very responsible job elsewhere. Many want to give something back to the community and help young people understand the world that they live in. Such people have much to give to young people, particularly those disaffected by the educational scene, because they know of a world beyond education that young people are interested in.

The first guidance for teachers on how to work effectively with teaching assistants came in 2000 from the Department for Education and Employment (DfEE). It identified the role of the teaching assistant as one that supports pupils, teachers, the curriculum and their school. The DfEE identified effective practice as that which fostered pupil participation, enabled pupils to be independent learners and helped to raise standards for all. Unfortunately, many schools did not use this document to inform practice. Schools at that time received several large documents each week, from one or other government agency, telling them what to do, so it was little wonder that this particular document had little impact. Some teachers thought that having a teaching assistant increased their workload, and some saw an opportunity to offload disruptive pupils into a corridor, out of sight and out of mind, with the teaching assistant in charge of them. Sometimes the partnership between teacher and teaching assistant worked, for the benefit of the children, the teacher and the school, and sometimes it did not. It was another responsibility for overloaded teachers leading to a poor work–life balance for teachers.

Since 2004, with the introduction of the changes to reduce the workload on teachers, teaching assistant and other support roles have undergone many changes, sometimes not for the better, and sometimes exploiting the lesser paid employees in schools. The workforce remodelling agenda required schools to have a clear plan for improving teacher workloads established by September 2005 (Training and Development Agency for Schools (TDA)/Workforce Agreement Monitoring Group (WAMG), 2003). The initial lack of support from some teacher union members created difficulties for teaching assistant developments in some schools. Despite this, the reforms have made changes, but not all benefitted the teaching assistants in the first two–three years. Workforce remodelling was intended to improve teachers' and head teachers' workloads. It provided guaranteed time for preparation and responsibilities in addition to a solution for covering teacher sickness by using teaching assistants employed at Level 3. However, during 2005, teaching assistants began to feel the pressures that the teachers previously felt; their work–life balance was being eroded. Their pay levels did not match the level of responsibility or the number of hours they had to work to fulfil their roles (Bold, 2010).

The introduction of the Higher Level Teaching Assistant (HLTA) status and advisory job profiles and pay guidelines for teaching assistants (National Joint Council for Local Government Services, 2003) has provided schools with the opportunity to establish different types of support. Covering classes to allow teachers to prepare and plan their lessons, that is, preparation, planning and assessment (PPA) time, is just one aspect of this support. Teaching assistants now have many and varied responsibilities and, along with these, a decent salary and great job satisfaction. In 2010, after a period of much government intervention and change, roles and relationships appeared to be reaching a more stable footing to the benefit of the children and young people in schools, and beyond. No longer are the teaching assistants the hourly paid 'helpers', but have often progressed to full-salaried positions. Many, who were teaching assistants in 2004, have now become fully qualified teachers, having studied through various degree routes and teacher training. Many are excellent in their roles, because of their previous experience in their teaching assistant role, and they are in a prime position to understand how to work in partnership with another person. Others have found that they prefer the pastoral side of the role in school and have opted to move into social work or social care involving young people.

In the next section Elaine tells the story of her development as a learning mentor and currently as inclusion manager in a primary school, and she outlines some of her main responsibilities.

Elaine's story

My education career started in 1996, when I started my training as a nursery nurse (NNEB). I was looking for a way to learn something new, something I would enjoy that would also fit in with family life. I was fortunate to gain a place at the local college and, while learning the theoretical perspectives about childcare, I gained practical experience through placements. I have since been employed at the same school for eleven years. During this time, I have built some excellent relationships with parents, carers and other professionals. I start my story having completed my nursery nursing training. I hope to show that professionals other than teachers can indeed make a difference.

Becoming a learning mentor

Gaining the NNEB was just the beginning. On completing my training, I gained employment at an inner-city primary school in Manchester. I supported Kosovan children who had recently arrived in the country in a Year 3 (ages 7–8) class. At this time, I mainly supported the children outside the classroom, rather than in class. I found this role an interesting and fulfilling one and was able to build good relationships with the Kosovan parents and carers. During this time, I gained confidence, especially as the role required me to visit the families at home. The visits to the home were usually related to attendance issues, but despite the potential for conflict there were many times when the families invited me and other professionals for dinner! I found that, by visiting families and offering support, rather than sending letters warning of fines, parents and carers appreciated the personal contact. After a year of supporting in this role, the school offered me the role of learning mentor. At that time, learning mentors were a new initiative in schools.

Learning mentors were introduced in 1999 through the Excellence in Cities (EiC) programme, initiated by the Labour government to improve standards and achievement in English schools. The government's aim was that learning mentors would recognise children's barriers to learning and introduce strategies to remove them. Schools identified children as having emotional, behavioural or attendance needs that the learning mentor had to support. Within the bigger plan, the government said it was to raise standards in education with an emphasis on the inclusion of all children and young people. This was a time of change for education in Britain with the government heavily funding the initiative. In 2001–2, £200 million was allocated, with an additional £300 million in 2002–3. Although the government claimed the EiC initiative a success, shown by EiC schools having a greater rate of improvement than those not included in EiC, the National Foundation for Educational Research (NFER, 2005) has reviewed the EiC outcomes to show that measuring the overall success of such initiatives is difficult. The Office for Standards in Education (Ofsted, 2003) praised the learning mentor initiative because the support to disaffected, underachieving or vulnerable pupils was much better than previously, and was considered good value for money.

Becoming employed as a learning mentor within an inner-city school was exciting but at the same time confusing. Some head teachers were unclear about the role of the learning mentor within the school plan. They had been given the financial support to employ mentors but found the job descriptions difficult to write. I believe I was fortunate to have the support of a head teacher and management team who allowed me to develop the role. They saw this as a positive opportunity for change.

To understand the concept of 'mentoring' it is first necessary to determine what exactly mentoring is. At first, I found it difficult to define what mentoring meant, as did staff I worked with. The online *Oxford Dictionary* defines a mentor as 'an experienced person in a company or educational institution who trains and counsels new employees or students' (www.oxforddictionaries.com). This is what I was doing, supporting and advising children, and their parents, so that they were able to learn more effectively. Initially, before receiving training, learning mentors had to find their own ways to understand the role. Since then, the Children's Workforce Development Council (CWDC), which was set up in 2005, has since provided clear information and even video clips that you might wish to look at (www.cwdcouncil.org.uk/learning-mentors/role).

For the first few months, learning mentors had difficulty identifying their focus within school, until they attended the training made available within the local authority. The training I received provided a wealth of resources and advice. Over a few months, it helped mentors understand what some of their role should be. However, there were still challenges, such as identifying children who would benefit from mentoring support. There were issues about when mentoring sessions with children would take place and whether mentors supported in class or out of it. In the first two years, my own experience was in supporting children with behavioural difficulties, both within class and out of class. This brought many challenges, as I was not trained to deal with some of the issues and behaviours that many children had. I attended training in behaviour management provided by the local authority. This helped me to offer quality support for children, and guided me in the programmes of work I could use with them. Monitoring attendance also became my responsibility. I would check the registers every morning and telephone any parents who had not contacted school about an absent child. I also had to track children's attendance, highlight any improvements made, and provide support if there were no improvements. I also met with the Educational Welfare Officer, who is a local authority social worker responsible for improving children's attendance at school.

I found after a year or so of mentoring children that parents began to trust me. I found that parents and carers would come to see me with concerns about their children. The concerns would usually be about their children's behaviour and safety within the community. I now also receive requests from parents to support them at health appointments for their children. This allows me to liaise with the class teacher should additional support be needed. For example, on attending a speech and language appointment with a parent and child, I will then discuss the strategies needed within class. This enables a positive relationship between professionals in school and parents, and ensures a good outcome for the child. I have also been involved in supporting parents with housing issues. This might mean contacting housing managers with concerns parents may have about repairs or neighbourhood disputes. Parents also meet with me for advice on how to deal with their children's challenging behaviour outside school. This has allowed me to visit parents and children at home in a more comfortable environment for them. I believe the positive relationships that I build with parents have a good impact on their children's achievements.

Because of the number of requests I began to get from parents for support, I began to contact other agencies to help me fulfil my role: the school health team, the local authority Behaviour and Education Support Team (BEST) and the local high schools transition coordinators. Cluster groups were set up to support learning mentors. The clusters allowed mentors to meet in each other's schools, to share good practice, or to discuss any difficulties they were facing.

Over the years mentors have found that their roles within each school may be different. Some mentors found that they were mostly in class working as classroom assistants. Other mentors were the 'behaviour person' and, for some, attendance was their main responsibility. After two years of mentoring in school, I had a number of duties and I had gained confidence and acquired other responsibilities.

A major influence on how learning mentors supported pupils and families was the introduction of the British government's Green Paper *Every Child Matters* in 2003 and the subsequent Children Act of 2004, which set the legislation for developing more effective and accessible services that focused on the needs of children, young people and families. For learning mentors this was a time of training and sharing good practice during cluster meetings. Mentors found themselves in a position of having access to up-to-date information on new government initiatives, such as the Social and Emotional Aspects of Learning (SEAL), introduced in 2005 by the Department for Children, Schools and Families (DCSF). I became responsible for this initiative in my school, along with the Healthy Schools Initiative, and Safeguarding and Child Protection.

SEAL is a government initiative that aims to develop underpinning qualities and skills to promote positive behaviour and effective learning. Resources are available to support pupils, focusing on five aspects of behaviour and emotional well-being: self-awareness, managing feelings, motivation, empathy and social skills. Schools include this through activities such as Circle Time, or as part of the Physical, Social and Health Education (PSHE) or Citizenship curriculum, buddy systems and the whole school ethos. Our school visits seven themes over the year:

- new beginnings
- getting on and falling out
- say no to bullying
- going for goals
- good to be me
- relationships
- changes.

The school holds an initial assembly at the beginning of the new term, and then a celebratory assembly at the end. There are also SEAL resources for the staff to use: year group packs, a resource file with photographs and posters, and packs to use for Family SEAL. My role is to support all staff in having resources available, leading assemblies, and assessing pupils' understanding and the impact the SEAL programme makes on the children's learning. Measuring the impact SEAL has on pupils outside school can be difficult, yet Ofsted want to see it.

Recently, Dimitra Hartas (2010) was very critical of the SEAL initiative in the education pages of *The Guardian*, suggesting that the therapeutic prioritising of emotions and the language used is limiting, and that learners should feel good through acquiring intellectual tools. I believe she has misunderstood the purpose of SEAL in presenting it in the way she has. It does not replace other learning. It aims to enhance the prospects of those who find learning in school a challenge for whatever reason. It certainly does not make us therapists and we do not think of ourselves in this way. Ecclestone and Hayes (2009) also discuss the therapy culture we are imposing on our children and young people, calling emotional literacy, SEAL and similar initiatives the 'new curriculum of the self'. In my experience, I believe we do have some children and young people in need of emotional support, who may, for whatever reason, not receive this within their own home setting. From my own observations, teachers within school need to have a young person ready to learn. If we can provide a support to enable them to access a positive learning experience, any initiative that recognises their emotional state at that time can only be a positive thing.

My responsibilities as Healthy Schools coordinator are varied and very rewarding. The National Healthy Schools Programme (NHSP) is a joint initiative between the DCSF and the Department of Health (DH) and has existed since 1999. There are various aspects to this role, one of them being as link person to other professionals such as the local Health Team. This team offers 'healthy eating', 'healthy bodies' and 'healthy relationships' lessons. I work closely with the local authority Healthy Schools coordinator and we meet regularly to work on national and local targets. For example, there is a national target for all authorities to reduce child obesity. This is challenging and, in my school, it is in the early stages. We are in the process of setting up a working party to examine how this agenda can best support children and families. We also monitor standards relating to healthy eating, safeguarding, PSHE provision and becoming a safe school. Using the Healthy Schools enhancement model provides us with rigorous health and well-being evidence. We will be able to audit our provision to stakeholders, and put in monitoring arrangements to see where we can improve. Also, in using this model, we will be able to assess that all policies are recent and relevant to our pupils and staff.

Being the designated Safeguarding Officer is a major part of my workload. In recent times, Safeguarding and Child Protection has been at the forefront of national debate. Keeping children safe is a major issue for any school. Within many schools there are looked-after children (LAC), families within the Family Action (FAM) process (see www.family-action.org.uk), children on a Protection Plan, or families receiving support from a member of staff. I work with families and children who fall into these categories, within the guidelines of the Common Assessment Framework (CAF).

The CAF is a standardised approach to assessing children's additional needs, and agreeing with parents and carers how these should be met. A range of services – education, health and social – all use the same framework, which focuses on the needs of children and young people. After an assessment of the child's needs, a decision is made about the support needed. It may be a simple health check or it may be an assessment from the Child and Adolescent Mental Health Services (CAMHS). Other referrals may be made to the Behaviour Educational Support Team, Youth Inclusion Service, National Society for the Prevention of Cruelty to Children (NSPCC), Educational Welfare Officer or an educational psychologist. Within this process there will be a lead professional (LP), who will usually be the person who has initiated the CAF process and completed the assessment of needs. It may also be that, in identifying a child's needs, parents or carers may also need support. For example, they may need drug and alcohol services, housing, the police or counselling services.

The LP will keep everyone informed, review progress and generally make sure good integrated working is happening between agencies. This is a challenging role. With reference to safeguarding children and passing information to children's services, professionals should always keep the children's needs at the forefront of their actions. When I have serious concerns about a child's welfare, I will always discuss this with a parent before deciding to contact children's services. I believe the best practice is to develop good relationships with all parents and carers. At times, this means accepting that some parental lifestyle choices do not match mine. However, for the best outcomes for the child, working closely with the parents is a major part of any integrated approach to supplying a service.

We have a Children's Centre at the school, which has many facilities for families and children. There are times when I have helped a parent access these, and sometimes advised on specialist support, such as meeting with an early years' worker. The support available varies at each Children's Centre according to the community needs. At our Children's Centre there are parents' coffee mornings, opportunities for back-to-work advice, college courses advice, baby massage, family outreach work, support for families accessing other agencies, breastfeeding groups, health visitors, dads' group, tots drop-in and, of course, nursery places for children from birth to five years.

In addition to being responsible for these core areas of practice, I am also an A1 Assessor. In this role, I have supported teaching assistants to acquire the Level 3 Teaching Assistant award. I am also a trained practice teacher for social worker placements and a member of the Senior Leadership Team in school.

Professional partnerships

Elaine's experience and that of many in similar positions has shown us that professional roles in schools are changing. Teachers spend their time more focused on activities related to learning and teaching, while other professionals can respond to the school's, the children's and their families' other needs. Sometimes this means that professionals work in partnerships of various kinds, within the classroom and with external agencies outside the classroom. Sometimes it requires the ability to take the initiative and work independently and, at other times, to become part of a team.

Elaine seems to have several responsibilities and her role seems to be rationalised as an important part of the school team, and the management team. This is typical of many teaching assistants' experiences over the past few years. They are a skilled and knowledgeable workforce. Despite this, some concerns still exist about the amount and nature of teaching that teaching assistants do and the level of underlying knowledge of pupil learning among the teaching assistant workforce (Gibson and Patrick, 2008). The HLTA standards (TDA, 2006) expect teaching assistants to engage in whole-class teaching and activities such as briefing the supply teacher. The HLTA standards use the word *professional* rather than *paraprofessional* in their description, suggesting that those with HLTA status should make judgements about learning and teaching, rather than just being a technical workforce delivering and monitoring with materials provided for them. Unfortunately, some teaching assistants may have acquired increased responsibility, but may not have the knowledge and understanding to engage in serious professional judgement about their pedagogy. In relation to working in partnership with teachers, teaching assistants may still suffer from power imbalances, with teachers responding negatively to teaching assistants' suggestions for change.

Groom and Rose (2005) would agree that Elaine's role enhances her ability to provide effective support to primary pupils with social, emotional and behavioural difficulties (SEBP). They identified the following important factors that ensure the teaching assistant role is effective:

- inclusion as a full member of staff;
- involvement in target setting, monitoring and in rewards and sanctions;
- involvement in planning and reviewing;
- training;
- involvement in a range of classroom activities;
- involvement in developing pupil self-esteem and social skills.

(Groom and Rose, 2005: 28)

These key factors create an enabling environment, such as Elaine's, in which teaching assistants can thrive as part of the school workforce. McVitie (2005) identified that clarity of role is important, something that Elaine also commented on. Early in her role there was a lack of clarity, but now she has a much clearer, albeit diverse, role. By incorporating her into the school management team they are fulfilling what Groom (2006) suggests that schools need to do: valuing her work, involving her in decision-making, planning and review.

In summary, through sharing Elaine's professional development story we hope we have provided some understanding of how many teaching assistants have progressed from their original role of 'assistant' to roles with significant responsibility. In these times of change, with school communities becoming more diverse and society responding differently to education than it used to, schools cannot justify having a workforce that consists only of teachers. Schools are now part of the wider integrated services agenda, supporting children in health and social care in addition to their main priority of education.

Discussion starters

1   Discuss the advantages and disadvantages of having learning mentors in schools.
2   Identify the challenges and constraints faced by the different teams when integrating their working practices in using the CAF effectively. What are the implications of budget cuts at either national or local level?

Reflecting on practice

1   Observe a teaching assistant or learning mentor working with children and other people in the school setting. Reflect on the demands of the role and the skills, knowledge and understanding required to fulfil the role effectively.
2   Offer to support a group of children in a school setting. Reflect on the children's learning needs, and their social and emotional needs. How well did you support them? What training might you require?

Useful resources

www.cwdcouncil.org.uk: Children's Workforce Development Council for information on learning mentors and the CAF (www.cwdcouncil.org.uk/caf).

www.education.gov.uk/schools/pupilsupport: Pupil Support section of the Department for Education. The DfE is just developing its website and making decisions about the initiatives it wishes to keep in schools and those it does not.

http://home.healthyschools.gov.uk: Healthy Schools initiative.

References

Bold, C. (2010) 'The diverse and changing roles of teaching assistants', in Sage, R. (ed.) *Meeting the Needs of Students with Diverse Backgrounds*, London: Network Continuum.

Department for Children, Schools and Families (DCSF) (2005) *Social and Emotional Aspects of Learning (SEAL): Improving behaviour, improving learning*, Nottingham: DCSF.

Department for Education and Employment (DfEE) (2000) *Working with Teaching Assistants: A good practice guide*, London: DfEE.

Ecclestone, K. and Hayes, D. (2009*) The Dangerous Rise of Therapeutic Education*, London: Routledge.

Gibson, H. and Patrick, H. (2008) 'Putting words in their mouths: the role of teaching assistants and the spectre of scripted pedagogy', *Journal of Early Childhood Literacy* 8(1): 25–41.

Groom, B. (2006) 'Building relationships for learning: the developing role of the teaching assistant', *Support for Learning* 21(4): 199-203.

Groom, B. and Rose, R. (2005) 'Supporting the inclusion of pupils with social, emotional and behavioural difficulties in the primary school: the role of teaching assistants', *Journal of Research in Special Educational Needs* 5(1): 20-30.

Hartas, D. (2010) 'Children do not get respect they deserve', *The Guardian*, 12 May. Available online at www.guardian.co.uk (accessed 10 February 2011).

McVitie, E. (2005) 'The role of the teaching assistant: an investigative study to discover if teaching assistants are being used effectively to support children with special educational needs in mainstream schools', *Education 3–13* 33(3): 26–31.

National Foundation for Educational Research (NFER) (2005) *Excellence in Cities: The national evaluation of a policy to raise standards in urban schools 2000–2003*, London: London School of Economics Centre for Economic Performance. Available online at www.education.gov.uk/publications/standard/publicationdetail/page1/RR675A (accessed 10 February 2011).

National Joint Council for Local Government Services (2003) *School Support Staff: The way forward*, London: Employers Organisation for Local Government. Available online at www.lge.gov.uk/lge/aio/778006 (accessed 10 February 2011).

Office for Standards in Education (Ofsted) (2003) *Excellence in Cities and Education Action Zones: Management and impact*, London: Ofsted.

Times, The (1999) '"Mum's Army" to start teaching', 24 May.

Training and Development Agency for Schools (TDA) (2007) *Professional Standards for HLTA Status*, Manchester: TDA. Available online at www.tda.gov.uk/support-staff/developing-progressing/hlta/professional-standards.aspx (accessed 12 February 2011).

Training and Development Agency for Schools (TDA)/Workforce Agreement Monitoring Group (WAMG) (2003) *Raising Standards and Tackling Workload: A national agreement*. Available online at www.tda.gov.uk/~/media/resources/national-agreement.pdf (accessed 10 February 2011).

2

The Changing Educational Scene

Alan Barrow

My background, beliefs and values

This chapter presents some of the changes that have taken place in education in the latter part of the twentieth century and the beginning of the twenty-first. Since it largely presents my perspective on those changes, it is important that the reader knows my background. I was head teacher of a village primary school (ages 4–11) from 1982 until 1988 – pre-National Curriculum. Then, in 1988, the year the National Curriculum became law, I was appointed head teacher of a larger primary school. Until my retirement in 2002, I oversaw a continuous flow of changes that affected every facet of school life. Since then I have attempted to keep pace with the continuing changes in education, partly through work for universities as a tutor and partly through my work as a consultant with a local primary school arts initiative. My experiences of these events and my thoughts on them provide the main substance of this chapter.

It is my intention that readers use my remarks as points for discussion and further enquiry. I aim to present a balanced view, but occasionally it will be biased in the light of my experiences. There are no simple truths in education and no single way forward, but there are signposts. These appear as you begin to make connections between what has gone before and what is occurring now. Wherever possible, I will attempt to make these connections and to explore the implications.

The beginnings – school life pre-1988

Cunningham (1990: 4) writes that the Education Act of 1944 did no more than define primary education as 'that suitable for the requirements of junior pupils'. Successive governments had failed to define a primary curriculum more clearly than that. The reasons for this are not obvious. With the growth of industrialisation in the late nineteenth century, some form of universal education had been needed to enable the population to cope with an increasingly complex world of automation, written instructions, balance sheets, buying and selling. There is some substance in the view that the ruling classes saw no need to furnish the masses with more knowledge than was absolutely necessary! The model set in place was sufficient – it enabled a workforce to function reasonably effectively. By the 1950s and 1960s, although there might have been schemes of work in core subjects that teachers were expected to follow, they had freedom to determine how they taught and the amount of emphasis they placed on any subject. There was no entitlement to a national curriculum – no generally accepted curricular model that parents might expect their children to learn.

Therefore, pre-1988 and the advent of the National Curriculum, the educational establishment in England and Wales had escaped without too much interference from government ministers for several decades. Schools immediately before 1988 were mainly autonomous institutions. Head teachers largely decided the content taught in their schools and, sometimes, the teaching method as well. Before 1988, children would encounter very different approaches from individual teachers in their local primary school. Teachers acquired reputations for subjects in which they excelled and children would know that, when they reached a particular class, they would experience geography, art, physical education or music taught with excitement and enthusiasm. This richness was good since children experienced enthusiastic, inspirational, knowledgeable and creative teaching free from the constraints of a closely controlled syllabus. However, there was a downside. Children would also encounter teachers who delivered only the rudiments in subjects they did not like. They might omit these subjects entirely from their plans. Moreover, educational fashions sometimes came and went. The teaching in some schools very often reflected the influential views of local authority advisers promoting their individual philosophies to schools. In fairness, some of these were exceptionally gifted educationists who enhanced teaching in many schools but, in the worst instances, their ideas were translated into repetitive, superficial and narrowly framed activities, catering for only a few children.

The snowball of educational reform

The Plowden Report was *the* document for trainee teachers in the late 1960s to read and consider before embarking on their careers. The report, *Children and their Primary Schools* (DES, 1967), was an insightful and balanced review of schools at that time. It made many excellent recommendations. It covered a range of topics and did not, as its critics were to state, fail to challenge the status quo where necessary. However, the reasoned and reasonable views of the authors were deemed too liberal and were out of tune with the mood of the times. Politicians disparaged it as being too indulgent. They wanted greater governmental control of schools than Plowden was recommending (Cook, 1972).

The Schools Council, formed in 1964, had the remit to unite teachers, local education authorities (LEAs) and the government in developing curricula, improving teachers' effectiveness and devising improvements for other areas of education. Throughout the country, Teachers' Centres emerged and many excellent initiatives were set in place by teachers for teachers. However, there was little coordination of ideas between these centres and the government perceived the Schools Council to be ineffective. It had, perhaps, been too subtle and not sufficiently clear in communicating its intentions. As Thomas (1990) suggests in his discussion of the Schools Council's work, it set out to 'fine-tune' the existing situation, whereas the government wanted broad and radical change. The government disbanded the Council in 1982.

In the late 1980s, teachers' unions remained unable or unwilling to embrace changes to the status quo, despite warnings that the Conservative government was intent on radical reform of the public sector. (Teachers in England and Wales did not have membership of a single professional body, capable of representing their views, unlike in Scotland where teachers were registered with a General Teaching Council from 1965.) If teachers had been prepared to accept the need for reform and had taken the initiative on debating some important issues (greater accountability, greater clarity in relation to what was taught in schools, better teacher–parent communication, etc.), they would have been more able to control the rate and direction of reform. They did not seem to understand that ministers saw the vast majority of schools as closed communities, not accountable, unclear in their objectives, and subscribing, in the main, to vague ideologies. This self-determining model of education was never likely to appeal to a government intent on strengthening its control over the public sector and over LEAs.

In the run up to the passing of the 1988 Education Reform Act, the Conservatives were mindful that a previous Labour government had launched the great educational debate as far back as 1976. In that year, James Callaghan, Labour Prime Minister, gave his Ruskin College speech. Using agricultural and horticultural analogy, he argued that the school curriculum should no longer be a *secret garden*, that there were no *holy cows* in education and no areas, therefore, that 'profane hands were not allowed to touch' (Brooks, 1991: 6). In essence, he asserted the right of central government to have a controlling interest in education and established the principle that government should be able to determine whether the education services were delivering value for money.

The Conservative government of 1988 received input from many and varied contributors – Her Majesty's Inspectors of Schools, for example. It acknowledged the difficulties in determining exactly what should be included in a National Curriculum and how best to do this (Thomas, 1990). Conservative Secretaries of State for Education, including Keith Joseph, Mark Carlisle and Kenneth Baker, had presided over a decade of educational debate. The government was not prepared to put off educational reform indefinitely and published *The National Curriculum – 5–16: A consultative document* in July 1987. After a short period of consultation, with very little change, it became law through the Education Reform Act (ERA) of 1988. It precipitated a continuous programme of change, imposed from government with little consultation of, or contribution from, teachers. Teachers had no control over the pace of the reforms heading the way of their profession and their school.

The impact of the National Curriculum

The 1988 Education Reform Act created the first National Curriculum as a statutory requirement. It established the subjects all teachers in all schools would teach. It stipulated levels of attainment all children would aim to achieve. It devised a national testing system (to begin in 1991) for all children and proposed publication of results to which all parents had access. A universally acknowledged, minimum entitlement for all children was born. In addition, the concept of public accountability in education was recognised. The Act established an inspection process with quality control by an independent body, the Office for Standards in Education – Ofsted.

Let us consider, again, what teachers knew before the National Curriculum. It is important to think about this, as the profession is poised for announcements of further changes from a new 2010 British government. Pre-National Curriculum, the best teachers had a clear grasp of the phases of child development and how identifiable stages influenced the growth of children's intellect and understanding. They were familiar with the works of Piaget (translated in the 1950s and 1960s) and Bruner (particularly from the 1960s and 1970s) – not abstract theorists but contributors of workable models for primary education on which teachers could construct a learning environment. As far back as 1926, the Report of the Hadow Committee recommended that a primary curriculum 'be thought of . . . in terms of activity and experience rather than knowledge to be acquired and facts to be stored' (Brooks, 1991: 89). The developing child was not a passive receptacle but an active participant at the centre of a learning situation. Teachers used their understanding of how children learnt to inform their teaching. Discovery learning, practical activity and group work (the social constructivist approach) often replaced a didactic model of learning. Teachers wanted to develop links between subject areas and very often placed a theme or topic at the centre of their planning. These things should have been defended by a united front of teachers using the support of educational research and examples of good practice, but the initiative had been lost. The government view was that it was not 'rigorous' enough and the National Curriculum was framed within subject boundaries. As a profession, primary teachers seemed to be incapable of presenting a reasoned and informed defence of those principles of primary education in which many believed. We need to return to this later in reviewing Labour's intended new curriculum for 2011 emanating from the Rose Review, its six areas of study, its emphasis on cross-curricular planning and its subsequent fate at the hands of the 2010 coalition government.

The government showed some sensitivity in its approach by introducing the three core subjects (Maths, English and Science) and, later, the seven foundation subjects over a phased period – two years in total. Schools assimilated the requirements for Mathematics, English and Science reasonably successfully within their existing long-term planning but found that, in making provision for the content within the programmes of study for those subjects, they had allocated insufficient time within the school day for history, geography, art, music, technology, physical education and religious education when they came on stream. The result was curriculum overload. Brooks (1991) examined some elegant alternatives to the curriculum. A different approach might well have fitted more easily into the existing primary school environment and resulted in reform with less upheaval.

Rethinking teaching and assessment

Schools increasingly perceived subject-specific teaching as the only way to deliver the content. Teachers sought new ways of planning and began to change how they organised their children. With the publication of Standard Assessment Tasks (SATs) results, teachers became concerned that the public would use the outcomes of these tests as a crude yardstick to measure schools' performance. Many became obsessed with maintaining grids for recording every child's encounter with every statement of attainment in every subject. Measuring performance almost became more important than teaching.

Testing and assessment became something that had to be done in many instances without sufficient thought. The report of the Task Group on Assessment and Testing (TGAT, 1987) was an attempt to respond to those critics who wanted a more accountable school environment with teachers reporting clearly to parents on their children's progress. Its recommendations were sensitive and balanced. It said that assessment should be formative. The task group suggested that tests at Key Stages 1 and 2 would integrate with normal school work. There would be selection from a bank of SATs, and the subject matter would be suited to the children. Parents and the LEA should have access to the results of the test. Most importantly, assessment would relate to profile components or clusters of attainment targets in the National Curriculum, not to every target individually. Results from Key Stage 2 onwards should be published in schools' own brochures but not published nationally (Thomas, 1990). The government ignored these last two recommendations. It wanted complete public accountability. Educational publishers therefore furnished schools with assessment charts that became covered in meaningless ticks and crosses in many colours. Many *advisers* came forward with suggestions on how to make assessment more manageable, for example the compilation of portfolios of concrete evidence to support teachers' assessment. It was generally thought that Ofsted inspectors would only be satisfied if schools could prove they were completing continuous and detailed assessments on every child. The government vigorously refuted this expectation in the mid-1990s. The government had little understanding of the impact of curriculum and assessment changes on those who had to implement them. It is worth noting here that change needs good management with all affected becoming involved in preparing for and implementing the changes.

Ofsted inspectors worked with an unfamiliar handbook when they began to arrive in schools in 1994, to judge the quality of teachers' work and pupils' learning. There were guidelines for Registered Inspectors (an interesting mix of LEA advisers, head teachers and deputies, and independent consultants). Some inspectors interpreted their guidelines rather loosely. These inspectors saw their role as one to seek out and expose teachers deemed to be *failing*. The worst inspected in a negative and aggressive fashion, causing distress and anxiety out of all proportion to the usefulness of their final reports. Several head teachers and class teachers resigned rather than face the brown envelope containing notification of an inspection for their school. Not all of these people were expendable. Many were a serious loss to the profession. Negative Ofsted inspectors were sometimes supported by a hostile press and by a Chief Inspector appointed in 1994, Chris Woodhead. Woodhead and his colleagues had previously produced a report (Alexander *et al.*, 1992) that was heavily critical of child-centred and topic-based curricula. They claimed there was clear evidence that much topic work led to fragmentary and superficial teaching and learning. The report also suggested that 'highly questionable dogmas' hampered pupils' progress in primary schools and its authors were critical of the devaluing of the place of subjects in the curriculum.

Local Management of Schools

An aspect of education reform few people outside the teaching profession understood was Local Management of Schools (LMS). Pre-1988, LEAs had controlled money used to resource schools and pay staff. Local authorities devolved funding to schools with the advent of LMS. Schools would pay their own staff, pay for repairs to their premises and pay for resources they used. The money was to be delivered to schools almost entirely through an amount per child – the age-weighted pupil unit (AWPU), that is, money per capita with greatest weighting for secondary pupils, some weighting in favour of nursery and reception infants, and the least weighting for all other primary children. LMS was one of the most revolutionary reforms of all. Part of the reasoning behind it was that successful schools (measured largely by the results of public tests) would attract more parents, more children and, therefore, more money. This would encourage schools to strive for excellence. Rewards for good schools would be tangible – the more children they attracted, the more money they received. This proved to be an over-simplistic equation.

Additional funding would be delivered through a register of free school meals (denoting deprivation and need) and still more money through other criteria, usually decided by LEAs charged with devising ways and means of apportioning money for heating and lighting and premises maintenance to individual schools. School governing bodies (composed of unpaid, co-opted citizens) would manage these budgets. The result would be openness not seen before in local government funding. Schools would have greater freedom to manage their money. Everyone would benefit.

The crucial document for everyone with responsibility for LMS was DES Circular 7/88. This offered guidance on the new system of funding. It suggested that funding should be based on objective needs rather than simply on historic spending (Coopers and Lybrand, 1988). The government asked LEAs to create a formula and not surprisingly most of them resorted to the use of historic factors that were no longer relevant. Many primary schools thus received inadequate funding. A source of funding statement went to schools to explain how the LEA calculated individual items of funding for their school. Scrutiny of a typical statement for my school for any year from 1990 to the present day highlights interesting perspectives on the LEA's interpretation of Circular 7/88. For example, they grouped the head teacher with class teachers to establish a lower pupil–teacher ratio. Assumptions were made about the staffing required, for example I had a part-time caretaker, school secretary and cleaner. There was funding for one part-time nursery nurse intended to support the reception teacher.

In many ways, LMS has been the change schools have found hardest to manage. From the start, LEA officers acknowledged that devolved funding would create winners and losers – an unacceptable aspect of the previously unregulated education system that the 1988 Education Reform Act intended to remove. Schools with falling pupil rolls found they could not adequately resource the curriculum. Over time, it has become obvious that schools generally have little control over pupil numbers – even schools that are recognised as excellent by any criteria Ofsted might care to use cannot always attract additional pupils. Perhaps the 2010 coalition government's free schools programme will improve this situation.

The new Labour governments of Messrs Blair and Brown from 2000 onwards adopted a compensatory approach to LMS. They supplemented school budgets with injections of cash direct from central government and usually ring-fenced for specific purposes that ministers determined as important – information and communications technology (ICT), facilitating disabled access to school buildings, improving school security, etc. While these injections of cash were welcome, they did not allow school governors freedom to direct funds to areas of greatest need, usually shortfalls in staffing. Other initiatives designed to raise standards did not reach all schools – Education Action Zones (EAZs), for example.

The impact on schools

Let us reflect on what has gone before. Some in government circles adhere to the view that to change an institution where there is entrenched resistance to change, it is best to be swift and incisive, allowing no time for opposition to mobilise. There will be some damage, some instability and confusion, perhaps, but out of that will emerge something better. The period from the 1988 Reform Act to the publication of the 1994 Dearing Report reflected this philosophy. It was unrelenting with short time scales, brief consultation periods, and the weight of the law ensuring statutory requirements were met. However, after the initial shock had worn off, those most directly affected by the reforms began to take charge of their own destinies. They began to learn how to manage the imposed changes. Teachers, advisers and LEAs generally went through fire but emerged better at doing many things. They were also forced to change certain entrenched attitudes, such as relationships with parents, planning and assessment, management structures, professional development and roles and responsibilities.

Relationships with parents

Pre-1988, it was possible for some schools not to hold parent evenings and/or provide written reports about children's progress. Some schools displayed signs informing parents that their presence in school was not welcome. Post-National Curriculum, teachers had to recognise that parents were partners in their children's education, something about which Plowden (DES, 1967) had previously expressed concern. Parents now had a minimum entitlement to an annual written report, but most schools were keen to offer much more. Teachers became inventive at creating home–school links and at making their aims clear. Schools organised workshops to show parents how they taught the new curriculum and evening meetings to explain the administration of national tests and the real implications of attainment levels. More and more teaching assistants engaged in direct communication with parents as they began to take responsibility for specific learning programmes or specific children.

Planning and assessment

Pre-1988, teachers' planning and assessment were not usually subject to inspection by an outside agency and many schools did little formal, written planning or assessment.

Teachers' use of assessment was intrinsic and some found it hard to formalise their thoughts on children's progress. Post-National Curriculum, teachers began to gain greater insight into the purposes of planning and began to understand the reason for assessment. They began to make assessment manageable and useful.

Management structures

Pre-1988, there was a management structure in place in primary schools but, in many, the head teacher ruled over his or her school like a (hopefully) benevolent despot. Amazingly, pre-1988, some teachers had rarely attended a staff meeting. Post-National Curriculum, head teachers realised that only by working with their staff as team leaders would they survive the legislation and be able to deliver the new curriculum. They had to learn new management strategies. Consultation, evaluation and delegation were unfamiliar terms to most head teachers. Now they had to use these terms, understand the implications of them for their schools and create staffing structures designed to put them into effect. Schools produced action plans and organised staff meetings with real agendas and real purpose.

Professional development

Pre-1988, teachers attended courses designed to improve their skills in a very ad hoc fashion. LEA advisers ran many excellent workshops, but they were usually projections of their individual philosophy. Teachers often chose to attend because they wanted to experience something for which they already had a great liking, such as art, poetry, science or mathematics, and sometimes their pupils did reap the benefit of the ideas and inspiration with which they returned. However, such courses rarely supported school priorities.

Post-National Curriculum, schools began to allocate money for training designed to plug gaps in teachers' knowledge and understanding. Priorities were linked to the needs of the school. In the best schools, a teacher who returned from a course was expected to give an account of it to his or her colleagues and to use new understanding for everyone's benefit. Moreover, advisers began to respond to the needs of teachers and a bottom-up model of in-service training was created in the most supportive LEAs, in place of the top-down one that had gone before. Twenty-day courses targeting specific subject areas were created and teachers were funded from government money to be released from school for extended study periods. Excellent advisory teachers were appointed as an additional tier of support for teachers desperate for help with the delivery of a science or technology curriculum. Higher education institutions organised courses in conjunction with schools to broaden teachers' understanding in areas such as technology, ICT and mathematics.

Today, teachers enter the profession with an entitlement to continuous professional development (CPD) contained in their Career Entry and Development Profile (CEDP). Professional development opportunities have continued to grow. There have been opportunities to gain credit for being excellent teachers, for example becoming an advanced skills teacher, or a mentor/coach to new colleagues, instead of all promotion being through management responsibilities. The New Labour government of the 1990s wanted to push this sharing of expertise between colleagues further by creating Accredited School Partnerships, where high-achieving schools would guide and support underachieving partners. Finally, the Labour government in 2009 wanted teachers to be 'licensed' with continual review and development to maintain the licence.

Roles and responsibilities

Pre-1988, the head teacher often controlled the budget and ordered resources in many schools, which was ineffective when it failed to address the priorities for the school. Large under-spends that LEAs instantly reclaimed sent out the wrong messages to those in charge of school funding.

Post-National Curriculum, schools began to recognise the value of the subject coordinator, whose responsibility for the successful teaching of a particular subject area included resourcing it. Cockcroft (1982) had previously recommended the development of the role of the subject coordinator or subject leader in mathematics and other subject areas copied this initiative. Above all, after 1988, schools recognised the need to be accountable and to adopt the notion of 'stakeholders'. Parents, governors, the local and wider community were all to become active partners in children's education. Schools had to learn to communicate their intentions to these different bodies, encourage their interest and solicit their opinion.

The impact on education for the under-fives

Before the introduction of the National Curriculum, the child-centred classrooms that flourished throughout the primary phase reflected good early years' practice. However, the changes wrought by the National Literacy and Numeracy Strategies, in particular, saw Reception classes (ages 4–5) become the last outposts of the holistic approach. Almost immediately a child moved from Reception, learning through play ceased to happen. Oral language development began to take second place to formal written language and the child's working day became much more formal.

Nursery (ages 3–4) and Reception classes were declared to be the Foundation Stage of the primary phase from September 2000 (now referred to as EYFS – Early Years Foundation Stage). They had a curriculum divided into six broad areas of experience. Children moved along 'stepping stones' towards Early Learning Goals (DfEE/QCA, 2000). The government handled early learning practitioners sensitively, allowing them to approach learning in ways they considered appropriate. Reception classrooms were usually stimulating and multi-sensory, with teachers nurturing different learning styles through interactive displays, making full use of the senses and integrated topics linking different subjects of the curriculum. Most classrooms would have a number of regular adult helpers, either paid or voluntary, at the Foundation Stage, engaged in small group activities with the children and actively encouraging discussion and debate about the tasks in hand.

A teacher in 1988 and today would understand the importance of play as a way of learning and for working out ideas or exploring feelings, often through well-constructed role-play areas. However, the Reception class teacher today is certainly more adept at recording the individual progress of each child and is particularly good at tailoring learning situations to suit each stage of a child's development. Most probably, the teacher recognises more readily the role of the child's parent or carer as a partner in his or her education and builds into each day a time for dialogue about each child. The teacher seeks to establish with these adults the recognition of each child's need to grow and develop in independence and confidence, moving through the same stages of development but at their own rate. Today's Reception teacher, or teaching assistant, actively makes contact with those adults who care for the child pre-school, including childminders and nurseries, for a seamless transition into school.

Sometimes, Reception teaching teams carry out home visits. They model approaches they intend to adopt with the children and convey to parents and other carers their expectations. They offer advice about the kind of support parents and other carers can offer children. When teachers and parents have similar goals, children are likely to feel more secure and achieve more. Teachers' work during pre-school sessions is designed not only to help young children settle more readily into school in September, but to exchange information on each child and begin the process of baseline assessment.

In 2003, all Reception teachers were using baseline assessment (replaced by the EYFS Profile in 2008) to establish a starting point for themselves and for colleagues throughout the school. Any future progress a child made was measured against this early assessment (a 'value-added' measure). The responsibility for establishing an accurate baseline of achievement for each child entering Key Stage 1 is one of the most significant changes to impact on early years' teachers. Despite its usefulness, the coalition government is preparing to review such aspects of provision in EYFS. Consultation is under way and it is intended to proceed towards a new curriculum in 2012.

The influence of ICT

Keeping pace with all the other changes to the curriculum has been information and communications technology (ICT), initially an unwanted and overlooked addition to the core subjects but now, increasingly, an enabling tool and a vehicle for curriculum enrichment. Computers found their way into schools well before the National Curriculum. Margaret Thatcher's Conservative government gave every primary school a computer, but these primitive machines were slow and uncertain, accessing programs from a tape recorder. With only limited software at their disposal, few teachers could see a role for them in their classrooms. LEAs were equally confused. I attended a session where I spent a whole evening learning how to program a computer to perform a simple addition. Many head teachers and teachers regarded the computer as a problem, rather than an educational solution. We often locked computers in cupboards or covered them with drapes in classroom corners. A few enterprising teachers did use them with their children, seeing their potential as teaching tools. As the technology became more sophisticated and tape recorders gave way to discs, the way forward was still not a clear, straight road but a track that wound uphill with many branching paths. Some LEAs put their resources into machines such as the BBC Acorn, ignoring the fact that PCs (personal computers) were taking over as the operating system in almost every office and household. Incompatability between types of software hindered progress. The problems associated with ICT in schools (and it was a National Curriculum Foundation subject almost from the very beginning) were:

- different and incompatible systems;
- software as dedicated teaching aids but boring, repetitive and unsophisticated;
- sophisticated software not suited to educational use;
- unreliable hardware;
- no effective technical support;
- not enough computers;
- inadequate training.

Not surprisingly, Ofsted inspectors began identifying ICT as a key issue in schools across the country.

Slowly and painfully, ICT has found its place in the scheme of things. The new Labour government of the 1990s directed large amounts of capital towards improving the situation. It recognised the huge potential for education that lies in the internet and its aim was to make ICT a powerful support mechanism in all schools.

For example:

- Teachers were given laptops. This enabled the computer-phobics to engage at home with *the beast* in comparative security, where they found it to be a powerful and friendly support that could produce labels and worksheets and reports far quicker and far better than any other means.
- Government funding provided better organised and more effective technical support for the school.
- PCs were installed in a computer suite, and were faster and more reliable than before.
- Compatibility of educational software was no longer a problem.
- Well-designed educational software was available and targeted towards areas such as special educational needs.
- Interactive whiteboards were installed in computer suites and sometimes in every classroom.

Most schools have plotted a way forward that ensures delivery of most strands of the statutory framework for ICT. The interactive whiteboard is now used more effectively in all teaching areas. It is the most powerful of visual aids. It enables teachers to demonstrate concepts clearly and to engage with learners using a wealth of resources from all over the world. In computer suites, children can learn skills in a supportive environment.

There is a range of technologies available to enhance children's learning in other subjects. These include digital cameras and photo-editing facilities that children may use creatively to enhance their learning, for example by filming their critical analysis of art works. The power of the internet continues to grow. Most teachers have recognised its effectiveness and encourage pupils to research topics either via websites or by downloading worksheets and articles directly on to a smartboard. Some schools experiment with videoconferencing and links with schools in other countries. With the advent of broadband, connections to the internet are quick and sure, but filtering the mass of information available is not easy. Most children of primary school age can find their way around the web with ease, but channelling their experiences into productive areas takes insight and ingenuity. Most significantly, many have access to smartphones that can handle applications of amazing sophistication, as well as being extremely powerful cameras. Schools have an uneasy relationship with mobile phones, which do have potential for anarchy, especially when linked with weblogs and sites such as Facebook and YouTube. However, children who can download music on to mobile phones and use applications on these phones to play a range of games and to share photos and texts do not always see how the school ICT curriculum relates to their use of them outside school. We need to find ways of using their awareness to greater purpose within our lessons. We cannot afford to allow children to be hijacked by media gurus who see them as ripe for exploitation. The impact of the media on even young children's lives is enormous (particularly the cult of *celebrity*) and schools sometimes fail to recognise this. Schools need to offer a culture in ICT that is viewed by children as rewarding, creative and exciting.

ICT is *the* area of curriculum that will need continuous government funding of a significant kind. Schools need to be able to commit to investment in training, renewal and expansion of hardware and software and on-site, effective technical support. I could argue that ICT needs to be moved centre stage. Should not a curriculum for the twenty-first century be organised more effectively around the new technology? At present, it remains an addition to most subjects – a bolt-on. Imagine if every child had a note-book PC, linked by wireless to the internet. Early acquisition of keyboard skills at Key Stage 1 would certainly need much more emphasis than at present, but teacher and pupil would eventually be able to interact in a way not possible currently.

New Labour, new changes

Writing about change in education is akin to attempting to chart the flow of a river. Somewhere around 1997 would have been an appropriate place to halt my chapter because, by then, teachers were taking ownership of the National Curriculum. They had become more effective at delivering its requirements and were promised a period of consolidation. However, a New Labour government in 1997 declared publicly that education was top of its agenda. It felt that the National Curriculum was still fail-ing children and saw the need for further, immediate change to secure their future. It decided to set national targets in literacy and numeracy – National Curriculum Level 4 in both subjects was the target for all Year 6 children. The government asserted that 85 per cent of all eleven-year-old children would reach Level 4 in English by the summer of 2002. There were to be no more vague aspirations. Instead, schools would set clear school targets linked to national benchmarks and be expected to achieve a year-on-year improvement in standards of attainment until they reached the government's objective.

To ensure they did so, they provided training of a very detailed nature. In fact, there was so much detail that the National Literacy and Numeracy Strategies (DfEE,

1998, 1999) were destined to become the long-term and medium-term plans for most primary schools in English and Mathematics. Few teachers recognised that the material contained in National Literacy and Numeracy documentation was non-statutory and did not constitute National Curriculum English or Mathematics. This was largely due to the way in which the strategies were introduced to schools by local authorities. The aim of the training delivered was to compensate for a perceived lack of subject knowledge on the part of teachers and their apparent inability to teach those skills required in core subjects. In many instances, however, instead of enabling teachers to teach better, the amount of prescriptive detail de-skilled them by not allowing them sufficient time to connect it to their own creativity.

The result of this over-prescription led to teachers, once again, losing control of their own classrooms. They attempted to become carbon copies of those colleagues whose lessons had been video-taped and used as teaching models in DfEE training packs. Many primary schools, faced with Ofsted inspections, adopted the infamous 'wheel' model for the literacy hour. This recommended very specific amounts of time for each element of the literacy lesson – shared reading, group activity, plenary, etc. Some teachers were extremely nervous at going beyond these recommended times. Others felt they had to use a 'big book' in every lesson. Most distressingly, the pace at which teachers felt obliged to go resulted in children rarely finishing a piece of writing. Completion of extended writing had to happen during some other part of the timetable. This had an impact on other subject areas – often the humanities and the arts.

The reader can relate this back to those symptoms that plagued teachers soon after the introduction of the National Curriculum. Experienced professionals were abandoning their own judgement in deference to a script they were afraid to edit to suit their particular situation. The 'one model fits all' philosophy of teaching that appeared to be recommended by the Literacy Strategy (DfEE, 1998) had a more traumatic effect on teachers' morale than did that designed for the Numeracy Strategy (DfEE, 1999). Perhaps the government felt that teachers needed more direction in the teaching of English. Certainly, the government continued for the next decade to send out more and more material to ensure they reached their targets. There was an intervention package for almost every year group from Year 1 to Year 6 (ages 5–11) and beyond. These packs were heavily weighted towards phonics-based materials designed to be used with small groups of children who were deemed to be 'vulnerable' – not likely to achieve a Level 4 at the end of Year 6 (age 11). This raft of intervention strategies by the Labour government, in a sense, was at least recognition that schools needed a differentiated support for those children for whom National Curriculum targets and formal tests were an uphill struggle.

Significantly, LEAs trained teaching assistants to deliver many of the intervention strategies the government devised, signalling a rapid growth in their numbers supporting Key Stage 2 (ages 7–11) and beyond. Government policy on inclusion was the other driving force for schools seeking to appoint well-qualified teaching assistants at all Key Stages.

Special schools and units attached to mainstream schools have always taken in some of the most severely physically and emotionally handicapped children, but a far larger number have remained the responsibility of the mainstream primary school Special

Educational Needs Coordinator (SENCO). In most cases, support takes the form of an individual education plan (IEP) or individual behaviour programme (IBP) – a programme of intervention tailored to an individual child's needs and delivered by the resources available within that child's school. One of the chief resources is a trained teaching assistant. Working in partnership with a class teacher and the school SENCO, he or she can deliver small group sessions or individual tutorials using a different approach and at a different pace from the main lesson. No mainstream school can discharge its responsibilities to those children who have significant difficulties coping with the National Curriculum without trained staff. Schools today are more accepting of children with conditions such as autism and dyspraxia, more informed of the wide spectrum relating to these conditions and capable of supporting them more effectively.

Enough time has passed for us to reflect on some of the results of New Labour's mantra of 'education, education, education'. The spotlight on teaching reading and writing revealed serious weaknesses in some teachers' understanding and their lack of subject knowledge and this helped improve things. Teaching within the core subjects of English and Mathematics, in the most effective schools, has developed a sharpness and purposefulness that was not so apparent before. Some of the most effective results have been the small innovations that have helped teachers communicate concepts more clearly and have helped children to interact with their teachers better, for example the increasing use of visual aids, such as number lines in numeracy, and the creative use of individual whiteboards in literacy and numeracy lessons. The 'learning wall' in classrooms is another – a dynamic, changing display of flip charts, post-its and labels, usually derived from a sequence of lessons, that serves to support, challenge and remind children. Pre-National Curriculum, teacher training had been focused on child development. The focus post-National Curriculum was on pedagogy. A balance has been achieved and knowledge and understanding of teaching methodology was very much enhanced during delivery of the Literacy and Numeracy Strategies.

Unfortunately, in some schools there has been a proliferation of worksheets brought about by a belief that differentiation can only be delivered in this way, resulting in mundane exercises being used to keep children occupied during group activities (frustratingly, these sometimes follow on from a purposeful and interesting introductory session). An overemphasis on literacy and numeracy has driven the arts and humanities (and even technology and science, in some schools) to the sidelines. Schools have to make a conscious effort to find room within their timetable for subjects that were once seamlessly integrated and valued. In many local authorities, the quantitative factor has led to qualitative experiences almost disappearing from view.

If schools are to design their own curricula, teachers must set down a justification for the inclusion of the arts and the humanities in qualitative and quantitative terms. The benefits that accrue from a study of the arts are not easily measured, but they need to be identified, as much to safeguard their inclusion as for any other reason. They tend to be long term and of an individual and personal nature. They can often seem to outsiders to be without immediate material value, but they are about problem solving, self-awareness, creativity, communication, personality development and the ability to create connections between subjects, among other things. There is still a tendency in many primary schools to import a quick fix of creativity after national tests are over, sometimes via external arts providers. However, education in the arts is a process. Children develop skills, insights and understanding over many years until they are able to use them with confidence, and are able to make informed choices.

Onward and upward – the end of the twentieth century and the start of the twenty-first

Every Child Matters

The Green Paper known as *Every Child Matters* (DCSF, 2003) occupied centre stage at the beginning of the new century. It led to the Children Act of 2004 and, ultimately, the renaming of the Department for Education and Skills (DfES) as the Department for Children, Schools and Families (DCSF) in 2007. It led to the creation of Children's Centres. It led to the reorganisation of local authorities with social services and education services grouped under one director.

On paper, *Every Child Matters* is a praiseworthy attempt to secure the rights of each child to a safe and nurturing environment. It establishes a need for early intervention where a child is at risk. It wants those involved in the care of children, at whatever level, to communicate and to ensure no repetition of the mistakes made in the Victoria Climbié case. It aims to unite parents and carers, recognised as having the greatest influence on children as their primary educators, alongside teachers, social workers and those in the medical profession as equal partners. Combining social services and education services under one umbrella has often proved unworkable in practice. Some directors of local authorities have found it difficult to be equally strong in both fields.

Teachers must not ignore the fact that lack of social skills and emotional trauma negatively affect a child's learning. We have known for a long time that learning something new can be either exciting or frightening. All learners are in a position that is not yet secure, ready to consolidate new skills and assimilate new knowledge. The publication of Social and Emotional Aspects of Learning (SEAL) materials in May 2005 recognised this. Vulnerable children find school hard to cope with. Effective learning behaviour is necessary or they will find alternative, possibly disruptive, coping behaviours. Labour recognised this and the Sure Start programme was their attempt to foster good parenting skills among vulnerable families and to help prepare their children for the learning culture of school. Good learning behaviour involves children in developing empathy, mastering social skills to succeed as part of a team, acquiring perseverance and acquiring the ability to accept failure and to benefit from constructive criticism. They have to be able to listen for extended periods and to respond to questions. Children from deprived or damaging backgrounds usually do not find this sort of learning behaviour easy to acquire. Teachers must seek to plan for individual differences and to engage each child.

However, teachers are not social workers, nor should they attempt to take on that role. A teacher has a primary aim – that of enabling each child to learn effectively. The eight principles of the General Teaching Council for England's *Code of Conduct and Practice for Registered Teachers* (GTCE, 2009) makes interesting reading. Pedagogy is not the first principle. The first principle spells out at length that teachers must use their professional judgement to do their best for the children in their care. Teachers must follow child-protection procedures and policies and demonstrate awareness for accessing help and support. In addition, when the need arises, they must raise concerns about the practice of other professionals, if this has a negative impact on children's learning or progress. Interestingly, the second principle has teaching standards assigned to it. Sometimes the school designated SENCO becomes a participant in endless meetings involving partner services. Teachers need robust, informed action from their partners in social services and, where necessary, the medical profession in dealing with situations that are beyond their prime remit, which is that of behaviour management within the classroom environment.

Academies and new free schools – the coalition government of 2010

In the nineteenth century, the church, philanthropic organisations or private enterprise, led by individuals who recognised the importance of educating the wider populace and were in a position to do something about it, created schools. Only at the end of the nineteenth century did the government authorise local councils to levy a rate and use the money to create state schools. This was a cost-effective way to create a universal education system. Local authority control of schools was thus established.

The 2010 coalition government is revisiting old ground, but with a new object in mind. It wants to free schools from local authority control. It sees this as a way of empowering head teachers who want to devise their own curriculum and run their schools to meet the individual needs of their pupils. Providing heads teach the National Curriculum in core subjects and avoid controversial approaches (fundamentalist teaching, possibly), the intention seems to be to allow them to plan their own route, answerable only to central government. In theory, groups of parents or teachers or other 'enthusiasts' from a wide spectrum could apply to establish a free school. It is important to acknowledge that academies run by businesses and various philanthropic organisations already exist, so this is not entirely a new scheme. It is important to note, however, that the launch of this initiative is set against a background of financial cuts in the public sector. At the time of writing, the school building programme is suffering from these, so the new free schools or local academies may exist in a variety of converted buildings rather than the shiny, purpose-built schools envisaged by New Labour. In addition to encouraging new institutions, the government has invited 1,700 existing schools with a record of solid educational attainment to consider becoming academies. The aim is for local academies to seek to reward success. Cynics might say that the middle classes will most likely take on these initiatives and that poorer areas will not benefit, an accusation levelled at Labour's 'Sure Start'. It will be interesting to see what happens.

A child's culture is often the prime factor in determining how successfully he or she can benefit from educational projects. By culture I mean shared ideas and beliefs – a common identity – which shapes the worldview and the aspirations of those who subscribe to it. There are cultures in our society where deferred gratification – working hard and doing without today in order to obtain greater rewards tomorrow – is an alien concept. Yet this philosophy lies at the heart of all educational initiatives. Some schools have to work within a culture where members want rewards now and cannot conceive of much beyond the immediate. Teachers in these schools have to use all their skills, sometimes *guile* would be a more apt term, to keep pupils on board the learning train. The National Curriculum, with the turning wheel of literacy and numeracy at its heart, can be an unattractive model that daunts many children and their families. Free schools could shape their curricula (and their timetables) to attract and sustain pupils for whom a learning culture is an unfamiliar ethos. I said at the outset that pre-National Curriculum schools were very individual, relying on the enthusiasms of their teachers to shape curricula. Having a common entitlement is desirable, but most educationists accept that curricula have become over-prescriptive. It is probably time for individuality to return to the classroom.

Stop press: item one

The Rose Review and a curriculum for the future

In 2009, Jim Rose handed his findings of a review of the primary curriculum to then Secretary of State, Ed Balls. His recommendations were to form the basis of a new, slimmed-down curriculum for primary schools in September 2011. The report examines all aspects of the curriculum, including the continuing discussion centred on the teaching of reading and the debate about phonics teaching. Importantly, it seeks to make the curriculum more manageable and to give teachers more flexibility in its delivery. It maps out six areas of learning and, while placing language, literacy and numeracy at the very centre of things (alongside ICT), it does not frame its recommendations within precise subject boundaries. It recognises that learning knowledge and skills is most effective within subject disciplines, but it wants learners to transfer this to other contexts. It wants teachers to plan for this, to make cross-curricular connections. It wants those child-centred activities encountered by children in the early years to be present further on. It wants Key Stage 1 teachers to become more involved in assessment in the EYFS. It presents heads with an opportunity to tailor a curriculum that works in their schools.

I was prepared for the new government to introduce changes in the fullness of time but was astonished to learn that, immediately upon the advent of a new coalition government on 12 May 2010, all plans to use the findings of the Rose Review to formulate a twenty-first-century curriculum were set aside. There will be further announcements from the new Secretary of State in the near future.

We might draw parallels between the suspension of Rose by this government and the mood following the Plowden Report in 1967. Then, a government that was largely unfamiliar with the holistic nature of a primary classroom and wanted the order that familiar subject disciplines would bring did not consider that report rigorous enough in its findings. It is probable that the present government has more insight, although its line-up of new education ministers reveals them to have almost entirely political backgrounds, one from accountancy but none from education. A glance at its website might cause alarm bells to ring. The coalition's rather subdued website for the Department for Education (DfE) has replaced the colourful DCSF. This recent change might indicate a reaction to what has gone before and a tightening of control, with any school wishing to develop a bespoke curriculum having to become one of Michael Gove's free schools.

Throughout this chapter, the prime mover for educational change has been (and will probably continue to be) central government. Proctor (1990) makes out a case for this not only being perfectly acceptable but actually desirable, since only government is in a position to balance the interests of all the stakeholders in education and ensure no single body has undue influence. From its vantage point, government can reach an accommodation between what children, schools and teachers can do, and what society offers and requires of its members (Thomas, 1990). This is a view I partially endorse. However, we have to rely on governments being completely objective and building on the previous achievements. There is always a danger that governments might change or reverse the work of their predecessors for ideological or political reasons. There have to be checks and balances. The question remains, 'Who is to provide these?'

Stop press: item two

The General Teaching Council for England

It might be that the answer to the question posed above lay with the GTCE, the professional body for teaching in England. However, it is proposed by the coalition government that the GTCE is to be abolished by March 2012. The GTCE states on its website that it aims to promote the highest standards in teaching. Currently, all teachers register with it as the guardian of professional standards through its *Code of Conduct*. Its website is a resource with links to several related sites, one of which, Research for Teachers, supports educational research and gives access to over fifty topics on subjects such as dyslexia, interactive teaching and special educational needs. It is a supporter and initiator of continuous professional development.

The reasons for disbanding the GTCE are unclear, but the move has been supported by teaching unions (Shepherd, 2010). According to Paton (2010) the new education minister, Michael Gove, regards the GTCE as one of several bodies that does not fulfil its expected role, that of improving standards. Apparently it is part of the new government's drive to reduce bureaucracy and give schools greater freedom. It used to alarm me as a college tutor when my PGCE students were not aware of its existence and of its role in their professional lives. The GTCE has appeared unquestioning of government initiatives, although greater scrutiny of its response to previous legislation suggests this is not entirely true. Perhaps it has not presented itself sufficiently strongly to teachers for them to recognise it as being the independent voice of a profession united under one banner.

If we return to the beginning of this chapter, we saw missed opportunities, and teachers unable or unwilling to challenge public perceptions and to have a voice in what was happening in education. It would be heartening to believe that they are in a better position now to influence what is going to happen next. According to the chief executive of the GTCE, Keith Bartley, the public has a greater respect for the profession. This, he believes is due partly to the work of his organisation and its efforts to raise awareness of their role in society. Certainly, the GTCE should have provided a conduit through which the profession could speak, both to government and to the public. Teachers as a group tend to be pragmatists, getting on with the job, assimilating changes and making things work – eventually. I believe they should take time out from that to fight for the retention of the GTCE and for a greater say in whatever changes are to be made to schools of the future.

Conclusion

- Change over which we have control is less threatening.
- Change to which we contribute is better understood.
- Change to which there is general agreement is better implemented and more effective.

Discussion starters

1   How has the National Curriculum changed since it was first introduced in 1988?
2   Are child-centred theories of learning relevant in primary schools today?
3   What subjects would you include in a core curriculum for secondary school children in the twenty-first century?
4   How might the roles of teacher, teaching assistant and other educational support workers change over the next decade?

Reflecting on practice

1   Reflecting on your own education, to what extent have you been aware of the changes occurring that might have affected your learning?
2   In your experience, how does the way in which ICT is organised in educational settings reflect the use of technology in the world beyond?
3   What choices should learners be given in relation to the subjects they study and the way they learn them? What is the feasibility of your ideas and what are the implications for local and national government policies?

Useful resources

www.atl.org.uk: Association of Teachers and Lecturers.
www.education.gov.uk: Department for Education.
www.educationengland.org.uk/index.html: History of Education in England, a personal website established by Derek Gillard.
www.guardian.co.uk/education: *The Guardian* Education section is useful for news.
www.historyofeducation.org.uk: History of Education Society.
www.nasuwt.org.uk/index.htm: National Association of Schoolmasters and Union of Women Teachers.

www.teachers.org.uk: National Union of Teachers.

www.telegraph.co.uk/education: *The Telegraph* Education section for news features about current issues in education.

www.tes.co.uk: *The Times Educational Supplement* – a paper devoted to all phases of education.

References

Alexander, R., Rose, J. and Woodhead, C. (1992) *Curriculum Organisation and Classroom Practice in Primary Schools*, London: Department of Education and Science.

Brooks, R. (1991) *Contemporary Debates in Education: An historical perspective*, New York: Longman.

Cockcroft, W.H. (1982) *Mathematics Counts*, London: HMSO.

Cook, K. (1972) 'The garden of Plowden', in Boyson, R. (ed.) *Education: Threatened standards*, London: Churchill Press.

Coopers and Lybrand (1988) *L.M.S. Report to the Department of Education and Science*, London: HMSO.

Cunningham, P. (1990) 'Primary education – early perspectives', in Proctor, N. (ed.) *The Aims of Primary Education and the National Curriculum*, Bristol: Falmer Press.

Dearing, R. (1994) *The National Curriculum and its Assessment: Final report*, London: School Curriculum and Assessment Authority.

Department for Children, Schools and Families (DCSF) (2003) *Every Child Matters*, London: DCSF.

Department for Children, Schools and Families (DCSF) (2005) *Social and Emotional Aspects of Learning (SEAL): Improving behaviour, improving learning*, Nottingham: DCSF.

Department for Education and Employment (DfEE) (1998) *The National Literacy Strategy: Framework for teaching English YR to Y6*, London: DfEE.

Department for Education and Employment (DfEE) (1999) *The National Numeracy Strategy: Framework for teaching mathematics Years R to 6*, Cambridge: Cambridge University Press.

Department for Education and Employment (DfEE)/Qualifications and Curriculum Authority (QCA) (2000) *Curriculum Guidance for the Foundation Stage*, London: HMSO.

Department of Education and Science (DES) (1967) *Children and their Primary Schools: A report of the Central Advisory Council* (The Plowden Report), London: HMSO.

General Teaching Council for England (GTCE) (2009) *Code of Conduct and Practice for Registered Teachers*. Available online at www.gtce.org.uk/teachers/thecode (accessed 7 February 2011).

Paton, G. (2010) 'General Teaching Council "to be scrapped"', *The Daily Telegraph*, 2 June. Available online at www.telegraph.co.uk/education/educationnews/7798333/General-Teaching-Council-to-be-scrapped.html (accessed 10 February 2011).

Proctor, N. (ed.) (1990) *The Aims of Primary Education and the National Curriculum*, Bristol: Falmer Press.

Rose, J. (2009) *Independent Review of the Primary Curriculum: Final report*, London: DCSF.

Shepherd, J. (2010) 'Gove to abolish General Teaching Council for England', 2 June. Available online at www.guardian.co.uk/education/2010/jun/02/general-teaching-council-england-abolished (accessed 10 February 2011).

Task Group on Assessment and Testing (TGAT) (1987) *National Curriculum: Report of the Task Group on Assessment and Testing*, London: DES.

Thomas, N. (1990) *Primary Education from Plowden to the 1990s*, Bristol: Falmer Press.

3

Learning and Teaching: What's Your Style?

Pat Hughes

My values and beliefs about learning styles

Steven Stahl (1999) wrote that he met with more disagreement about learning styles than anything else. The major dichotomy was between practitioners and researchers: the former being positive that there were different styles of learning and that they needed to heed this, and the latter suggesting that there were no good scientific data to support this claim. In this chapter, we try to step back and look objectively at some of the evidence about teaching and learning and link this with work on learning styles.

The evidence is from a number of sources. It involves examining our own learning as well as providing a brief history on learning and teaching theories. Historical data are useful as a means of predicting what may happen due to the introduction of specific policies and practices. Most of all they remind us to be critical of any theory and data linked with the theory.

Educational politics are also involved and this is often a very simple matter of different educational spokespersons making statements based on little more than the current educational fad within their own political party. Most recently, this resulted in a large-scale 'experiment' in the English primary state sector involving the teaching and learning of literacy and numeracy. Specific beliefs about effective learning and teaching underpinned the 'National Strategies', reinforced by central government for almost ten years. Yearly tests and assessments measured their success with results published to assure accountability. Both the tests and the practices advocated were strongly criticised by many educationalists. Unfortunately, no large-scale, independent piece of data collection evaluated the whole experiment and such politically driven initiatives will continue to influence the English education system.

Introduction

The terms 'learning' and 'teaching' imply two separate activities. The term 'lifelong learning' challenges this separateness. We are all learners, just as we are all teachers. Some people may have a job with the title of teacher but, in their daily work, they are also learning. Learners also teach – themselves and others. 'Teaching' covers a number of activities – presenting, authenticating, directing, leading, training, facilitating, developing, mentoring and coaching (www.alite.co.uk). The stereotyped image of teaching tends to concentrate on presenting, but this traditional view of teaching has been challenged, has been found wanting and is being replaced by a greater variety of teaching strategies than ever before. Personalised learning, as outlined by the Department for Children, Schools and Families (DCSF) in 2008, is part of this ongoing revolution and is linked with transformational learning. The political concepts of exactly what is meant by personalised learning are muddled and confusing; and politicians are determined not to use the term 'child-centred learning' (DES, 1967). Yet government department guidance makes it clear that personalised learning should be possible in a class of 30 and should involve teaching tailored to pupils' needs. Readers need to make their own judgement on the practicality of this, based on both their reading and experience in schools. This section aims to look at some of the theories about the ways children learn, and identify useful sources of information for further study. We will examine some of the research into how people learn and the obvious implications for how to support and develop this learning.

Starting points: ourselves as learners

What sort of learner are you? It is tempting to think that we all learn in the same way. Indeed, this *was* the assumption behind the Department for Education and Employment frameworks for literacy (DfEE, 1998) and primary mathematics (DfEE, 1999) in England. They identified core content for each year and term of a child's primary school career and advised on lesson structure and teaching strategies. This contrasted with the Australian approach to a literacy programme known as First Steps (McDonald, 1999). The designers based this on observation of children learning and identified effective teaching strategies to move them forward. In the guidelines that followed, non-age-related learning continuums in reading, writing and spelling developed. In theory, the recent move in England towards teaching led by the 2008 launch of the Assessment for Learning (AfL) Strategy and, in 2009, Assessing Pupil Progress (APP), discussed further by Christine Bold in Chapter 11, should reinforce a more personalised and holistic approach to learning. Indeed something that resembles the Australian First Steps approach.

Much of the research over the past century makes it clear that we learn in different ways and at different speeds. For example, you may be reading this, sitting in a comfortable chair with the television on. Someone else might need to sit in silence at a table or desk. Another person might prefer to listen to someone else reading it aloud. You may or may not make notes, create a learning map or devise a diagram to help you remember what you have read. The growth in digital technology to provide interactive media support for learners indicates that there is a growing market for different types of presentation. The Barsch learning style audit in Table 3.1 provides a useful and easy way to determine your own learning style (DfES, 2001). It is important to remember that such simplistic tests are heavily criticised and you should be able to see huge loopholes in the thinking behind their construction. When completing the audit, remember that no particular style is best and each style makes its own demands on the learning and teaching environment. There are also a growing

TABLE 3.1 Barsch Learning Styles Audit

Place a check on the appropriate line after each statement. Then score, following the directions after the questionnaire.

STATEMENT: I . . .	OFTEN	SOME-TIMES	SELDOM
1 Can remember more about a subject through listening rather than reading			
2 Follow written directions better than oral instructions			
3 Like to write things down or take notes for visual review			
4 Bear down extremely hard with pen or pencil when writing			
5 Require explanations of diagrams, graphs or visual directions			
6 Enjoy working with tools			
7 Am skilful and enjoy developing and making graphs and charts			
8 Can tell if sounds match when presented with pairs of sounds			
9 Remember best by writing things down several times			
10 Can understand and follow directions using maps			
11 Do better at academic subjects by listening to lectures and tapes			
12 Play with coins and keys in pockets			
13 Learn to spell better by repeating the letters out loud than by writing the word on paper			
14 Can better understand a news article by reading about it in the paper than by listening to the radio			
15 Chew gum, smoke or snack during studies			
16 Feel the best way to remember is to picture it in my head			
17 Learn spelling by 'finger spelling' the words			
18 Would rather listen to a good lecture or speech than read about the same material in a textbook			
19 Am good at working out and solving jigsaw puzzles and mazes			
20 Grip objects in my hand during learning periods			
21 Prefer listening to the news on the radio than reading about it in a newspaper			
22 Obtain information on an interesting subject by reading relevant materials			
23 Feel very comfortable touching others, hugging, handshaking etc.			
24 Follow oral directions better than written ones			

VISUAL – Number of points	AUDITORY – Number of points	TACTILE – Number of points
2	1	4
3	5	6
7	8	9
10	11	12
14	13	15
16	18	17
19	21	20
22	24	23
Total VPS (Visual preference)	Total APS (Auditory preference)	Total TPS (Tactile/Kinaesthetic preference)

Scoring procedures:
Place the point value on the line next to its corresponding item number.
Often = 5 points; Sometimes = 3 points; Seldom = 1 point
Next, sum the values to arrive at your preference scores under each heading.

number of such audits for children and they should be used with great care, since some argue that there is no such thing as a learning style and, if it does exist, others ask how it is measured (Markham, 2004). Traditional psychology texts provide plenty of research on learning and indicate clearly that no single answer exists.

Therefore, this audit should be used lightly and discussed with others; make comparisons between different individuals, but also consider the variety of individual learning.

Historical overview

There is much literature on how people learn, covering cognition, learning, development, culture and the brain. The influence of the nature of the subject is sometimes explicit, for example Blyth (1990) considers whether five year olds are too young to learn history. More recently, subject influence is implicit in much of the material that has come from central government for the use of schools.

In the beginning

In Ancient Greece, philosophers adopted a question and answer approach, which has remained the traditional teaching structure for many years. Greek philosophers and teachers such as Plato and Socrates (Cahn, 2009) would ask questions for which they would teach their followers the answers. Their followers would in turn transmit their learnt knowledge in the same way. The basis of much formal education is this presentation approach, with a question and answer technique employed to assess learning.

Early years

It was not until the nineteenth and early twentieth centuries that people questioned the Socratic method of learning. In the area of early years' education, formal presentations were particularly inappropriate. Educators such as Froebel, Montessori and Steiner looked more closely at the children themselves (Bruce, 1987). Such educators and their followers no longer saw children as blank slates. They did not consider that failures in learning are the child's fault, but examined other relevant factors. They viewed learning as holistic, rather than separated out into subjects. These educators accommodated other factors, such as differences between learners in terms of their motivation, self-discipline and individual development. They observed children as they learnt, looking at implications for changing designs of formal learning environments such as schools. A visit to any good nursery today shows how the learning environment has changed from the traditional question and answer approach to stimulating and exciting indoor and outdoor play provision. Informed and talented adults support and extend learning. They are also prepared to continue to observe and learn from their children.

Children's learning: the traditional approach

Until quite recently, the work and ideas of three people – Jean Piaget, Lev Vygotsky and Jerome Bruner (Whitebread, 2002) – have influenced most of the thinking about children's learning in schools. Many educational texts and websites refer to their work, for example Alfrey and Durell (2003) and Hughes (2008). I like the websites because they provide photographs, hyperlinks on difficult terminology and, in some cases, spoken extracts. As we have seen from the learning styles audit above, this is more to do with my preferred learning style than a statement about which is the most effective method of further informing yourself about their work. Here is a brief summary:

- *Piaget* alerted educators to the child's active role in their own learning and the importance of mental activity. He emphasised the importance of the child interacting with the physical environment and produced a series of age-related stages through which children progressed in an apparently linear fashion.

- *Vygotsky* explored the role of language and social interaction in learning. He argued for a much more central role for the adult that could extend children's 'level of actual development' into the 'zone of proximal development' (ZPD). Figure 3.1 provides a visual explanation of this.

- *Bruner* looked at the relationship between language and thought and the need to provide children with a relevant and appropriate vocabulary so that they could use this in thinking, talking and exploring ideas. He also coined the phrase 'the spiral curriculum' and demonstrated the importance of revisiting topics at different levels of understanding. This translates very easily into school curriculum terms, when children learn about a specific thing at one stage, for example playing with blocks and learning about the way in which cubes are different from cuboids when building a tower. Later in their school careers, they learn how to make nets of different types of cuboids and cubes and discover additional different properties such as edge sizes. Bruner also used the term 'scaffolding' as a metaphor for how adults should encourage and extend the child's search for understanding (Whitebread, 2002).

The work of all three provided different views on learning that had an impact on teaching at all levels. Piaget's developmental approach suggested that teachers needed to be facilitators and organisers. Vygotsky and Bruner both gave more importance to

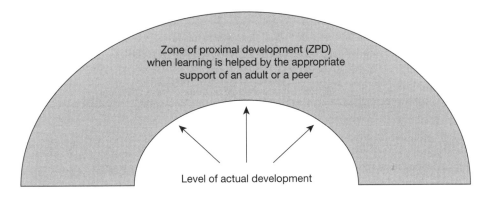

FIGURE 3.1 Vygotsky's zone of proximal development

language and the adult (and peer) role in teaching. Bruner's 'scaffolding' metaphor is the rationale behind the guided reading and writing parts of the Literacy Strategy and the 'thinking aloud' element of the mathematics lesson.

Other factors influencing children's learning

Once compulsory education came into force in the UK in the nineteenth century, it became obvious that other factors influenced children's ability to learn. Maslow's hierarchy of human needs, shown in Figure 3.2, summarises these very effectively. The most effective learners are those at the top of the pyramid. Clearly, if you are starving, that is, at the base of the pyramid, you are unlikely to be able to think of more than how you can fulfil your basic need for food. This does not make you an effective learner in a formal situation.

When looking at the pyramid, you might like to think of two different children, or indeed adults, whose particular needs at specific levels hinder effective learning. This initial hierarchy is from over sixty years ago, but its importance in identifying basic physical and emotional needs remains. Indeed, much of the work on emotional literacy/intelligence stems from Maslow's initial identification of basic needs (Hughes, 2008). The growth of breakfast clubs in schools, the role of learning mentors and

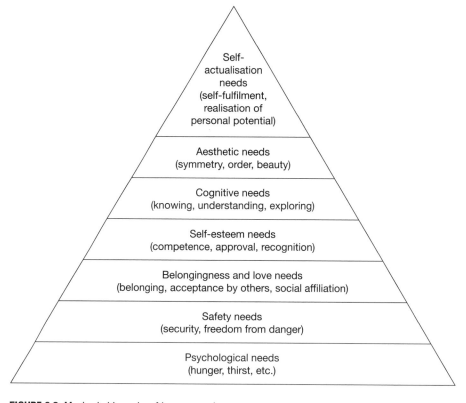

FIGURE 3.2 Maslow's hierarchy of human needs

policies on bullying and anti-racism demonstrate the practical ways in which many educational institutions are addressing some of these needs for specific children (Hughes, 2010). The Social and Emotional Aspects of Learning (SEAL) programme was an overall pastoral care programme designed to provide a framework for helping children to understand more about their emotional as well as physical needs.

The approach has its critics. Ecclestone and Hayes (2008) and Furedi (2009) raise important issues about the growth of an all-pervading therapy culture in our schools. They explore whether the emphasis on feelings ignores the more important needs of children to access formal education and disempowers those most needing to gain qualifications. Certainly, the overemphasis on *self-esteem* leaves many questions unanswered, such as who defines whether a child has poor self-esteem. A non-academic achiever may have very high self-esteem within their peer culture and be unconcerned about *doing well* in a conventional sense.

Teaching styles

There is less research on teaching styles in the UK than in the USA. The question and answer approach has dominated teaching in educational institutions. As long ago as 1976, Bennett and his research colleagues set out thirteen characteristics of what they termed *progressive teachers* and contrasted these with *traditional teachers.* For example, the progressive teacher would act as a guide to educational experiences, where the traditional teacher was a transmitter of knowledge. Pupils had an active role in the progressive teacher's classroom, whereas they had a passive one in the traditional teacher's classroom. The most controversial finding was that children were more successful with a traditional teacher. This seemed to conflict with other research evidence about children's learning, which required interaction such as Bruner described, but it did fit in with the political agenda at the time. Galton (1980) actually went into primary and secondary classrooms, while Bennett had simply gathered his data through questionnaires. Galton found much less progressive teaching than the government had feared and the media had announced! Some years later, Bennett revisited his initial data and came forward with different conclusions. However, by this time the damage had been done and his initial findings continued to be used as a rationale for traditional teaching, which completely ignored children's different learning needs and styles.

Although there were several other studies on teaching styles in the UK, later studies supported a political agenda of more centralised control, both in the classroom and from the centre. For example, Alexander *et al.* (1992), in their documentary enquiry on primary education – called the 'Three Wise Men' due to its publication at Christmas – reaffirmed the need for more 'traditional' presentation-type teaching. In parallel, increased centralised control over the contents of the curriculum and teaching methods arose, as discussed by Alan Barrow in Chapter 2. In the mid-2000s Alexander was asked to look at primary education again and gathered together an impressive array of research literature that included work on both teaching and learning. *Children, Their World, Their Education: Final report and recommendations of the Cambridge Primary Review* (Alexander, 2009) was the most comprehensive enquiry into English primary education since the 1967 Plowden Report. What it shows most clearly is not that it has become easier to understand how learning takes place, but how many other variables need to be taken into account.

Summary

This historical review has noted the work of a few key *traditional* researchers in the area of children's learning, and has suggested how their findings fit in with a particular view of teaching. It has very briefly reviewed two major studies into teaching styles in the UK that were carried out at a key period (the 1970s and 1980s), when central government (both Labour and Conservative) determined to take a tighter hold on education in order to make educational institutions more accountable for the money spent. Later, both the Literacy and Numeracy Strategies for primary and secondary schools gave specific recommendations to increase the use of a whole-class interactive teaching style. Only later did *Curriculum Guidance for the Foundation Stage* (DfEE/QCA, 2000) release Reception classes from the literacy hour and daily mathematics lesson, where so much whole-class teaching is inappropriate. Towards the end of the first decade of the new millennium it was clear, yet again, that the answers to how to provide more effective learning and teaching seemed no easier than they had in the past. It also became more obvious that political expediency was more important than honestly evaluating the impact and outcomes of new initiatives.

The UK is not alone here as we are living at a time when global changes are forcing all governments to re-examine their approaches to education at all levels. There is a genuine understanding by most key UK policy makers that we all need educating, whatever our age, to live and cope with such a rapidly changing world. The 'learning revolution' – a term used by Dryden and Vos (2005) – is here, fuelled by international changes in communication and revolutionary changes in identifying how people learn. It also challenges four myths of learning that:

■ School is the best place to learn.

■ Intelligence is fixed.

■ Teaching produces learning.

■ We all learn in the same way.

The learning revolution

Dryden and Vos (2005) claim that everyone now has to become a self-acting manager of one's own future. However, much education still resembles the declining industrial method of production: a standard assembly-line curriculum divided into subjects, taught in units, arranged by grade, and controlled by standardised tests, that no longer reflects the world we live in. Dryden and Vos have written a book you will either love or hate. There is no modesty in its blurb; it promises to be a catalyst to change the way you think, live, learn, work, teach and act. Most importantly, it is great fun to read. This is an inspirational text, rather than an academic one, and summarises research in a popular format from a wide range of disciplines. It reports how knowledge is already bringing about revolutionary breakthroughs in learning, education, business and families. It presents current findings crisply and clearly and the layout helps easy reading. You may disagree with some of the evaluations and find the hype off-putting, but it is a book worth reading, either as a starting point to challenging conventional views about learning or as a popular review to some of the work being done on translating new ideas about teaching and learning into practice round the world. Already many of the findings in their work are outdated – for example, the contrast between learning that takes place in the left/right sides of the brain. Yet this is still presented as fact in many education texts.

There has been a revolution in the study of the mind over the past fifty years, resulting in amazing findings about the power of the brain. So far, most of the practical outcomes of this are for business and personal growth. In the past ten years, however, the implications of these new ideas have been developed and adapted for education. In both the United States and the UK, much of this work is through commercially based professional development organisations (alite.co.uk, for example). Their initial success with practitioners, pupils and students led to a change in many local authorities, which recognised the need to vary teaching styles and encourage creativity in both learning and teaching. This was deeply embedded in the Building Schools for the Future (BSF) programme, where an ambitious building programme for schools in England was closely linked to designs to transform learning (Hickton Madeley Architects, 2008; Hughes, 2010).

A new science of learning

On a more academic note, a new science of learning continues to emerge that has important implications for education. This new theory of learning leads to a very different approach to the design of curriculum, teaching and assessment. It involves a growth of interdisciplinary inquiries and new kinds of scientific collaborations. This integrated approach to research has helped make the path from empirical research to educational practice more visible. In particular, neuroscience is beginning to show how learning changes the physical structure of the brain. This starts at conception and is heavily concentrated in the first four years of life. However, for those of us who are a little older than this, neuroscience provides some useful findings about ways in which the brain fixes itself. There are also strategies to keep the brain sharp as we age.

The American National Research Council (NRC, 2000) summarised the work of two of its committees, linking the findings of research on the science of learning to actual practice in the classroom. They consider the latest research in the field and explore the development of a variety of research approaches and techniques and ways in which evidence from many different branches of science is beginning to converge. Here is their summary:

- Research from cognitive psychology has increased understanding of the nature of competent performance and the principles of knowledge organization that underlie people's abilities to solve problems in a wide variety of areas, including mathematics, science, literature, social studies and history.

- Developmental researchers have shown that young children understand a great deal about basic principles of biology and physical causality, about number, narrative, and personal intent, and that these capabilities make it possible to create innovative curricula that introduce important concepts for advanced reasoning at early ages.

■ Research on learning and transfer has uncovered important principles for structured learning experiences that enable people to use what they have learnt in new settings.

■ Work in social psychology, cognitive psychology and anthropology is making clear that all learning takes place in settings that have particular sets of cultural and social norms and expectations and that these settings influence learning and transfer in powerful ways.

■ Neuroscience is beginning to provide evidence for many principles of learning that have emerged from laboratory research, and it is showing how learning changes the physical structure of the brain and, with it, the functional organization of the brain.

■ Collaborative studies of the design and evaluation of learning environments among cognitive and developmental psychologists and educators are yielding to new knowledge about the nature of learning and teaching as it takes place in a variety of settings. In addition, researchers are discovering ways to learn from the 'wisdom of practice' that comes from successful teachers who can share their expertise.

■ Emerging technologies are leading to the development of many new opportunities to guide and enhance learning that were unimagined even a few years ago.

(NRC, 2000: 4)

Blakemore and Firth (2007), in *The Learning Brain: Lessons for education*, provide some excellent practical examples of this and their book is an excellent starting point for well-referenced research findings.

Research findings, however effectively based in practice, are often given little opportunity for wide dissemination. And those working in schools have little time or opportunity to test out new findings about learning. The move towards having a Masters level teaching profession may help to empower practitioners to be more critical about the heavy political influence in some research findings, and to be bolder about trying out ideas found in such handy publications as Greenhalgh's (2002) book on 'mind friendly learning'. Many research findings have little opportunity to influence education, particularly since the 1998 introduction of the National Strategies from Key Stage 1 to Key Stage 3, which relied on a delivery input. This teaching style, particularly the Literacy lesson format, has permeated into other curriculum areas as well at Key Stages 1 and 2; for example, history and geography lessons starting with the 'Big Book' for information, followed up with five ability groups doing short-term tasks.

The National Literacy and Numeracy Strategies from Key Stage 1–3 were supported by a vast quantity of central government and commercial publications that set out generic planning for these two subjects. This planning included very detailed lesson plans telling the teacher what to do, say and practise. Similarly, central government standards outlined for the some Foundation degrees, Initial Teacher Training (ITT) degrees and the Masters in Teaching and Learning (MTL) are similar, in that they encourage writers of texts – such as this – to write for specific standards. The danger is that the standard then has a defined and fixed content, which does not take account of the learning needs of individuals studying the course, the placement situations in which they work and changes in technology that may have occurred in the lapse of time between writing and reading. This is to some extent inevitable, but the important task of both the reader and writer is to acknowledge that this is taking place.

Research into the brain and improving learning

According to Kotulak (1996, in Dryden and Vos, 2005), anything you learnt two years ago is old information. Neuroscience is exploding. The pace of research related to the brain is phenomenal. Methodological advances have been made in the field of developmental psychology and much of what is known about how the mind works comes from the study of how infants learn. For example, it is now possible to use non-nutritive sucking as a means of showing that infants from five to twelve weeks of age can learn how to control a projector lens, so that the images shown come into focus more clearly (NRC, 2000). Clearly, new knowledge about the working of the brain has important implications for learning and teaching if we now have the techniques to see into the learning process of a five-week-old baby.

Dryden and Vos (2005) provide a quick overview of the potential for learning. Your 'magic brain' as they dub it:

- has a trillion brain cells;
- can grow up to 20,000 branches;
- has four distinct brains in one;
- has two sides that work together;
- runs a 'telephone exchange' that shuttles millions of messages a second between the left and right sides;
- has many different intelligence centres;
- operates on at least four separate wavelengths;
- controls a transmission system that flashes chemical-electrical messages instantly;
- holds the key to your own personal revolution.

Popular authors such as Tony Buzan use such findings to provide learning self-help manuals for us all. Buzan and Buzan (2003) have produced many books, audio cassettes and videos on the brain and how to improve memory, Mind Map®, develop thinking and creativity, and speed read. These are easy-to-follow 'handbooks' about improving the working capability of your own brain. They have produced several for children. Like Dryden and Vos, Buzan and Buzan provide a useful reminder that finding out more about our own learning style informs our knowledge about learning and teaching.

The Educational Kinaesthetics movement looks directly at strategies using simple movements to integrate the whole brain, the senses and the body to prepare people with the physical skills they need to learn more effectively. It originally came from the United States and was the result of research into learning and brain function by Paul Dennison (Dennison and Dennison, 1986; see also www.braingym.org). Originally, its aim was to help adults and children with learning difficulties such as dyslexia, dyspraxia and attention deficit hyperactivity disorder (ADHD). It has now developed into a more generic action programme to improve everyone's life. The benefit claims are extensive and the Healthy Schools programme in the UK made use of them. The Brain Gym® movements are claimed to help with:

- academic skills – reading, writing, spelling and maths;
- memory, concentration and focus;
- physical coordination and balance;
- communication skills and language development;
- self-development and personal stress management;
- the achievement of goals, both professional and personal.

The Brain Gym philosophy has been used very successfully in many UK schools and practical strategies such as drinking water in classrooms and 'brain breaks' are now quite common. Smith and Call (1999) provide several examples of this and link it closely to their accelerated learning approach. Ginns (2002) provides examples for secondary pupils.

As Brain Gym became more popular in the UK, its claims were scrutinised. Jeremy Paxman, in a *Newsnight* interview with Paul Dennison (2008; available on www. youtube.com), highlighted some of the more extreme claims made for it. This illustrates the dangers of commercial institutions making claims that cannot be substantiated. This interview should not take away some of the very obvious advantages of some of the practices involved, including using physical exercises to take a break from formal learning.

Multiple intelligences

Howard Gardner (1983) devised a non-scientific theory of learning, based on the idea of multiple intelligences. He has now moved on from his original thinking: he has extended his theory of seven intelligences (linguistic, mathematical, visual, musical, bodily, interpersonal, intrapersonal) to nine intelligences, including 'naturalistic' and 'existential', and has speculated on including another two: 'spiritual' and 'moral'. Whatever Gardner may now feel, the idea of multiple intelligences has certainly taken on a life of its own, although there is very little scientific evidence for it. Measurements of different types of intelligences, however attractive, have failed to produce valid results.

Gardner's work was linked with other more simplistic work on learning styles. For example, the DfES (2002) used his visual, auditory and kinaesthetic theories of particular intelligences to suggest that they were linked with visual, auditory and kinaesthetic (VAK) learning styles. Gardner identified specific centres of the brain, and the VAK process claims to be a summary of the six main pathways to the brain through which we learn:

- by what we see;
- by what we hear;
- by what we taste;
- by what we touch;
- by what we smell;
- by what we do.

The senses of taste, touch and smell link with the practical activity of 'doing' to make the preferred kinaesthetic learning style. When looking at all these ideas, it is important to remember that, just because you *may be able to* identify yourself as having a specific learning style, this does not mean that all your learning must take place in this way. Translated into 'teaching' styles, it means that teachers need to take account of and value different learning styles, while working to extend the opportunities that we all have to develop other styles.

Accelerated learning/mind-based learning/brain-friendly learning

It is possible to use all of these terms to describe the practical strategies for learning and teaching that some research developments have indicated are necessary. Rose (1985) originally coined the term 'accelerated learning'. Initially, the American management training system used the concept but, more recently, it has come as an educational package into the UK education system. This is largely through the work of Alistair Smith, the organisation Alite and publishing houses such as Network Educational Press and Continuum. The Alite website (www.alite.co.uk) contains useful readings, case studies, bulletin boards and courses. It suggests an accelerated learning cycle to aid learning, which teachers and learners share. Strategies include:

- work on physiology and learning linked to Maslow's work on a 'hierarchy of needs'; these strategies acknowledge that learners have to be in a good physical state for learning, which includes learners having:
  - constant access to water to avoid dehydration, which can lead to drowsiness, inattention and poor learning;
  - a good diet;
  - a room to work in with the appropriate temperature;
  - physical breaks, also known as 'brain breaks';
- teaching specific skills such as listening, paying attention, concentrating, good sitting, etc.;
- providing a good, secure and purposeful working environment.

The accelerated learning strategies also draw on Goleman's (1996) work. Goleman refines what it 'takes to be smart'. In the UK, the initial learning mentor training encouraged such strategies and they became embedded in the SEAL philosophy, to give support to 'underachieving' and 'non-productive' pupils (DCSF, 2005). Many schools use the term 'emotional literacy' to describe a 'good, secure and purposeful learning/working environment'. Again, it is worth reminding ourselves that some people question this approach as 'dumbing down' education to a form of therapy and failing to give children/pupils the type of formal instruction to which they are entitled.

The twenty-first-century learning society

Dryden and Vos (2001: 42) cite Negroponte (1995, *Being Digital*): 'You can expect to have on your wrist tomorrow what you have on your desk today, what filled a room yesterday.' This is the age of instant communication, which is changing the shape of the future. Educational institutions are already changing to accommodate this, but they are changing slowly. One of the main features of the learning revolution is that the internet can change your life and your learning because it is global, personal, interactive, low cost and forever growing and changing. The personal computer (PC) initially and now the mobile phone have revolutionised individual learning and provided access to electronic, interactive, multimedia software, which, coupled with the internet, can provide almost unlimited potential for learning and education.

It is always dangerous to predict what sort of technological changes will take place and how they might significantly alter learning and teaching. We might ask how the massive growth of texting and e-mail should alter what is taught and how it should be taught. After all, we no longer teach children to write with quill or fountain pens, so how do we adapt and respond to writing needs in the future? We can question how the very restrictive access to the internet available in schools holds back transformational learning and teaching. The answers to such questions are unpredictable. What we can be sure of is that such changes will take place and all of us will need to learn to swim with the tide, or otherwise drown.

Conclusion

This chapter reviewed some of the work that has been done on how people, particularly children, learn and how all of us, including babies, are both learners and teachers. It points out that we are now in the challenging position of being part of a learning revolution, which is changing nearly all our assumptions about effective learning and teaching. Effective teaching teams recognise this and seek to change their practice. This chapter has identified texts, individuals and groups who have tried and tested different strategies to support those teams in supporting learning. Many of these make inspirational reading and will help us all face the challenges ahead.

Discussion starters

1 What factors make it easier for us to learn?
2 How are nurseries/schools/colleges/universities changing to encourage a more positive working environment for their pupils/students?
3 How is technology changing current practice in teaching and learning?

Reflecting on practice

1   Identify five ways in which you have learnt something from reading this chapter, or by using further reading. Compare your five points with those of a colleague and discuss how they can help you develop your practical skills in an educational setting.
2   What is your favourite approach to learning? Why? How can you improve your learning strategies?

Useful resources

Websites

www.alite.co.uk: Alite website.
www.braingym.org: website giving an overview of Paul Dennison's work.
www.mindfriendlylearning.co.uk/whatpeoplesay.asp: a selection of comments and feedback from teachers, head teachers and local authorities on the Mind Friendly Learning website.
www.Mind-Map.com: Buzan Centre for details of books, software, audio and videotapes.
www.nwlink.com/~donclark/hrd/styles.html: an online lecture by Don Clark on learning styles.
www.skeptic.com: the Skeptic's Dictionary website provides some fascinating descriptions and insights into specific theories.
www.youtube.com: various video clips related to brain gym.

Other resources

Teaching and Learning Research Programme (TLRP) (2007) *Neuroscience and Education*, London: Institute of Education. Available online at the www.tlrp.org/pub/documents/Neuroscience%20Commentary%20FINAL.pdf (accessed 10 February 2011).

Audio cassettes

Goleman, D. (1996) *Emotional Intelligence*, Thorsons Audio.
Tracy, B. with Rose, C. (1995) *Accelerated Learning Techniques*, Simon & Schuster Audio.

References

Alexander, R. (ed.) (2009) *Children, Their World, Their Education: Final report and recommendations of the Cambridge Primary Review*, London: Routledge.
Alexander, R., Rose, J. and Woodhead, C. (1992) *Curriculum Organisation and Classroom Practice in Primary Schools*, London: Department of Education and Science.
Alfrey, M.A. and Durell, J.A. (2003) 'How children think and learn', in Alfrey, C. (ed.) *Understanding Children's Learning: A text for teaching assistants*, London: David Fulton.
Bennett, N. (1976) *Teaching Styles and Pupil Progress*, London: Open Books.
Blakemore, S. and Firth, U. (2007) *The Learning Brain: Lessons for education*, Oxford: Blackwell.
Blyth, J. (1990) *History in Primary Schools*, Milton Keynes: Open University Press.
Bruce, T. (1987) *Early Childhood Education*, London: Hodder & Stoughton.
Buzan, T. and Buzan, B. (2003) *The Mind Map® Book*, London: BBC Worldwide.
Cahn, S. (ed.) (2009) *The Philosophy of Education: The essential texts*, London: Routledge.

Dennison, P. and Dennison, G. (1986) *Brain Gym*, London: Body Balance Books. Available online at www.braingym.org (accessed 31 August 2010).

Department for Children, Schools and Families (DCSF) (2005) *Social and Emotional Aspects of Learning (SEAL): Improving behaviour, improving learning*, Nottingham: DCSF.

Department for Children, Schools and Families (DCSF) (2008) *Personalised Learning: A practical guide*, London: DCSF.

Department for Education and Employment (DfEE) (1998) *The National Literacy Strategy: Framework for teaching English YR to Y6*, London: DfEE.

Department for Education and Employment (DfEE) (1999) *The National Numeracy Strategy: Framework for Teaching Mathematics Years R to 6*, Cambridge: Cambridge University Press.

Department for Education and Employment (DfEE)/Qualifications and Curriculum Authority (QCA) (2000) *Curriculum Guidance for the Foundation Stage*, London: HMSO.

Department for Education and Skills (DfES) (2001) *Mentor Training Modules 1–4*, Liverpool: DfES and Liverpool Excellence Partnership.

Department for Education and Skills (DfES) (2002) *Key Stage 3 National Strategy Learning Styles and Writing* series of guidance documents for different subject areas. Available online at www.standards.dfes.gov.uk/keystage3/strands/publications (accessed September 2003; no longer available).

Department of Education and Science (DES) (1967) *Children and their Primary Schools: A report of the Central Advisory Council* (The Plowden Report), London: HMSO.

Dryden, G. and Vos, J. (2001) *The Learning Revolution*, Stafford: Network Educational Press. Partly available online (free) at www.thelearningweb.net (accessed 12 February 2011).

Dryden, G. and Vos, J. (2005) *The New Learning Revolution: How Britain can lead the world in learning, education, and schooling*, Stafford: Network Educational Press.

Ecclestone, K. and Hayes, D. (2008) *The Dangerous Rise of Therapeutic Education*, London: Routledge.

Furedi, F. (2009) *Wasted: Why education isn't educating*, London: Continuum International Publishing Group.

Galton, M. (1980) *Inside Primary Classrooms*, London: Routledge & Kegan Paul.

Gardner, H. (1983) *Frames of Mind: The theory of multiple intelligences*, Oxford: Heinemann.

Ginns, P. (2002) *The Teacher's Toolkit: Raise classroom achievement with strategies for every learner*, London: Crown House Publishing.

Goleman, D. (1996) *Emotional Intelligence*, London: Bloomsbury.

Greenhalgh, P. (2002) *Reaching Out to All Learners: A mind friendly framework for learning*, Stafford: Network Educational Press.

Hickton Madeley Architects (2008) Exemplar Studies for the Provision of New Build Primary Schools, Telford.

Hughes, P. (2008) *Principles of Primary Education Study Guide*, London: Routledge.

Hughes, P. (2010) *Breaking Barriers to Learning in Primary Schools: An integrated approach to children's services*, London: Routledge.

McDonald, S. (1999) 'First steps to improving literacy', *Literacy Today*, 21.

Markham, S. (2004) *Learning Styles Measurement: A cause for concern*, Monash: Monash University Computing Educational Research Group.

National Research Council (NRC) (2000) *How People Learn: Brain, mind, experience, and school*, Washington, DC: National Academic Press.

Rose, C. (1985) *Accelerated Learning*, New York: Basic Books.

Smith, A. and Call, N. (1999) *The Alps Approach: Accelerated learning in primary schools*, Stafford: Network Educational Press.

Stahl, S. (1999) 'Different strokes for different folks: a critique of learning styles', *American Educator*, Fall: 27–31.

Whitebread, D. (ed.) (2002) *Teaching and Learning in the Early Years*, 2nd edn, London: RoutledgeFalmer.

4

Supporting ICT: Control Technology in the Primary School

Anthony Barnett

My beliefs and values about ICT

The encounter with the rapidly changing world of information and communications technology (ICT) is firmly established as part of everyday life from the earliest years and throughout adult life. It is therefore essential for children to be developing ICT capability during their time in school. The value of ICT is in its capacity to support curriculum learning objectives, to enhance the quality of the children's learning experience and to transform the learning and teaching process in order to bring the previously unachievable within reach. The huge potential of ICT for making both learning and teaching more effective needs to be constantly actualised.

Introduction

This chapter aims to develop understanding of the value of children's engagement with control technology as part of their learning experience; to provide an overview of the important areas of progression and differentiation; and to consider broader issues including cross-curricular themes. The intention is to provide a context for managing and supporting learning and to stimulate reflective thinking about themes and issues in order to enhance the quality of teaching and learning related to control technology. At certain points in the text I have placed activities for the reader to complete, signified by the 'To do' prompt.

ICT refers to all manner of digital technology and technology used for communication. The list is lengthy and includes computers and interactive whiteboards, as well as all the software that runs on them. Then there are the peripheral devices such as printers, scanners, digital cameras, graphics tablets with pressure sensitive pens and digital microscopes. The scope of ICT also encompasses both more traditional and modern methods of communication: telephone, mobile and Smart phones, pagers, the internet, e-mail, news groups, chat rooms and videoconferencing, television, video and sound recorders, OHT projectors, pocket calculators and calculators that work with an OHT.

ICT also includes all the automatic electronic devices that regulate and control other devices. This includes artificial intelligence and robotics and comprises the domain of control technology. Learning objectives relate to operating programmable toys, developing ideas, learning how to plan, giving and refining instructions, modelling ideas and asking 'What if . . .?' type questions. In addition, they include talking about, investigating and comparing the way ICT is used both within and outside school. Control technology in primary school (ages 4–11) typically involves, for example, Reception class children (ages 4–5) playing with remote control cars; Key Stage 1 children (ages 5–7) giving instructions to Roamers, Bee-Bots or even Pro-Bots; and Key Stage 2 children (ages 7–11) using a computer to control a fairground ride or movement of a buggy.

To do

Look in current curriculum documents for different age groups. Identify learning objectives that relate to control technology.

The historical context of control technology

Historically, control technology in primary schools has been an area of weakness identified in Ofsted subject reports for both ICT and Design and Technology (D&T).

Weaknesses continue to manifest themselves in recent reports. In 2008, Ofsted reported a need to improve primary school teaching teams' overall understanding of D&T and control was cited as a particular area of weakness:

> Satisfactory rather than good achievement was often associated with teachers' limited competence in the subject and a narrow curriculum. In particular, pupils' access to aspects of the subject such as food technology, systems, control and electronics, or work with the more resistant materials such as wood, were restricted.
>
> (Ofsted, 2008: 11)

In 2009, Ofsted noted that pupils had some strengths in using ICT for communicating and presenting their ideas but were weaker in handling data and control: 'The pupils observed generally used ICT effectively to communicate their ideas and to present their work, but they were less skilled in collecting and handling data and in controlling events using ICT' (Ofsted, 2009: 4). This correlated with teachers' continuing weak subject knowledge in data logging, manipulating data and programming.

Clearly, judging by these reports control technology is an area in need of development! Of course it is not possible in a single chapter to do more than begin to address the identified issue of subject knowledge, and practical experience would be essential in any case. However, by thinking about the value of control technology in the primary curriculum, learning support assistants and teachers will develop more insight about ways of developing this important area of learning and will be encouraged to try out new ideas.

The value of control technology in primary school

The various claims made for the value of control technology are as follows:

1 It helps children understand applications of technology in the wider world.
2 It provides a context for the development of skills, particularly investigation and problem-solving skills.
3 It supports a more authentic learning experience.
4 It contributes to the development of curiosity, perseverance and collaborative group work.
5 It contributes to mathematical development, for example measurement, spatial awareness and estimation skills.
6 It stimulates motivation: children love building and experimenting with robots.
7 It provides opportunities to develop vocabulary and conversational skills.
8 It supports the development of technical writing and sequencing skills as well as creative writing.
9 It speeds up the learning process and supports hands-on learning that is appropriate for pupils at the concrete operational stage of development.

Let us now look at each of these claims in turn.

(1) *Control technology helps children understand applications of technology in the wider world*:

Learning about control technology in school will help children develop their understanding of the social, economic and environmental implications of technological developments in the world. This cross-curricular theme draws on various subjects including ICT, Science and D&T and it involves learning to appreciate the contribution technology makes to the quality of life, being able to work with emerging technologies and being able to assess their practical value. As Druin and Hendler write: 'The purpose is not to teach children to become extraordinary robotics experts, but to engage, excite, and compel them to learn, among other things, about values, communication, teamwork, science and math' (2000: 163).

To do

Think about the range of curriculum subjects and consider how they can contribute to understanding applications of technology in the wider world.

(2) *Control technology provides a context for the development of skills, particularly investigation and problem-solving skills*:

Control technology fits neatly into a project-based learning format, which integrates different subjects of the National Curriculum. This can help make learning more coherent and meaningful. Literature and history can be productive starting points, with links to D&T, Art, Maths, Music and even RE. Working with control problems will certainly engage a variety of process skills, particularly where the cross-curricular project includes elements of designing as well as investigative science. Extract 4.1 illustrates a conversation at the beginning of a control project, where children were designing and making a riding stable.

The focus when operating the control equipment is likely to be related to decision making and sequencing of instructions. A group of Reception class children might be solving the problem of moving the floor turtle to a variety of map coordinates. The question 'I wonder what would happen if . . .?' may arise, predictions will be made, a plan formulated, decisions taken, results interpreted and the outcome will be a sequence of instructions.

To do

In Extract 4.1 – an extract of a conversation – children were working independently. How might a teaching assistant contribute to the learning experience in this sort of group activity?

(3) *Control technology can support a more authentic learning experience*:

Authentic learning experiences are more meaningful, perceived as more relevant and more exciting than learning based on answering questions on worksheets. Whereas playing with programmable toys would be an authentic learning experience in the early years, solving a traffic flow problem by programming a set of traffic lights would provide a more authentic learning experience for an older child.

A useful model of computer use was included in Futurelab Report no. 4 (Loveless, 2006), which regards ICT as a set of generic and subject-specific tools functioning in instructional, revelatory, conjectural and emancipatory modes. ICT may help with the actual learning of a subject (instructional mode), with the interpretation of data through data-handling programs and simulations (revelatory mode), with the development of ideas through modelling (conjectural mode) and with the workload (emancipatory mode). Conjectural and emancipatory uses, in particular, support authentic learning experiences. Another useful and simple model is the Tutor/Tool/Tutee model (Taylor, 1980). Control technology fits into the conjectural mode of wondering what would happen if . . .?, as well as computer as tutee, where the child teaches the computer by programming it to follow instructions.

EXTRACT 4.1 Designing and making a riding stable toy

A group of three boys and two girls had decided to design and make a riding stable toy, where lighting and other effects were to be controlled by a computer control program. The model itself was intended to be a Christmas toy, where the horses or reindeer came into view by rising behind the stable doors on a lift until they appeared in the stable windows. There would then be lights, including flashing coloured lights, like fairy lights, to illuminate the stable. The children's conversation focuses on problems encountered during the initial modelling of the riding stable design. When reading through the conversation, notice the different effects mentioned and identify the specific problems encountered by the children at this stage in the project.

Boy 1:   Do we need this?

Boy 1:   I don't know. What could we use that for?

Boy 2:   J, that thing needs to go up a bit more because it's not shining . . .

Girl 2:   Well, it's shining okay . . .

Boy 1:   Unless we have another torch there . . .

Boy 1:   Shall we have one on there?

Girl 2:   Yeah

Boy 1:   That's mean, that one

Boy 2:   How are we going to make the door open and close?

Girl 2:   I don't know. What do you want to . . .?

Boy 2:   . . . because look, I'll show you mine . . . right, look, here's the centre line . . . Does that look okay? . . . I said does it look okay? (The others are busy exploring possibilities and ways of connecting bulbs to the stable)

Girl 1:   We need a buzzer

Boy 3:   I'll do the buzzer, I'll do the buzzer

Boy 2:   . . . 'cos look, there's mine . . . the lift can go up and down

Girl 2:   How are we going to do that then?

Boy 3:   We need another battery (Not realizing batteries and bulbs could be connected in parallel)

Boy 2:   All . . . the lights go on (Having now moved on to help Girl 2 with the lights)

Boy 3:   Can you go and get the battery please?

Boy 2:   Look, J, all the lights go on

Boy 3:   I'll do the battery equipment . . .

                    . . . I do the battery stuff

Boy 2:   I do the sellotaping

(???):   Here it is, here it is, here it is.

Boy 2:   J, I'm doing the battery equipment

(???):   There's the end plugs for the buzzer

Boy 3:   Right, I'll do it

Boy 2:   Sellotape

Girl 2:   No just try it, see if it works

Boy 3:   Try the other one

Boy 2:   No it didn't work

Boy 3:   J, I know what to do . . . change the batteries

(4) *Control technology contributes to the development of curiosity, perseverance and collaborative group work*:

Cognitive engagement in an activity is influenced both by the situation-specific factors of the classroom context and by the enduring interests and values of the individual children. Mastery goal orientation is to be preferred as it involves deep thoughtful engagement with the activity in a way that facilitates conceptual change, in contrast to performance motivation, which is driven by external rewards and competition.

Research evidence suggests that significant classroom factors include the nature of the activity, the authority structures and the evaluation procedures (Pintrich and Schunk, 1996). Activities that are challenging, meaningful and authentic can lead to the adoption of mastery goal orientation. In addition, where activities are open-ended, with sufficient time allocated, pupils are discouraged from opting for any answer or avoiding an answer altogether in case it is the wrong one. There is increased attention, persistence and the application of previous experience. Where authority structures are such that pupils have some control over what they do and how they work, they may be more willing to get involved, engage with and resolve problems. Negotiated assessment is a preferred evaluation procedure, rather than social comparison and competitive performance.

Pupils' more enduring interests and values also contribute to the willingness to engage in and persist with cognitively challenging activities. This is enhanced where learning activities are seen as useful and important for some personal goal as well as being intrinsically interesting. Evidence from a small-scale research project undertaken by the author provided several illustrative examples of pupils' cognitive engagement and persistence when solving open-ended problems related to their own designs. One eight-year-old child was observed experimenting with different ways of attaching a motor for the tail in a model Cat design, persevering with the report writing and then exploring modifications to the control program to include forward and reverse at different speeds. Another child was absorbed for an extended period with the problem of connecting a motor to the inside of his helicopter model, in the process eliciting and organising the support of another child. Yet another child persevered with the connections in his fan-assisted 'oven' model and was finally rewarded with an ingenious solution.

(5) *Control technology contributes to mathematical development, for example measurement, spatial awareness and estimation skills*:

Extract 4.2, from an interview with a Reception class teacher focusing on the use of Roamer and Logo, demonstrates the link with mathematics.

Opportunities for mathematical development are also present in the Data-Harvest Go control program. Apart from the sequencing and use of flow charts, there is the option to use simple percentages. As flow charts become more complicated, they begin to take up space on the computer screen. The flow chart can be reduced in size using the scale view. It is also possible to control the speed of a motor by specifying the percentage of full speed.

EXTRACT 4.2 Control technology and mathematics

Int: Do you ever use Roamer in the Reception class?

T: Yes, definitely, yes . . . particularly when I'm doing direction. Sometimes I've used it when I'm doing 'more than' or 'less than'. And I will programme him . . . too much . . . too little, and then the children . . . have got to do 'more' or 'less'.
. . . and also with the very young ones, I would have a number line. I've got some big number line tiles and I would put the number line out and Roamer would go to a different number . . . so you're getting your consecutive numbers and your counting as well as the . . . Roamer experience, as it were . . . with the numbers.

Int: Is Roamer used in other parts of the school or is it only used in Reception?

T: No, no, they've used it for the angles further up the school although they have also got the Logo program and that on the . . . computer.

---

(6) *Control technology stimulates motivation: children love building and experimenting with robots*:

Here, a few quotes from teachers and children taken from a small-scale research project conducted by the author illustrate the motivational nature of control technology:

(a) A Reception class teacher's response to a question about using Roamer:

'Oh yeah, yeah. They love it. It's exciting. And I mean I think they understand . . . they can understand, a bit of science comes in with energy and that you've got to switch them on and off. It's all part of your science . . . as well as the maths that can come in. But it's a good way to deliver it. It's a good way of delivering the whole curriculum in many ways really . . .'

(b) Responses of nine- to ten-year-old children when asked about their experience of control technology:

'I think it's great because it's cool.'

'I think it's interesting but it's quite fun as well because you can make things happen that you are not actually going along and doing . . . It's just fun.'

(7) *Control technology provides opportunities to develop vocabulary and conversational skills*:

Control technology group work also provides ideal opportunities for the development of conversation skills. Groups typically talk continuously as new ideas begin to emerge and they confront problems. Children ask questions of each other, listen and respond, issue instructions, explain their ideas and even congratulate themselves. Some of the conversation is likely to be friendly social chatter, but most of the talk will be purposeful and task related as the group engages with the activity.

(8) *Control technology supports the development of technical writing and sequencing skills as well as creative writing*:

There are opportunities for writing sequences of instructions and explanations of how the control problem was solved; storyboarding the development of the project; and contextualising the project within a narrative storyline.

(9) *Control technology speeds up the learning process and supports hands-on learning that is appropriate for pupils at the concrete operational stage of development*:

> new robotic technologies can make learning more concrete and physically active ... traditional educational environments are transformed into constructivist, problem-centred learning experiences.
>
> (Druin and Hendler, 2000: 163)

Stephenson (1997) raised the question of the contribution of control technology to children's conceptual development:

> [control IT] ... provides not only an enrichment at each level that has benefits across the curriculum, but can accelerate conceptual development and process skills such as predicting, hypothesising, testing, problem-solving and so forth in a way that more traditional methods fail to do.
>
> (1997: 48)

Shared use of language and familiarity of context are key factors supporting the development of children's reasoning ability. The role of the adult quite clearly involves interacting with children working within their 'zones of proximal development'. Whereas for Piaget the teacher's role is to observe and wait for the right moment, for Vygotsky the teacher's role is more active and involves scaffolding the learning situation 'in order to' move the children on in their learning. In addition, the neo-Piagetian view suggests that significant cognitive gain comes when children are engaged in socio-cognitive conflict. It seems, therefore, that control technology activities can accelerate conceptual development because such activities are an ideal way of developing collaborative group work situated in real and meaningful contexts.

Progression and differentiation

Effective teaching requires attention to elements of progression and differentiation when planning. Children will make more progress when the planned activities match appropriately to their experience and abilities. There are various ways to think about progression within control technology. Phillip Stephenson (1997) separated procedural understanding (i.e. skills) from conceptual understanding. Skills progression in control technology is the development of independent problem-solving ability. This relates to the process skills and includes the ability to recognise and formulate problems, to suggest ways of solving problems, to devise fair tests and to evaluate results, repeating the problem-solving cycle as necessary. Conceptual progression in control technology relates to the ideas of giving commands, giving sequences of commands, and using command procedures to repeat instructions, including the use of recursive programs. Helen Smith (1999) focused on introducing control technology simply, in a relevant context and progressively. She identified progression as moving on from operating a simple switch through giving single commands and sequences to writing procedures, then incorporating sensors and evaluating and refining procedures. See Table 4.1 for a more concise view of these approaches.

Although the curriculum in England may change in the next few years, the current National Curriculum (NC) level descriptions do still provide a useful way of identifying progress. Table 4.2 helps make the NC levels clear by providing a simplified view of the main characteristics and linking them to control technology as a specific area for development.

TABLE 4.1 Conceptual and procedural progressions

CONCEPTUAL UNDERSTANDING	PROCEDURAL UNDERSTANDING
1 simple commands	Planning structured investigations:
2 simple sequences	■ identifying and formulating the problem
3 simple procedures	■ recognising and planning possible approaches to solving the problem
4 complex procedures	■ reasoning and making decisions
5 use of sensors	■ evaluating results
6 procedures refined to improve efficiency	■ reframing the problem as necessary

TABLE 4.2 Characteristics of 2010 NC level progression

NC LEVEL	MAIN CHARACTERISTICS OF ICT LEVELS (NC)	CONTROL TECHNOLOGY
Level 1	Exploratory	Awareness
Level 2	Purposeful with specific outcomes	Simple sequences
Level 3	Develop ideas and solve problems	Procedures
Level 4	Combine and refine information, interpret and question plausibility	Include digital sensors
Level 5	Combine use of ICT tools and evaluate fitness for purpose of ongoing work	Precise instructions and use of analogue sensors
Level 6	Integration and efficiency in use of ICT tools, increased range and complexity of information	Monitor, measure and control events in an efficient manner

Hammersley-Fletcher *et al.* (2006) drew attention to several different approaches to differentiating in order to match challenge to ability and learning needs: resources, activities, support, presentation, time, outcomes, content and grouping. Although there is inevitably some overlap between these categories, they are a useful way of thinking about differentiation in relation to control technology.

Resources

Control technology software typically allows different levels of access, so that younger, less experienced or less able children using CoCo software work at level one, two or three, moving on to level six as their capability increases. Control technology hardware also supports differentiation by resource. For example:

- Bee-Bots allow for simple left/right/forward/back.
- Pro-Bots include a complete range of Logo-type programming possibilities.
- Roamers allow hands-on programming suitable for younger children, whereas Logo involves programming an onscreen turtle.
- Data Harvest's Learn and Go allows direct control of models compared with the more advanced control box hardware for use with nine- to eleven-year-old children.
- Crystal Rainforest V2, produced by Sherston software, is a very engaging adventure game for seven to eleven year olds, which provides a staged introduction to the Logo programming language.

Activities

Inputting simple instructions is an activity that even five-year-old children are able to manage. Sequences require thinking ahead, estimating and spatial awareness, although still within the ability of able five- to six-year-old children. Creating and refining procedures are more suitable for able children aged seven to eleven once they have been introduced to the Repeat function (using CoCo or Logo) and/or the loop concept (using Data Harvest's Go control software, which uses a flow chart approach). Within the seven to eleven age group some children may benefit from the further challenge of using inputs and sensors.

Programming the control software to operate a set of traffic lights would be more challenging than operating a model Ferris wheel that starts, turns for a specified number of seconds and then stops. Both of these activities would be more challenging than making a clown blink one of its eyes and smile. Programming a robot to say 'Turn on the light' when it gets dark involves using a light sensor as an input. This would be quite straightforward for an able nine- to eleven-year-old child; programming an authentic pelican crossing, with flashing 'Wait' sign coordinated with the red and green light, would be more challenging.

Support

Teaching assistants or teachers may work directly with an individual or small group of children, helping them become more familiar with the operation of the software or hardware. Teaching teams might also focus on helping children engage with problem solving, for example how to approach programming the traffic lights.

Children are likely to find prompt sheets particularly useful either to support use of the software/hardware or as a way of supporting the activity. Various prompt sheets are possible, such as:

- reminders of the meaning of control terms;
- Logo commands, e.g. fd = forward, cs = clear screen, pu = pen up;
- Go control software symbols, e.g. Wait symbol, Output symbol, Decision symbol, Edit symbol;
- planning frameworks, e.g. to support storyboarding the control idea or to support trying out programming ideas;
- writing frameworks; for example, where the control activity is part of a larger project, differentiated writing frameworks will support related written work.

Presentation

It is worth considering learning styles when introducing ideas and developing activities. Numerous construction kits are available and can be very useful for kinaesthetic learners for modelling their ideas at the start of a topic; for example, ideas related to a fairground topic can be modelled with K'Nex (Ferris wheels) and Lego (rides). Images and video clips are readily available on the internet and can be presented to the class using the interactive whiteboard. Some children might benefit from seeing onscreen demonstrations or guides that can be produced using screen capture software.

Time, outcomes and content

Realistic expectations will ensure that all children are able to achieve the experience of success. Some children will need more time and it is important to be aware of the impact of resource availability when planning control technology activities. The value of an ICT suite or laptops in the classroom is that every child can have appropriate access while programming the software. However, the control technology project is also likely to include designing and making a model to be controlled. A local neighbourhood project, for example, could include investigating the local area, producing design drawings for buildings, using construction kits for modelling, doing focused practical 'To dos' to develop the D&T skills needed to make buildings, street and traffic lights, as well as controlling the model or group of models using a computer program. Consideration of content, time and outcomes is relevant here also.

Broader issues

From machines to robots . . . issues that affect children, and society, now and for the future?

Karel Capek, the Czech playwright, introduced the word 'robot' into popular usage with his play *Rossum's Universal Robots* in 1920. The play begins by extolling the virtues of robot machines but ends by highlighting the ensuing social ills. A simple search in google.com using the phrase 'robot android' finds numerous and amazing video clips of lifelike androids that are able to perceive the world around them, answer questions including weather reports based on up-to-date information from the internet, read in different languages, walk and manipulate objects, and learn. Project Aiko reports the development of a very lifelike female android that can do all the above, from the first video showing only the head in 2007 to the complete android in 2010. Chang *et al.* (2010) report on a study of class-based teaching using humanoid robots acting as teaching assistants in second language teaching. An interesting and useful source of information, including a history of robots timeline and robot videos, is accessible at www.inventors.about.com. Figure 4.1 provides an example of such a timeline, which can easily be enhanced with copyright-free clipart.

Cross-curricular themes

In 1990, the National Curriculum Council published guidance for the following cross-curricular themes: economic and industrial understanding, environmental education, health education, careers education and education for citizenship. Later, these were reformulated as financial capability, enterprise education, education for sustainable development, career-related learning, PSHE and citizenship. In 1998, the government established the Sustainable Development Education Panel, which led to the theme of education for sustainable development being included in the curriculum. Such inclusion aimed to support pupils in developing the ability to participate in decision making about developments at individual, local and global levels. The sustainable

[INSERT CLIPART]	[INSERT CLIPART]	[INSERT CLIPART]	[INSERT CLIPART]	[INSERT CLIPART]
1886	1918	1919	1926	1956
First automatic dishwasher (J. Cochrane)	First refrigerator with temperature control (General Electric)	First pop-up toaster (Charles Strite)	First automatic traffic lights (Wolverhampton, England)	First robotic company (G. Devil and J. Engelberger)

FIGURE 4.1 A timeline of technological development

development theme was developed further in 2005 with the Securing the Future strategy.

A useful framework for thinking about control technology in relation to education for sustainable development is in terms of the key concepts identified by the Sustainable Development Education Panel: interdependence, citizenship and stewardship, needs and rights of future generations, diversity, quality of life, equity and justice, sustainable change, and uncertainty and precaution.

A brief review of the history of technological change for the last few hundred years will help to put these themes into a control technology context. Developments in ICT have broad economic and social implications. We have now moved from the industrial society of the nineteenth century, through the modern era of the twentieth century, and into the postmodern world spurred on by the development of the 'information superhighway' and the 'information society'. The Industrial Revolution introduced major changes to the methods of production, driven by the Protestant work ethic, fuelled by the ambitions of the entrepreneurs, with scant regard for social justice and the quality of life in general. Factories, machines and mass production methods, including child labour, replaced traditional methods. Even as early as 1811, the Luddites recognised the threat to their existing lifestyle when they destroyed the stocking frame machines during the riots. One hundred years later Henry Ford invented the assembly line, considerably reducing the cost of producing his famous Model T Ford car. Production line methods, including division of labour, led to considerable economies of scale and improved standards of living. In the twentieth century, the motor car industry introduced automated production techniques to the production line and the labour market changed to meet changing needs. By the beginning of the twenty-first century, advanced robotic machines are in widespread use in industry and the wider economy. There are now questions of deskilling, changing skills, the pace of technological change, environmentally sound technology, structural unemployment and the more general information society issues of social control, access and choice.

Work patterns are changing and employment continues to shift away from the primary and secondary sector to the tertiary sector, that is, from agriculture, fishing, mining and industry to the services sector. Ancillary, administrative and professional occupations are continuing to increase. Developments in ICT and robotics are having far-reaching effects. New technologies bring closer links between production, remote markets and the head office, greater decentralisation and growing treatment of information as a commodity. Stockpiling of products is no longer a necessity. Rapid communication of the results of market research is now possible. Robotic machines can be rapidly reprogrammed to produce small batches to match market demands.

Control technologies such as robotics are part of an interlocking interdependent system. Production on a much larger scale is possible and becomes necessary because of improved methods of communication. Boundaries of time and space are merging. With developing multinational corporations there is the question of the information superhighway being public led or market led. The current issue of 'net neutrality' involves the question of restriction of access where information is regarded as a commodity. Access to the 'best' content may eventually be by subscription or influenced by those companies willing to pay for preferential network speed of access.

Something similar is already with us in the form of pay per view Premier League football matches on digital television. The increased freedom of choice offered by digital multimedia may also turn out to be a force leading to social isolation and fragmentation of society. Interactive television, for example, provides a vastly increased range of programmes. The choice available through the internet is almost infinite. Whereas some may regard it as a liberating force, it may also mean that people have a more restricted common basis for participation. On the other hand, people readily establish online communities through websites such as facebook.com, where boundaries of time and space are less significant.

Control technology is a deeply embedded feature of the world we live in. The implications reverberate in all directions. Without control technology, driving to work would be difficult. At another level, geographic and cultural boundaries are being surpassed, the world is shrinking, and even the concept of 'literacy' is changing where the universal power of the visual image is more impelling than a cacophony of different languages. There is also the unremitting question of personal freedom with 'trojan horses', electronic tagging and government policies regarding surveillance of e-mail throughout the world.

These are complex issues and seemingly far removed from a group of six-year-old children working with a floor robot, or ten year olds controlling a set of traffic lights and buggy using a computer program and control box. However, a major part of the value of control technology in the primary school is that it can provide a context for learning and help to provide for a more authentic learning experience. Consider a geography unit of work on how to make the local area safer, or an issue such as whether the High Street be closed to traffic, or other environmental issues. The issues associated with control technology arise repeatedly.

Discussion starters

1   Consider the aims, values and costs involved in including control technology across the primary school age range. How much of a claim does control technology have on curriculum time?
2   Control technology software allows children to work in a simulated environment, e.g. writing the program to control an onscreen washing machine. What are the advantages and drawbacks of computer simulations?

Reflecting on practice

1   Identify examples from your own experience where you have observed children showing curiosity and perseverance in collaborative activities. Consider the characteristics of the activities and their impact on the children.
2   Prompt sheets and other resources can provide a useful way of supporting independent learning. Identify the various learning needs of a small group of children. Produce and evaluate resources to support independent learning.

Useful resources

Story books

Brown, Heather (2010) *The Robot Book*, Pan Macmillan Australia (12 pages – includes moving gears and cogs).

Griffiths, Andy (2009) *Robot Riot!*, Pan Macmillan (age 8+; 168 pages – Roberta Flywheel, a new girl at the school, is mistaken for a robot because she is so well behaved. Is the school being invaded by robots?).

Lucas, David (2008) *The Robot and the Bluebird*, Macmillan (age 4+; 32 pages – broken-hearted robot is befriended by a bluebird).

Parker, Andy (2010) *Robots*, Kingfisher (8 pages – includes popups and press-out robots, e.g. to explore the surface of Mars or the crater of a volcano).

Varon, Sarah (2007) *Robot Dreams*, First Second (age 8+; 208 pages almost entirely without text: 'Varon's masterful depiction of Dog's struggles with guilt and Robot's dreams of freedom effectively pull readers into this journey of friendship, loss, self-discovery, and moving forward' (http://us.macmillan.com/robotdreams; accessed 23 October 2010).

Other books and articles

Brooks, R. (2002) *Robot: The future of flesh and machines*, London: Penguin Press.

Penfold, R. (2000) *Introducing Robotics with Lego Mindstorms*, London: Babani.

Pritchard, A. (2001) 'Computer control in Key Stage 2 Design and Technology: massed or spaced, which is best?', *Journal of Design & Technology Education*, 6(2). (This article considers the advantages and drawbacks of 'blocked' time compared to a series of shorter sessions.)

Siraj-Blatchford, I. and J. (2006) *A Guide to Developing the ICT Curriculum for Early Childhood Education*, Stoke-on-Trent: Trentham Books.

Whitbread, D. (1997) 'Developing children's problem-solving: the educational uses of adventure games', in McFarlane, A. (ed.) *Information Technology and Authentic Learning: Realising the potential of computers in the primary classroom*, London: Routledge.

Websites

www.bbc.co.uk/cbeebies/littlerobots: this website is part of cbeebies and includes some robot games for early years children.

www.dataharvest.co.uk: the home page for Go control software, Learn & Go, Bee-Bots and data loggers.

http://el.media.mit.edu/logo-foundation/logo/programming.html: the Logo programming language was developed by Seymour Papert in the 1960s and is still in use as a central element in control technology in primary schools today. The Logo Foundation provides a portal to all things Logo.

www.kenttrustweb.org.uk/kentict/kentict_home.cfm: Kent ICT is a well-developed website with lots of ideas, resources and examples for all aspects of ICT.

www.logiblocs.com: Logiblocs are an interesting alternative to the usual control box interface. This website includes information about Logiblocs and illustrative examples.

http://matrixmultimedia.com/coco/CoCo-60-3.pdf: this webpage provides an overview of CoCo3 control software and interface.

www.rogerfrost.com: this website focuses particularly on data logging.

www.valiant-technology.com: the home page for Roamer, containing lots of practical advice and ideas.

References

Chang, C.-W., Lee, J.-H., Chao, P.-Y., Wang, C.-Y. and Chen, G.-D. (2010) 'Exploring the possibility of using humanoid robots as instructional tools for teaching a second language in primary school', *Educational Technology & Society*, 13(2): 13–24.

Druin, A. and Hendler, J. (2000) *Robots for Kids: Exploring new technologies for learning*, San Francisco, CA: Kaufmann Publishers.

Hammersley-Fletcher, L., Lowe, M. and Pugh, J. (2006) *The Teaching Assistant's Guide*, Abingdon: Routledge.

Loveless, A.M. (2006) *Report 4: Literature Review in Creativity, New Technologies and Learning.* Available online at http://archive.futurelab.org.uk/resources/documents/lit_reviews/Creativity_Review.pdf (accessed 12 February 2011).

McFarlane, A. (ed.) (1997) *Information Technology and Authentic Learning: Realising the potential of computers in the primary classroom*, London: Routledge.

Ofsted (2008) *Education for a Technologically Advanced Nation: Design and technology in schools 2004–07.* Available online at www.ofsted.gov.uk (accessed 12 February 2011).

Ofsted (2009) *The Importance of ICT: Information and communication technology in primary and secondary schools, 2005/2008.* Available online at www.ofsted.gov.uk (accessed 12 February 2011).

Pintrich, P. and Schunk, D. (1996) *Motivation in Education: Theory, research and applications*, Englewood Cliffs, NJ: Prentice Hall.

Smith, H. (1999) *Opportunities for Information and Communication Technology in the Primary School*, Stoke on Trent: Trentham Books.

Stephenson, P. (1997) 'Children's learning using control information technology' in McFarlane, A. (ed.) *Information Technology and Authentic Learning: Realising the potential of computers in the primary classroom*, London: Routledge.

Taylor, R.P. (1980) 'Introduction', in Taylor, R.P. (ed.) *The Computer in the School: Tutor, tool, tutee*, New York: Teachers College Press, pp. 1–10. Available online at www.med8.info/cpf/taylor/index.htm (accessed 12 February 2011).

5

Language and Literacy for Learning

Jean Clarkson

My values and beliefs about literacy

The successful teaching of literacy is a controversial, yet crucial, aspect of the curriculum. To make sense of the world today everyone requires a high level of literacy. Literacy is the litmus of being educated. Teaching literacy is not just to enable children to read books but to enable them to read print in the environment and access information to function in society. Language skills are critical in an information-laden society that is dependent on communication both electronically and in real time.

Skill with language gives power. Moreover, communication with others is vital and not just to find success in careers – the social skills created by literacy are important to good mental health and a feeling of well-being. Children of all ages who are poor readers and show a poor understanding of language are more likely to experience disadvantage than children who are more literate from an early age. Illiteracy produces high dropout rates from school, behaviour problems, high pregnancy rates, high truancy rates, high criminal rates, and a life destined for low incomes.

The World Wide Web has become the most important tool for nearly everything we do. Paying bills, doing research, catching up on news, and shopping are just a few of the things that are rising in popularity on the internet. By the time a child of eight is an adult, the internet will be the main venue for nearly all of our transactions and activities. As we move forward with technology, the gap between the literate and illiterate will continue to divide society. Those who cannot utilise the internet and other forms of technology because they are unable to read will potentially be living on the fringes of society.

Introduction

This chapter aims to support educationalists by exploring the integrated areas of speaking, listening, reading and writing, and the important role language plays in integrating the child into the social world. The chapter will describe the theoretical underpinning of children's language skills as the framework for the chapter and will discuss the social process of language and the relationship between language and thought. I will invite the reader to explore the role literacy plays in concept development in other curriculum areas. There is an overview of some methods commonly used to teach reading and writing and exploration of the harsh reality of assessment. In addition, the role of the teaching assistant as a member of the teaching team is acknowledged.

From the beginning

Communication skills develop in the child from birth. Babies hear and recognise their parents' voices before they can clearly focus. Interaction is vital for children's survival, so we need to support their innate skills for literacy for them to flourish. In 2004, when the first edition of this text was written, most schools used the recommended documents as appropriate for the age range:

- *Curriculum Guidance Foundation Stage* (DfEE/QCA, 2000);
- *National Literacy Strategy Frameworks for Key Stages 1–3* (DfEE, 1998; DfES, 2001).

Since 2004, the guidance documents have changed, after increasing criticism of the over-prescriptive nature of those particular documents, and there has been an ongoing debate about the best ways to teach reading. In particular, there has been an emphasis on establishing the use of synthetic phonics. All documentation published since 2004 is available on the internet, but a new curriculum is destined to arrive soon due to the 2010 change in government and the establishment of the Department for Education (DfE). This chapter aims to focus on the important concepts and practices, rather than government policies and guidance documents that change at a very quick pace for political rather than educational reasons.

Language is a crucial element in our life chances. We need to be skilled communicators to play our rightful role in society, at home and in the workplace. We need communication skills to live in harmony with our fellow beings; we need language to love, to dream and have a sense of well-being. Any person unable to communicate successfully in all of the interrelated language activities – speaking, listening, reading and writing – suffers emotionally and socially (Crystal, 1987). Therefore, it is imperative to teach children to communicate with others to give them a sense of power and to enable them to take command of their lives academically as well as socially. A literate person is a powerful person. There is a great deal of literature that discusses the acquisition of language before children arrive at school and the importance of an interactive environment to support children's innate ability to communicate (for example, Crystal, 1987; Wells, 1987; Wray and Lewis, 1997). The following section will focus on the development of the language elements developed *after* a child reaches school and how an interactive adult can foster the child's inherited ability to communicate.

Teaching reading

Most primary schools in England still adhere to the original recommendations of the 1998 National Literacy Strategy, but adapt it to their needs in the light of subsequent changes to the curriculum. Most secondary schools chose to audit their practice against the Key Stage 3 Strategy recommendations, and chose the most effective teaching approaches and content for their situation. Despite the criticisms of the National Strategy and the formulaic approach, there was a reported increase in children's achievements as evidenced by the national test results, but in most recent years there has been little improvement in English test results and much controversy about expectations, marking and standards achieved in national assessment tests.

The literacy hour was (and still is in some primary schools) highly structured to include three teaching strategies: whole-class teaching, group work and independent activities. Shared reading and writing manifests itself through whole-class teaching, where the teacher or teaching assistant provides a 'role model' for the children to copy and will demonstrate how to do both. Writers such as Southgate *et al.* (1981) and Holdaway (1979) advocated an 'apprenticeship' approach such as this. The method draws from the work of Clay (1972), who suggested that teachers could replicate the sharing of a book, such as a bedtime story, in a kind of mass-produced version of parent–child bonding at bedtime. The cosy setting of gathering children around your knee in an intimate style and relaxing to enjoy a book could encourage children to consider books and reading to be a pleasurable activity, thus creating the beginning of a positive engagement with literature sustainable throughout life. In addition, the teacher is providing the opportunity to extend the child's own reading skill level into the 'zone of proximal development' (Vygotsky, 1978) as described by Pat Hughes in Chapter 3. Group work and independent activities following the class shared reading ensure that children have a variety of ways to learn and practise skills at their own level.

The importance of creating positive attitudes as well as teaching reading skills is a feature of the strategy that teachers sometimes overlook. Teaching reading is the balance of the skills needed to 'decode' (Smith, 1973) and understand the text, and the pleasure of understanding the story or information motivates the children to conquer this extraordinarily complex task. To be able to mentally process symbols representing sounds and speech into meaning, quickly and fluently, sometimes when a child is but seven, is nothing short of a miracle. The content of the book is always the reward for the effort of processing reading and provides the major motivation for a child wanting to read independently.

The 'big book' and the interactive whiteboard

Publishers from 1998 onwards, delighted at a new marketing initiative, began to manufacture the 'big book' as a convenient way for teachers to use a communal text big enough for all to see during the literacy hour. Creative teachers made their own enlarged texts using the names of the children as players in the story, or photographs of the children's world as a basis for non-fiction. Children were involved in the construction of their own books through word processing and illustration. Some classroom action research had ten- and eleven-year-old children writing designer books, based on the adventures of Reception children, for the library (Clarkson, 1996). The big book is not the only way to share texts and, with older children in particular, the interactive whiteboard is very useful, especially when making comparisons between two different types of reading texts. However, let us not forget the use of class texts, from which everyone has the opportunity to read individually and develop debate. We recommend a range of age-appropriate methods, not just the big book or interactive whiteboard. While these can be engaging and appear to involve everyone, they cannot provide the individual experience and practice provided by individual texts.

Learning how to read

Children learn to read by using their linguistic, cognitive and experiential knowledge of the text. They use their letter and word recognition skills and text-level cues, such as the context of the text and illustrations, to help them comprehend the text. Here are three main strategies that children use when they decipher text:

- semantic knowledge (including contextual influences);
- sight vocabulary;
- phonics.

We will explain each one in the following paragraphs.

Semantic knowledge – the understanding of the text

Semantics is knowledge about meaning, a term often used in relation to the structure of the language, that is, how words are put together to make meaning, but children most often interpret text using their prior knowledge of the world. In other words, they often take a pragmatic (common sense) approach to interpreting meaning. Pragmatic knowledge about meaning takes into account the contextual, often non-linguistic, factors such as pictures and the whole setting of the story. A word changes its 'sense' in various contexts (Wertsch, 1991) and as children progress through school they need to develop an awareness of this, for example *volume* in the everyday context of the television, and *volume* in relation to the mathematical concept of three-dimensional space at Key Stage 3.

Children are able to read a book with much more ease if they have experiential knowledge of the content. For example, if a child has been to the zoo they can read text about the animals in the zoo with greater confidence. They will read the word 'elephant' without difficulty, especially if the book uses illustrations as visual clues. Knowledge of the content with a good grounding of oral language can allow the child to use their 'psycholinguistic' skills to have a good educated guess at the words. Smith (1973) called this a 'psycholinguistic guessing game'. Thus, the semantic structures that determine meaning are understood through the application of contextual clues that help children make sense of the words. Discussion about the book is vital to develop semantics or understanding and meaning. This crucial act links the spoken language to the symbolic form in reading. Adults in the classroom and beyond, teachers, teaching assistants and parents are ideal people with whom children can discuss their reading books.

Sight vocabulary

Most children have a good memory of the written word and can recognise the image of the whole word, especially if it has enough ascenders and descenders to make it distinctive. Again, *elephant* is a good example. This is a distinctive pattern with enough shape to make it instantly recognisable. Key words and high-frequency words on cards help children create a mental image. When they see a word repeated on the page, they remember it. This applies also to word patterns, words with the same endings or beginnings, suffixes or prefixes. Imagery is a powerful tool when learning to read at any age. Unfortunately, targets for achieving at-sight vocabulary at specific ages have resulted in an approach to teaching such vocabulary out of context, which was not the intention and is not the best approach for all-round development of reading capability. It is possible for young children to read all the at-sight words they should know for their age and still not be able to read a suitable text effectively. The development of at-sight vocabulary should occur within the context of developing the ability to use semantic cues, and to analyse and synthesise phonically.

Phonics

Graham and Kelly (2000) state that phonics is the association between symbols, that is, letters and letter combinations, and sound and how they are represented by the written form. When first teaching children phonics they learn to listen and distinguish individual vowel and consonant sounds in speech and to identify the written symbols used for these sounds. Knowledge of analytic phonics gives the child an additional support to decode the words. To use the example of 'elephant' again, the 'e' is a good starting point to guess the rest of the word using sight recognition and a knowledge of the context. Research supports the use of phonics in teaching learning and Haigh (1996) wrote about classroom research in Tower Hamlets that claimed that children and adults both sound out unknown words phonically.

One of the mainstays in teaching phonics is reading schemes. Campbell (2002) describes reading schemes as a collection of books written with the sole intention of teaching children to read. Teachers who advocate schemes say they offer structure to the teaching of reading because of their graded levels of difficulty. It could be argued that this structure is a weakness, too, as it does not facilitate adaptation and can be perceived to be too rigid. The key feature of schemes includes a natural increase in vocabulary, with regular repetition and a systematic introduction of letters and letter combinations. The major criticisms of reading schemes are by the children themselves, who claim they are boring, especially as children move through the primary years and become more discerning in their tastes. Many children will use the reading scheme books and some remain in schools sometimes for decades. Modern children have interests in contemporary issues and thus some schemes, currently used, are dated and are not sufficiently modern to appeal to the child of the twenty-first century. Most English primary schools use a mixture of scheme materials, particularly at ages seven to eleven, to provide a range of graded materials with different features and interest levels. At secondary level, some children have difficulty with phonics and there are specially designed schemes for more mature readers, with appropriate contextual content while at the same time providing the necessary phonic development.

Hofkins (2003) criticises phonic teaching, claiming that schools teach phonic skills too slowly and that we should teach the letter sounds and digraphs quickly in Reception and leave the complicated decoding and analytical phonic methods until later on when the child is more fluent. The recent focus has therefore been on the development of synthetic phonics – using the letter sounds and digraphs to build up words rather than to decode them. The debate about teaching reading has been with us for many years and no doubt will continue for many more. Unfortunately, children (and their teachers) become caught in the fads of the time, while people fail to recognise that readers need to develop all the skills; they need semantics, at-sight vocabulary and both analytic and synthetic phonics to become fluent readers. These skills develop in parallel, with no need to focus on one method as being better than another. Using one method to the exclusion of the others is to deny children and young people the opportunity to develop their reading skills in a way most appropriate for them.

Developing decoding skills

Phonics, sight recognition, semantics and innate syntactical knowledge, that is, grammatical knowledge, all contribute to the younger child learning to read. Consider the dialogue in Extract 5.1. You should be able to identify the different strategies children are using to decode words.

Different levels of work often permeate today's primary and secondary classrooms: text level, sentence level and word level. However, such work might not be described in these terms, which come from the original National Strategy guidance for teaching English. Text-level work focuses on the whole text, developing reading and compre-hension skills, often through whole-class discussion activities, but increasingly at individual level as children move through the years. Sentence-level work focuses on punctuation and grammar and can occur in whole-class, group or individual activities. Word-level work focuses on developing at-sight vocabulary, phonic synthesis and analysis. Intervention strategies, of which there have been several developed over the past few years, focus on identifying the gaps in learners' skills, knowledge and understanding at each of these levels and aim to enable children to catch up to their

EXTRACT 5.1 Strategies for decoding text

TA:	So what strategies do we use when we come across a word we don't understand?
Bilal:	We can go back to the start of the sentence and read again.
Aisha:	We look at the pictures for clues Miss.
TA:	Yes, good . . . and is there anything else that you do?
Bilal:	I skip the word Miss and read to the end of the paragraph and then we can guess the word.
Aisha:	We can sound it out Miss by breaking the word down into . . . parts.
TA:	Great – you have remembered all the things we have been practising this term!

peers. Unfortunately, the intervention strategies have had little success in achieving catch-up as envisaged by the government, thus highlighting that teaching and learning are much more complex than providing a learning diet for teaching teams to deliver.

Shared writing

Shared writing creates text in a communal process as the whole class contributes to the writing. Books written by the children together in groups are often well produced using word processing, and are stored in the library for all to read. Long after leaving a class, children will read a book they have made years before and reminisce with friends on the process of writing for the public. Indeed, once children have read texts together, they will return frequently to the same text, confident they have an understanding of the gist of the text. Confidence cannot be overemphasised in any form of learning. A confident child who believes they can achieve will 'have a go' and not be afraid of making mistakes because, with confidence, they will take a few setbacks without giving up.

Shared writing with a more competent adult role model shows the messy process of writing and how a writer constructs a good piece of writing as an artist crafts a piece of sculpture. It demonstrates explicitly the process of composing and redrafting. It allows thinking out loud to occur on the page. It demonstrates the activities that writers do while composing:

- Deletion: the elimination of false starts and unnecessary or wrongly chosen words.
- Rearrangement: changing the logic or word order and adding or expanding materials.
- Consolidation: making the text more compact or streamline while retaining the content.

Children understand the structure of the writing when they see it emerge on the page and, in turn, begin to comprehend how speaking and reading all interrelate. Non-fiction writing across the curriculum introduces children to different vocabulary. The teaching team can usefully display key words to support writing in any classroom.

Writing is a creative process and children have an innate ability to be creative in language. Pinkerton (1994) writes about the fascinating way children learn and use language creatively. The biggest drawback to using this creativity in shared writing is the size of the class. If children cannot see or do not feel involved with the creative process, they will lose motivation. With two adults in a class working in partnership, the children have more chance of an interactive experience. Active involvement of all pupils during shared writing should directly contribute to pupils' oral language development. There is a need to plan carefully to allow for extended speaking and listening opportunities.

Assessment

Have the children learnt what you wanted them to? Assessment is a time for harsh realities. For a professional in the world of teaching the child's learning is solely the responsibility of the adult, particularly in primary school. No longer can you blame the child for lack of understanding, intelligence or application to the task; the responsibility lies with the adult in the classroom. An analogy sometimes used is that of firemen reaching a fire in a house and finding that the reason for the fire is that a person fell asleep while smoking; firemen do not leave and say 'Well, it's your own fault, you caused the fire.' In teaching, a child not learning or making progress is directly the responsibility of the adult. That is why assessment has to be honest and effective. To discover that the child has not learnt despite your best efforts is frustrating and means that you have to find another more effective method. It is daunting and assessment can be painful as it also measures the adults' competence. Small group work is an opportunity for assessment when an adult can identify and record individual children's achievements. Teaching assistants are often in a privileged position when working with a small group and can provide excellent feedback to the teacher about a child's performance on a task, thus enabling the teaching team to make professional judgements. Read Extract 5.2 and compare it with your own experiences in educational situations.

From the extract, you will notice how the teaching assistant and teacher are working as a team, using the feedback to modify teaching approaches in the next lesson. This type of formative assessment is the most important as it has a direct impact on the teaching and learning process. Assessment of individuals takes place when observing a small group closely. The reading conference motivates children as they have the undivided attention of an adult who is evaluating their reading progress. Keeping records is a task for the end of the week, at which time the teacher writes an overview of the individual child's progress over the week.

The supporting adult questions the child's understanding of the text, encourages and gives positive feedback. It is essential to keep careful records of the child's errors and, when appropriate, use miscue analysis for a focused assessment of reading skills. Miscue analysis consists of recording the child's reading errors on a copy of the text, and allows the adult to analyse the patterns of mistakes the child is making. Many school schemes contain miscue analysis models to use. Diagnosis of mistakes leads to development of focused teaching strategies to rectify them.

EXTRACT 5.2 Sharing information and making judgements

T: How do you feel blue group are progressing in their guided reading?

TA: They love the new non-fiction materials and have been very keen to carry out wider research into 'sharks' this week. Adnan and Halima have really struggled to scan the text for key vocabulary prior to reading.

T: Well, I can emphasise scanning in the shared reading tomorrow. Why don't you join in and ask them questions in that part of the lesson. I'll watch to see how Adnan and Halima respond and whether they've remembered.

TA: Yes, I'll sit them at the front and prime them before the lesson starts and it should really give a boost to their self-esteem.

T: Yes, and on Friday, we'll spend some time together filling in our 'Reading Records'.

Planning to maintain an interest in reading

To create a balance between each of levels – text, word and sentence – requires careful planning and depends very much on the individual children within the class. The professionalism and skill of teaching staff lie in assessing the needs of each child and in providing the best method by which they will become a fluent reader. Thus, teachers approach reading in several ways because children are individual and learn differently and to use only one method can be demotivating. One method will suit some children better than others. When a variety of methods is used, eventually they all mesh and the result is a fluent reader.

Essentially, it is important to maintain interest in learning to read because, if laboured teaching gets in the way of the motivation, a child will reject reading for life. Teachers maintain children's interest through well-chosen books that are appropriate to the children's interest level. We have to remember that these children will grow into a future world that we cannot comprehend. Children are the next generation and they will be motivated by books that reflect the culture in which they live. Make reading appropriate to the modern world. In Extract 5.3, the teaching assistant is helping a child choose a book to read.

The teaching assistant acts as an *opportunist ally* in recommending the text for individuals to read in their own time. In this way, the child chooses a book with content similar to that he was looking for. Without an adult intervening here, he might well have chosen nothing. We can see that adult support is important in discussing the choice of books, too. Relating learning to the children's experience and the modern world is important for motivation. To understand the purpose of reading and the benefits it brings are part of the reason why children continue to learn (Campbell, 1998).

Gender issues

Research has shown that some boys are underachieving in reading, causing them to be disadvantaged in all other subjects (Millard, 1997), but there has been some criticism of this research and others claim that the concerns are unfounded. Motivating

EXTRACT 5.3 Appropriate interventions

TA: Can you find a book that you think will be interesting, Ehsan?

Ehsan: No, there's nothing here I like. I want a book about wrestling, Miss.

TA: You're interested in wrestling are you? What about this book? It's not about wrestling but it is about martial arts and there are some lovely photographs with captions in it.

Ehsan: Thanks Miss, I'll read it tonight.

TA: Tell me tomorrow what you think of it. If you like it you can show it to the class. But remember, karate is for experts only and can be dangerous!

Ehsan: Yes Miss.

---

boys to read has the additional difficulty of overcoming the image reading has of being an 'uncool' activity and not sufficiently masculine. We can overcome this. Experienced teachers use non-fiction books, science fiction and other non-traditional reading material to encourage boys to read. They use magazines, football programmes, computer literature, and any reading matter that has 'street credibility' and that boys do not consider feminine. Skelton (2001) suggests that we should look for different ways of being male, instead of trying to feminise their nature. They like to be best at what they do, and if they cannot be the best they will drop out. In other words, we must appeal to their styles of learning and the need for a competitive challenge. The interim report from the 'Raising Boys' Achievement' (RBA) Project appears to support the notion of working with the preferred learning styles of boys in literacy (DfES/RBA, 2003). They found that boys from the seven to fourteen age group responded well to an integrated approach to literacy, with less emphasis on the technical aspects of literacy learning and more on the processes. They found drama highly motivating in this respect.

Peer group pressure has considerable influence on this age group, many of whom are pre-pubescent at a much earlier age than even a decade ago and thus are motivated by a different range of reading matter. The Harry Potter series has encouraged all children to read and added cult status to the skill of reading. We can capitalise on this with other books of a similar nature. Many boys are particularly interested in the concept of the 'superhero'. They will read literature to which they can relate in this type of fantasy. Teachers and teaching teams can share their own reading interests, from their childhood or in adulthood, and this can be a motivating factor.

The connection between language and thought

Vygotsky (1978) thought that children only begin to have memories at about the age of eighteen months, when they have the words to enable thoughts and thus memories. He studied the relationship between language and thought, and their roles in further developing language skills. Crystal (1987) agrees that language facilitates much of our thinking; in other words, language creates thought. There is clearly a complex interrelationship between the two and Vygotsky was interested in the processes by which thoughts became language. To set this into the classroom context, there is no doubt that if children discuss a piece of writing together first before they commit to paper they produce writing of a higher standard. The kind of thinking that involves language is the reasoned thinking that helps us to work out problems. Thought production and language are dependent on each other and one informs the other. In other subject areas such as science, children who are performing an experiment gain greater understanding if they discuss the concepts together and move towards their own understanding. Consider how these ideas might have an impact on planning for an activity in the classroom by reading Extracts 5.4 and 5.5.

In Extract 5.4, the teaching assistant is making a useful suggestion to develop a role-play situation, possibly because it will be particularly useful for a specific group. The teacher agrees to the suggestion and proposes that the teaching assistant can have a role in determining children's understanding of the pollination process. They are capitalising on the relationships between thought and language to provide opportunity

EXTRACT 5.4 Working in partnership 1

> *TA:* What about developing a role-play for this work on pollination?
> *T:* Yes, we could ask groups to present their work to the class to include a demonstration of the pollination process.
> *TA:* That will give them the chance to collaborate and learn from each other.
> *T:* Yes, you could observe their contributions and let me know who you think has a good understanding of the concept.

EXTRACT 5.5 Working in partnership 2

> *T:* How could we create a speaking and listening opportunity with the letter writing?
> *TA:* What about a debate where pupils are assigned roles so that we fully explore the issues relating to the change of use of the school playground for car parking?
> *T:* Yes, but we might need to help some pupils develop their arguments in advance.
> *TA:* I'll plan a guided group session with 'blue group' next week to develop their roles well in advance.

for secure development of conceptual ideas. In Extract 5.5, they decide on a debate to explore an issue fully before the children write a letter (presumably a letter of complaint). Such an approach is much more interesting than simply planning a letter on paper with no real exploration of the issues. Thus, speaking and listening in all subject areas creates a better understanding of concepts and creates new knowledge in addition to helping children form important social relationships.

Reading with ICT

A key Labour pledge at the 1997 election was to connect every classroom to the internet. All schools now have established access to the internet and the potential to use ICT for a range of teaching and learning activities. The level of popularity among teachers for computer-based instruction in reading may vary, but few will dispute the fact that computers have won a permanent place in educational establishments. The motivation of reading and writing on a computer cannot be overemphasised for all children. Research studies (e.g. Reinking, 1988) indicate that computer instruction is effective for a wide variety of reading skills. The emphasis should not be on using computers to increase reading and writing achievement, but rather on using computers within the context of the curriculum for purposeful reading and writing activities. This is more motivating for pupils than computer-based drill and practice software. Pupils need opportunities to use the computer to apply reading strategies. Programmes related to science, humanities and numeracy will all require the use of reading strategies.

Many pupils now have computers at home. Parents and carers need to be aware that most games can be educational, developing skills and reading for meaning, but should be set up for two or more players, with the parents taking an active role to create important social and language interaction.

Partnerships in literacy learning

In partnership with teachers and parents, teaching assistants have a crucial role to play in the development of young people's literacy skills. This chapter creates a picture of how that relationship might look in the context of literacy teaching. Teaching assistants usually have a very good insight into pupils' reading and writing development, and are involved directly in the evaluation of teaching and learning. They are an integral part of the literacy team, with a wide range of skills and the ability to take initiative in response to issues as they arise. It is an exciting model that assumes ongoing opportunity for career development for all parties who care about young people's literacy development. Since 2004, teaching assistant roles have changed in all sectors of education. They no longer just deliver the latest government 'catch-up' literacy programme, with minimal training, but instead they are well-trained professionals working in partnership with teachers to ensure that children's literacy skills develop effectively.

Discussion starters

1   What are the disadvantages of being unable to express one's thoughts effectively? Consider the main aspects of language: speaking, listening, reading and writing. Consider personal as well as professional issues.

2   What motivation is there for a child to learn to read and write?

3   Some educators believe that teaching children to read by breaking words down into pieces and teaching strategies to sound out the letters can be tedious and turn children off reading. They claim that children learn to read more effectively without intervention if they are given motivational books – 'real' books – and they frequently 'read' with an adult. What is your view on this?

4   Some children leave school at sixteen less able to read than they could at age eleven. Why might this happen? And what can we do about it?

Reflecting on practice

1   Consider ways to value children's culture through their reading and writing experiences in school.

   (a)   List all the approaches you can think of.

   (b)   If possible, try some of your ideas and evaluate the impact on the quality of the children's work.

2   Explore the benefits of ICT in supporting reading and writing skills. How may ICT improve the development of these skills? If possible, use and evaluate your ideas.

3   Choose a selection of books from the school library that you think will appeal to a specific group of children. Share your choice with some children and observe their responses.

   (a)   Was your choice a good one, or were the children's preferences different from what you expected? Give reasons.

   (b)   Consider the criteria you used to choose the books and compare these with the criteria the children would choose.

Useful resources

www.bbc.co.uk/schools: various materials and resources for literacy.

www.informationliteracy.org.uk: the Information Literacy website provides useful perspective about the range of literacies needed for the modern world.

www.learn.co.uk: teaching resources and information.

www.literacy.lancs.ac.uk: the Lancaster University Literacy Research Centre.

www.literacytrust.org.uk: a charity that supports the development of literacy.

www.ukla.org: a charity for the advancement of literacy.

References

Campbell, R. (1998) 'A literacy hour is only half the story', *Reading*, 32(2): 21–33.

Campbell, R. (2002) *Reading in the Early Years Handbook*, Buckingham: Open University Press.

Clarkson, G.J. (1996) 'Designer books for Reception children', *Language and Learning*, 12–18.

Clay, M.M. (1972) *Reading: The patterning of complex behaviour*, Auckland: Heinemann Educational Books.

Crystal, D. (1987) *The Cambridge Encyclopaedia of Language*, Cambridge: Cambridge University Press.

Department for Education and Employment (DfEE) (1998) *The National Literacy Strategy: Framework for teaching English YR to Y6*, London: DfEE.

Department for Education and Employment (DfEE)/Qualifications and Curriculum Authority (QCA) (2000) *Curriculum Guidance for the Foundation Stage*, London: HMSO.

Department for Education and Skills (DfES) (2001) *Key Stage 3 National Strategy: The framework for teaching English: Years 7, 8 and 9*, London: DfES.

Department for Education and Skills (DfES)/Raising Boys' Achievement (RBA) (2003) *Raising Boys' Achievement Project Interim Report/Key Findings*. Available online at www.standards.dfee. gov.uk/genderandachievement – link to the project report (accessed 10 September 2003).

Graham, J. and Kelly, A. (2000) *Writing under Control*, London: David Fulton.

Haigh, G. (1996) 'This is the way they learn to read', *The Times Educational Supplement*, 6 September.

Hofkins, D. (2003) 'And then there was phonics', *The Times Educational Supplement*, 21 February.

Holdaway, D. (1979) *The Foundations of Literacy*, Sydney: Ashton Scholastic.

Millard, E. (1997) *Differently Literate: Boys and girls and the schooling of literacy*, London: Falmer Press.

Pinkerton, S. (1994) *The Language Instinct*, St Ives: Penguin Books.

Reinking, D. (1988) 'Computer-mediated text and comprehension differences: the role of reading time, reader preference, and estimation of learning', *Reading Research Quarterly*, 23(4): 484–98.

Skelton, C. (2001) *Schooling the Boys: Masculinities and primary education*, Buckingham: Open University Press.

Smith, F. (1973) *Children's Reading*, London: Holt, Rinehart & Winston.

Southgate, V., Arnold, H. and Johnson, S. (1981) *Extending, Beginning, Reading*, London: Heinemann Educational Books.

Vygotsky, L.S. (1978) *Mind in Society*, Cambridge, MA: Harvard University Press.

Wells, G. (1987) *The Meaning Makers*, London: Hodder & Stoughton.

Wertsch, J.V. (1991) *Voices of the Mind*, Cambridge, MA: Harvard University Press.

Wray, D. and Lewis, M. (1997) *Extending Literacy*, London: Routledge.

6

Conversations and Creative Resources: A Recipe for Success

Sue Cronin

My values and beliefs about teaching

Teaching is an essential human activity. Nearly everyone will at some time have experience of teaching a skill: a child to ride a bike; a teenager to drive a car; or a colleague who is new to the job. What makes the job of a teacher or teaching assistant different? Those who make a deliberate choice to teach have the responsibility to do so through considered thought and reflection. We must consider carefully how best to teach – what are the right prompts and resources, and what is the appropriate stimulus that will challenge and engage? How best can we help the learner negotiate meanings and make sense of the mathematics they are engaged in? Teaching is about good communication and relationships. The teaching assistant plays a key role in developing communication with the learner, building up a relationship of trust and safety, and allowing the learner to articulate emerging thoughts and ideas. Good communication and relationships between the teacher and teaching assistant are also vital in establishing a secure learning community in which pupils can flourish.

Introduction

Brown (1998) noted that the adults who work with children are their most valuable resource. This is true of all subjects, but is particularly relevant for mathematics. For many children who have trouble with the subject, the presence of a teacher or teaching assistant to support their mathematical development and understanding is crucial. This chapter will try to explore some of the issues involved in ensuring effective learning support in the mathematics classroom. It will consider the importance of the supporting adult's own perceptions and attitudes, and their awareness of the issues and current thinking on the effective teaching of mathematics. The chapter will also consider the importance of a resource-rich environment that will take account of a range of children's learning preferences to facilitate understanding and develop children's interest and capabilities in mathematics.

An emotional experience?

For many people the word 'mathematics' evokes an emotional response. Adults often have strong negative feelings about their school experiences. These include anxiety, panic and an inability to see any connection between the mathematics they learnt in the classroom and the real world they live in. Haylock (2001) notes that, even among academically highly qualified individuals, there is commonly a feeling of guilt that they are unable to do mathematics as well as they should.

It is interesting to reflect on some of the words that are associated with and describe mathematics by completing the task shown in Box 6.1.

It is important to reflect on any feelings that emerge, as they may reflect the attitudes and feelings of some of the children you might work with in the mathematics classroom. Those supporting children's learning should aim to understand the children's feelings towards mathematics. Understanding can provide a window into the necessary motivation and incentives required to ensure the child is stimulated and engaged. The teaching assistant's role is extremely valuable, as they will often form closer links with particular children who experience difficulties and will have a greater chance of finding the key to unlocking the children's barriers to successful learning. The nature of the relationship with the teaching assistant is often different from that with the classroom teacher, providing complementary knowledge of the children. Communication between members of the teaching team and the children is vital. Ensuring good communication within the teaching team is not easy, particularly in secondary schools, where the assistant may move from class to class with a child and thus not have time to discuss learning. It is important to find a working solution that maximises the chance of a successful learning experience for the child. For example, some schools use a link sheet, which is designed to promote a close dialogue between the class teacher and teaching assistant.

Before supporting children's learning it is important to consider one's own attitudes to mathematics and their origins. This helps us to empathise with the children, understanding their fears and anxieties. More importantly, we begin to rationalise why we feel the way we do. This process is a necessary start to feeling more positive and confident about one's own mathematical abilities as a teacher. It also ensures that we do not necessarily teach and support the learning of mathematics in the same way that we were taught (Smith, 1999). Through reflection, we can begin to evaluate the good and bad teaching and incorporate effective strategies into our own repertoire.

BOX 6.1 What do you think about mathematics?

Work with a colleague.

On a sheet of paper write down as many words as possible to describe mathematics. Compare and discuss with other groups any areas of commonality and differences in the words used. In particular, consider any emotive language used and reasons for its inclusion.

The supporting adult's feelings towards the subject will be transmitted to the child. If the adult admits to not enjoying mathematics or never having been any good at mathematics, this may contribute to and reinforce negative attitudes in the child. That is not to say that we should pretend that the subject is easy and that it has always been our favourite at school! Children are very quick to recognise the truth and respond accordingly. Nevertheless, by analysing our own experiences and image of mathematics, we can begin to understand why we feel the way we do towards the subject and this can help to develop a more positive attitude. Lim and Ernest (1999) suggest from their research that adults did not differentiate between their image of mathematics and their image of learning mathematics. They found that learning mathematics related more often to a negative experience rather than a positive one. Thus, if our own learning experience of mathematics at school was poor, not only will we have a negative attitude to the subject, but the prospect of being involved in a similar school process of mathematical learning may be uninspiring and itself generate negative expectations.

Carvel (1999) cites a primary school teacher recalling her public humiliation in front of the class by her 'sadistic' teacher for failing to understand a problem. This is often a common recollection and, if not a reality, many adults recall an anticipated fear of failing in mathematics. The outcome is the same – a very negative attitude towards mathematics and poor self-esteem. It is easy to suggest that the cause is simply and largely the result of poor, uninspired mathematics teaching, but the underlying reasons for previous poor learning experiences are complex and varied. It is not simply a case of weak teachers. Fraser and Honeyford (2000) refer to 'sum stress' and give a list of typical reasons, which include past failures or a particularly bad experience in a lesson, parental attitudes, relationships with mathematics teachers, and physical problems such as dyspraxia and dyslexia. They also cite Skemp (1986), who suggested that the underlying cause was rooted in the traditional methods used to teach, with the emphasis on rote learning rather than on understanding. Smith (1999) refers to a 'virtual mathematics' experience for children whose teachers perpetuate an image of mathematics as a set of unrelated routines, which he calls 'mathematical rituals' based on their own learning experiences. They unintentionally pass on the concept of mathematics as an 'arbitrary collection of meaningless procedures', rather than a real understanding for the rich interconnections that form the subject.

In primary schools, this has partially been a result of teachers' own lack of confidence of their subject knowledge. Bibby (2002) found that many primary teachers lacked confidence and were ashamed to admit any lack of proficiency. It is only by acknowledging that there is a problem in the first place that we can begin to successfully address it and resolve the underlying issues. Research carried out by Askew *et al.* (1997) found that even the most effective and enthusiastic teachers had in the past experienced 'arid' teaching and admitted to having had negative feelings towards the subject. Words describing their experiences included extremes such as 'traumatic' through to mundane feelings of boredom. However, it is encouraging that they survived and moved on to enjoy the subject and to share their enthusiasm and knowledge of mathematics with their children. Perhaps a result of their experiences was that they understood how not to teach mathematics! They recognised the need to make connections in mathematics, teaching strategies rather than sets of techniques and rituals, and engaging children in thought and discussion about their mathematics. Haylock (2001) relates that, by tackling these anxieties and confusions head on with trainee teachers, he has been successful in creating primary teachers who have a much more positive attitude to teaching mathematics and are able to employ more effective strategies than those they themselves experienced.

Teaching trends

The various trends in teaching methodologies and content in the past decades have also played a significant part in the largely negative view of mathematics held by the adult population. From the late 1960s to the early 1990s, primary mathematics (and some secondary) moved away from whole-class teaching and, based on the theoretical ideas of the time, there was a strong emphasis on a 'child-centred' curriculum. The practical result of this approach in the classroom was the evolution of published individualised schemes. There were many advantages of such schemes. They included many well thought out, stimulating activities for children and covered a wide range of mathematics, lending themselves easily to a differentiated curriculum that could meet the needs of a wide range of abilities. However, the disadvantages included the fact that many children were often teaching themselves, and by choice of booklets dictating, to some degree, the content of the work covered. The teacher's role was more of a facilitator and resource than classroom expositor. For many children this was not successful, since they required greater direction and whole-class teaching to learn many of the concepts effectively. As Haylock (1991) points out, the inherent feel-good factor of mathematics comes from learning with understanding and making connections reinforced by whole-class teaching.

More recently, there has been a swing back towards an increased proportion of whole-class teaching. Cockcroft (1982) published a report, which indicated the beginning of a significant change in approach to teaching mathematics, with a recommendation of a variety of teaching styles and integration of problem solving and investigation. It acknowledged the need for exposition by the teacher, but stressed the need for a dialogue between teacher and child. It referred to the need for teachers to take account of and respond to children's answers. The introduction of the National Strategies for primary and secondary schools between 1999 and 2001 reflected the changes in educational and political attitudes during the 1990s, with a main emphasis on the importance of whole-class *interactive* teaching and a clearly prescribed age-related curriculum. There is now greater stress on developing problem-solving strategies and thinking skills – important transferable skills that need to be developed in children. There is now a great deal of generic literature and a number of subject resources produced by organisations such as the Association of Teachers of Mathematics (ATM) and NRICH (http://nrich.maths.org/public), which provide ideas and strategies to improve thinking skills.

A review of research by Mujis and Reynolds (1999) suggested a greater degree of agreement between the different research bodies about effective ways of teaching and learning mathematics. There is a correlation between whole-class interactive teaching and mathematical achievement, but essential group and individual activities play an important role in developing the child's higher-order thinking skills. Mujis and

Reynolds noted that many countries blended these approaches, as reflected in the *National Numeracy Strategy Frameworks for Teaching Mathematics* (DfEE, 1999; DfES, 2000) and implicit in the new secondary curriculum (DCSF, 2008) and proposed revised primary curriculum (Rose, 2009). Teaching teams have an important role to play in assisting children to exploit this blend of methods. As we know, some children, for example those with Down's syndrome, require additional guidance to participate in the main whole-class activities and need focused support in smaller group work or individual tasks. In both cases, the use of questions, discussion and selection of suitable resources by the adult are key to teasing out misunderstandings or misconceptions. Together we can help the child to start thinking about the best way to tackle a problem or approach a task. This principle holds true for children of all ages and abilities. All children require challenge at an appropriate level.

Learning styles

Learning styles are simply the different approaches or ways of learning. They are the preferred sensory route to processing and making sense of the information. Some people have a visual preference, others auditory and others kinaesthetic or tactile. Although most people have a preferred learning style, it does not mean that they are unable to access and process information via a different sensory style. There is no one style that is better, but for some children their preferred style will be their most effective method of learning. Obviously, within the classroom, the teacher needs to employ as many different stimuli and resources as possible to cater for all the different learning styles of the children. For example, opportunities for learning visually arise through using 100 squares, number fans, empty number lines, posters of mathematical ideas and vocabulary, seeing the objectives of the lesson written up on the board. An emphasis on discussion and interactive questioning is important for auditory learning, as are opportunities to repeat aloud various procedures and facts, not just tables. For kinaesthetic learning, wipe boards, the chance to come out and demonstrate, and apparatus such as multi-link cubes to investigate patterns are examples of suitable learning experiences. If teaching teams provide a wide range of resources involving visual, auditory and tactile experiences, they will benefit all children and improve their overall learning approach.

Taking account of preferred styles is important when consolidating the children's learning and developing revision techniques. Learners with a visual preference might find a mind map useful for learning about a topic, while one with an auditory preference might revise effectively by making up a rap. Within the lesson, it is important to provide the children with lots of stimuli, but when helping children to revise and embed their learning it may be that a particular method is more successful and will play the major role in children's learning. Teaching teams might usefully discuss with the children their feelings about the best way of learning for a test or exam and encourage them to try some new techniques. For example, auditory revision techniques could include recording notes on tape, saying key ideas aloud, playing soothing background music, or an oral test. Visual techniques might include making a poster, chart, diagram or cartoon, as well as writing notes on key ideas and highlighting the main points/key words. Kinaesthetic techniques may include cutting up revision notes and rearranging them, or using sticky notes. Other techniques include tracing over key words and moving around, writing ideas in the air. Children need to be aware of the methods that they find most useful in helping them realise *how* to learn the mathematics as distinct from the content of *what* they have to learn. Using a range of personally effective learning techniques can increase their success in mathematics.

Thinking skills and metacognition

Becoming aware of how we learn is an important element of developing thinking skills. Becoming aware of effective learning techniques helps us capitalise on our knowledge and maximise our capacity to learn and retain information. Metacognition – thinking about your thinking – is recognised as an important element of the effective learning process. Tanner *et al.* (2002) cite research that indicates that good problem solvers display high levels of metacognitive knowledge and skill. They are able not only to think about the problem but to reflect on their approach and evaluate their own methods of tackling the problem. In mathematics these are particularly important skills. For children to succeed, they need to reflect on their mathematical knowledge and be confident in their ability to tackle a new problem. They need to be able to plan and select the knowledge and skills required by the task and reflect and evaluate the process and outcomes. We can help children become aware of how they are thinking and learning through guidance and discussion. This is often a teaching strategy promoted in relation to gifted and talented children, but it is not a strategy suitable only for the higher attaining children. Teaching lower-attaining children thinking skills has a positive impact on their mathematical learning. Some children may require more help to consider what they already know and what they need to know to solve a problem. They will need guidance to decide on the best strategies to tackle a problem and will need to talk through their planning, execution and evaluation of a task. Teaching teams play an important role in developing these higher-order thinking skills by engaging the learners in a dialogue, encouraging them to articulate their mathematical ideas. Creating opportunities for learning conversations, learner–learner and learner–adult, is important for the development of mathematical understanding. Questions, which can prompt the children into the metacognitive process, could include in the initial phase 'What is the task/problem all about?', since many children in mathematics lessons have misconceptions about the task or problem. Thus, they are unlikely to make much progress and be successful tackling the task. Once children understand the task, it is useful to ask if they have tackled anything like it before. Making connections to other areas of mathematics and previous work is critical, requiring constant reinforcement. With small groups, teachers and assistants can encourage children to share ideas and, where possible, consider the merits of different approaches, and can then let them try their ideas. Lower-attaining children will need adult or peer support with suitable prompts to help them organise their thoughts and actions. Vygotsky (1978) saw a difference between the child's capacity to solve problems on their own, and their capacity to solve them with assistance. He referred to this difference as the 'zone of proximal development'. This area included all the activities that the learner could only perform with assistance. He saw the need for an active dialogue between the 'senior learner', the supporting adult, and the 'junior learner', the child, to bridge this gap in potential between what the child already knows and what they were capable of achieving with a suitable level of *non-intrusive* intervention. This is not an easy task for the teaching team – finding a balance to ensure that the intervention is not giving the child directions rather than allowing them to think for themselves. With some children, progress in developing their thinking skills will be very slow. However, with practice and the use of appropriate prompts and questions, children can develop thinking skills that will have a considerable impact on their performance.

Learning conversations and dialogue

As mentioned above, helping children to develop thinking skills, and particularly the higher-order thinking skills of analysis, synthesis and evaluation (Bloom, 1956), involves talk. The teaching team needs to be involved in dialogue with the children, familiarising and modelling the language of the subject, encouraging them to realise that talk is a valuable tool for thinking. Cockcroft noted that one of the outcomes of good mathematics teaching was the ability of children to 'say what you mean and mean what you say' (1982: 72). Helping children to be able to talk mathematically about their ideas with the teacher, teaching assistant and other children is essential. Lee (2006) notes that teachers can help to develop pupils' mathematical abilities by helping them to express their ideas using appropriate language. In some classrooms the teaching assistant is particularly well placed to engage in a mathematical dialogue with the learner in order to help them develop their understanding. This takes time and scaffolding, since many pupils will display low levels of oral literacy and will find it particularly challenging to talk about mathematics. Dowker's (2009) research found that problems with language exacerbate difficulties and are an essential area of focus. Her research suggests even mild language difficulties will have a negative impact on the mathematical development of the learner. By sustaining regular learning conversations with the learner, progress may be made in addressing levels of both literacy and numeracy.

One of the dangers of working on individual programmes with children is that they never have the opportunity to discuss their work with others in a group. The teaching team must strive for a balance between whole-class, group and individual activities and conversations for all children. Such conversations will usually involve questioning both by the adult and by the child. It is possible to assess the child's grasp of the problem by the quality of the questions they ask. Getting children to form their own questions can be enlightening, providing an insight into their understanding of the mathematics and forcing the metacognitive process. For example, simply asking a child to supply a question/story for the division $12 \div 3$ can reveal if the child has a full understanding of the operation.

Research (Bauersfeld, 1988; Wood, 1994), cited by Tanner Jones and Davies (2002), identified two different forms of questioning: 'funnelling' and 'focusing'. Funnelling questions do not develop a child's thinking. They are usually short, closed questions requiring recall of facts, such as 'if n is 2 what is n^2 (n squared)?' They may be appropriate in certain situations to ascertain children's existing knowledge but, in terms of developing a child's problem-solving abilities and thinking skills, focused questions are required. These are usually more open-ended, requiring reflection and thought by the child. For example, 'Is n^2 always greater than n?' Supplementary prompts to assist the children to think about the answer may be required. Suggesting the substitution of simple numbers to start with, such as 'If n is 3, what is 3 squared?', can ensure the child understands how to square a number and is not doubling to obtain 6 for the answer instead of 9. Follow-up questions may then include 'What happens when n is negative?' or '. . . a decimal?' or '. . . a fraction?' Choosing appropriate questions requires a great deal of skill and judgement, and relies on the teaching team having good subject and pedagogic knowledge.

Many teachers have difficulty using focused questions. It is far easier to tell a children how to do something than to extract from them how they have tackled something themselves. If the child is 'stuck', altering the question, so that it provides clues, can help the child find an answer. It is useful to build up a bank of such questions that can help children reach the learning objective. A good starting point is often 'How did you get that answer?', or 'Explain how you worked that out.' From their responses, the teacher or teaching assistant can frame a supporting question, which will help the child think through the task. It may be a case of spotting where the child has made a mistake and saying 'Can you explain this bit again?' Explaining a second time may be sufficient to enable the child to spot a mistake or at least to realise which mathematics is not understood. If not, it may be that the child needs more guidance, perhaps by suggesting 'Have you thought about trying this?' or, where possible, bringing in another child, 'Sarah, how have you done this? Can you explain it to us?' Sensitive and appropriate questioning will ensure the self-esteem of the child is maintained and strengthened. The teaching team should establish a secure interactive environment. Children need to know that their peers value their responses. The Assessment for Learning (AfL) materials (DCSF, 2009) for the current primary and secondary strategies provide useful examples of rich and probing questions that can be used to help assess their level of understanding.

Connections

Research by Askew *et al.* (1997) found that the most effective primary teachers of numeracy were those who had a connectionist orientation of teaching. This was the most important factor, more so than their classroom organisation or their mathematical subject knowledge. They found that teachers across the range of effectiveness, from highly effective to moderately effective, were using whole-class teaching and group work. In other words, it was not the teaching organisational styles that made teachers highly effective, but their ability to share mathematical connections with their children.

The teachers in the research sample made these connections on many levels. They included the connections made between different topics, such as decimals, fractions and percentages, stressing their equivalence. They also made connections between the different representations used, that is, symbols and diagrams, words and objects. For example, in secondary school, connections to previous work in the multiplication of two digit numbers can be used when considering algebraic multiplication of two brackets (x +2) (x +3), by considering a rectangle of sides (x + 2) and (x + 3) and

BOX 6.2 Making connections using the 'grid' method of multiplication

	x	+ 3	(x + 2) (x + 3)
x	x^2	3x	$= x^2 + 2x + 3x + 6$
+2	2x	6	$= x^2 + 5x + 6$

finding the sum of the internal areas (see Box 6.2). This connects to the child's previous experience, building on their understanding of the grid method and providing a visual interpretation of multiplication in terms of area. This approach provides a way into multiplication of two brackets, which gives a greater insight than simply teaching children a rule such as FOIL (first pair, outside pair, inside pair, last pair), which may become a useful routine later, but only when the children's underlying understanding of the operation is secure.

Connections with the children's own methods of thinking and working out were also important to effective teachers. The teachers discussed these methods with the children and linked them to their own. Askew *et al.* (1997) found that the connectionist teachers worked more actively with their children. Their primary belief was that the process of teaching mathematics depended on a two-way dialogue between the teacher and child (this echoes the earlier views of the Cockcroft report (1982)). The child's work was valued and discussed. The class shared issues about methods and considered ways to improve.

Other connections are also important for effective learning. Making links to other curriculum areas can help children to see the transferable nature of mathematical skills. Tanner *et al.* (2002) refer to children and adults holding two sets of parallel mathematical knowledge. One is for use in school, in the classroom, the other for the real world, and these sets do not overlap. For many children at secondary school, the situation is worse. They do not even see the mathematical overlap into other subjects. They compartmentalise their knowledge, unable to recognise its applications in areas such as art, geography, science or technology. The teaching team is in a position to remind children of these links as they arise in other subject areas by pointing out to the child that this is a skill they have used before in their mathematics lesson. For example, children may have a quicker way of multiplying 460 x 5 than their geography teacher, who may suggest using a calculator when the child could use an appropriate mental strategy: find ten lots, and then halve it to obtain the answer. Constantly reminding children of the links and connections can help to embed the importance and relevance of the skills they are learning in the mathematics lesson and, for some children, this can be an important motivating factor. In a secondary school, the teaching assistant, especially one who moves from lesson to lesson with a child, has an important role in making these connections explicit. Some secondary subject teachers might not always know the connections, but in the primary school the generalist nature of the class teacher, who is largely covering all subjects, gives her or him a greater overview of the child's learning experience.

Resources

Connections and questions are essential for successful teaching and learning in mathematics, alongside the use of appropriate practical resources. As mentioned already in this chapter, children have different learning styles and require different incentives to engage their enthusiasm and understanding. A resource-rich environment provides the range of visual, auditory and kinaesthetic stimuli required to promote understanding and links to children's previous experiences. A good resource can spark a child's interest, generating questions and interactions between the children.

Newspapers and comics are a rich resource. They can prompt many different jumping-off points. The television page in a magazine or newspaper can be a revelation to children looking at time. They can consider the number of hours they watch television on a typical day, which can develop into work on fractions, percentages, pie charts, bar charts and more. Comparisons across the class to see if they watch more than an average child can produce more work on statistics and data handling. At a simple level, they may convert programme times to 24-hour time and calculate the length of time spent watching one or two television programmes. A more advanced piece of work may be to investigate statements such as 'There are far too many soaps on TV and not enough news programmes.' This work can involve groups discussing the validity of the statement and deciding on what evidence they have to argue for or against, and on a suitable presentation of the facts to support their point of view. Children can develop mensuration skills by finding the dimensions of the pictures/ images or columns of text and by comparing areas of text and images on a typical page. This can lead to work on ratio or comparisons of data to investigate what is a typical page, for example 'How much space is occupied by headlines, text, adverts, or pictures?' 'Magazines are bad value for money. They are just full of adverts' may be a statement that can provoke interest, argument and mathematics. House prices or car prices from a paper or a specialist magazine such as a motorbike or sports magazine, for example, can provide opportunities to look at range and averages, not to mention football and cricket scores! Consideration of annual percentage rates (APRs) on advertisements from loan companies can initiate essential discussion of money management and an increased awareness of the need for careful financial planning.

Books are also valuable for stimulating interest. Data can be collected from reference books that interest children, such as *The Guinness Book of Records* or encyclopaedias of animals, birds, history or geography. Number work emerges from comparison of facts. For example:

- How much bigger is the world's biggest bird than the world's smallest bird?
- What order would the animals be put in according to weight?
- For how much of his life was Henry VIII married?

If they enjoy the topic, children can answer such questions without realising they are working on mathematics. With imagination, adults can use these topics to develop resources that engage the children, by being relevant to their experiences and interests.

Topical characters and popular media events can prove an ideal motivational medium, particularly with younger children. Events such as the Olympics or the football World Cup lend themselves easily to mathematics. Using a current hit film or cartoon character can make a less than exciting activity come to life. For example, the use of the characters from *The Simpsons* to illustrate a worksheet on basic number skills or problem solving can create some humour in a task – 'How many Duff beers can Homer buy for $10 if they cost 75 cents each?'

The Harry Potter books have provided a source for many great worksheets on 'Muggle Mathematics', covering topics such as ratios, exchange rates, number bases or directions. The correct recipe for a polyjuice potion that lasts one hour for one child over three years, one and a half hours for a child under three, and so on, can lead on to a series of problems:

- How much boomslang is required for two ten year olds for three hours?
- If we only have twenty leeches, how much polyjuice can we make?

Foreign exchange based on 29 knuts = 1 sickle and 17 sickles = 1 galleon can be a more interesting alternative to the euro for some children. Working in the different bases of 17 and 29 when finding the cost of spell books and wands can stretch a child's numeracy skills and provide an unexpected appreciation and understanding of the advantages of the metric system and base 10! With squared paper and coordinates, a map of Diagon Alley can be used to discuss directions from one shop to another, such as the 'Leaky Cauldron' pub.

With older children, these stimuli can still play a part, but the presentation needs to be more sophisticated and may need to look less contrived. This is where newspapers and magazines can come into their own. Playing cards can also work well with older children; simple games such as 'Twenty-one' and variations can be used to consolidate number bonds, as can a memory game based on selected cards that pair up to ten. Cards are also useful to look at simple probabilities through the game of 'Higher and Lower'. For older children this could involve simple fractions – what is the probability of the next card being higher than the seven of diamonds? If there are only five cards left to turn, and three are greater than the seven, then it must be 3/5.

Games are a rich resource in mathematics and teaching assistants might find them particularly useful for the children they support. They are motivational, often adaptable and thus are ideal for differentiated work. They can have a different focus according to the desired learning objectives. The focus could be on the language and vocabulary of mathematics. Bingo is an example of an easily adaptable game to base on a current topic of work, such as area. The children may pick four areas, from ten possible areas, for example 12cm^2, 15cm^2 etc., and then in turn a series of shapes given with dimensions, for the children to calculate the area and check whether the units match the square filled in. The first person to obtain four matching answers has a full house and wins. Board games are also easy to adapt. If a game focuses on moving around according to number bonds up to twenty, this can be changed and the cards be simplified to make moves with number bonds up to ten. Once the children's understanding is secure, the rules could be changed to involve multiplication. We can develop thinking skills through games by asking children to analyse and evaluate the rules, and to suggest their own changes to a game.

In fact, all of the existing numeracy resources in the classroom, such as the dry-wipe boards, dice, cards or counting sticks, are ideal for supporting children in smaller groups. The whole-class activities based on these numeracy resources may need adapting to suit the child's capability. Sometimes certain children simply require more thinking time than the majority of the class. They may need to repeat the whole-class activity, for example, by physically moving their finger along the counting stick (a kinaesthetic approach) rather than just watching the class teacher. A teaching assistant can support a child in doing this during whole-class teaching, thus helping the child to benefit from it. Wipe boards are extremely powerful resources with lower attainers – children who gain confidence in knowing that any mistakes may be wiped away and will not remain a permanent reminder, unlike work in ink in their class books. The key is to be flexible in the creation and use of resources, adapting them to meet the specific needs of each child and designing them to build on any existing knowledge or interest the children already have so that the resources stimulate and engage.

A recipe for success

This chapter set out to discuss some of the issues concerning supporting mathematical learning effectively. A resource-rich learning environment is the key. By providing children with appropriate stimuli and resources, we can help them to break down the barriers and develop a greater understanding and appreciation of mathematics. However, it is important to remember, as mentioned earlier, that the greatest resource existing to support the child is the classroom teacher and the supporting adult. It is the adult's presence, personality, knowledge and experience that will determine the conditions for successful learning. A classroom where there is a positive, enthusiastic atmosphere and an expectation for children to enter into a dialogue about their mathematics, and to not only answer questions but to pose their own, is essential. Children need to explore mathematics; they need support in making connections between different but related areas within mathematics itself, such as fractions and decimals, and between mathematics and their real world, such as the use of statistics in newspapers. Making these connections requires adult help through discussion and questioning but also the use of concrete, practical resources.

There is no single recipe for the correct amount of each of the above 'ingredients', for in every classroom and with each child the proportions required will vary according to their attitudes and abilities. Figure 6.1 shows the range of ingredients that add up to effective mathematical learning – a recipe for success. Finding the best recipe for each group of children or individual requires a mixture of careful planning, patience, persistence and professionalism, but the rewards are high. The value of seeing a child suddenly understanding a new mathematical idea is just as satisfying for the adult as it is for the child. The reward of helping the child to unlock the door to a new and better understanding is the greatest job satisfaction and worth all the hours spent finding those right ingredients.

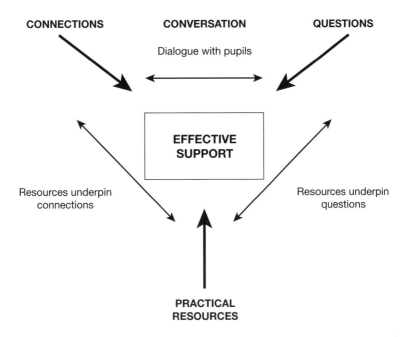

FIGURE 6.1 A recipe for success

Discussion starters

1   Reflect on your school experience of mathematics. What teaching and learning approaches did you experience? Which did you prefer? Did you expand your repertoire of approaches to learning?
2   Should all children follow the same mathematics curriculum?
3   What are the potential difficulties faced by mathematics teachers when a child with special needs is in the class? How can the teacher overcome the difficulties?
4   How can dialogue between the teaching team maximise the children's learning?

Reflecting on practice

1   Record examples of questions used by teachers in mathematics lessons (don't forget to ask the teachers' permission first). Sort the questions into 'open' and 'closed'. What was the purpose of each question?
2   Various research projects suggest that most questions asked by teachers are concerned with children's factual recall and comprehension. Few questions tackle the higher-order thinking skills such as analysis and evaluation. What is your experience? If possible, work with a group of children or peers on a mathematical investigation, aiming to challenge their thinking with appropriate questioning.

Useful resources

www.atm.org.uk: the Association of Teachers of Mathematics site has plenty of resources for primary and secondary pupils.

www.e-gfl.org/index.cfm?s=1&m=1&p=37,index: Essex Grid for Learning has a section called Maths at the Movies.

www.ex.ac.uk/~PErnest: to access *Philosophy of Mathematics Education* journals online.

www-history.mcs.st-and.ac.uk: the MacTutor History of Mathematics archive, which includes historical and cultural resources.

www.kangaroomaths.com/index.php: useful teacher-friendly guide to assessment and free resources.

http://nrich.maths.org/public: a project run by practitioners with free resources to enrich mathematics for primary and secondary pupils.

www.painsley.org.uk/mathsmirror: resources for secondary mathematics.

www.primaryresources.co.uk/maths/maths.htm: resources for primary mathematics.

References

Askew, M., Rhodes, V., Brown, M., William, D. and Johnson, D. (1997) *Effective Teachers of Numeracy: Final Report*, London: Kings College.

Bauersfeld, H. (1988) 'Interaction, construction and knowledge: alternative perspectives for mathematics education', in Grouws, D., Cooney, T. and Jones, D. (eds) *Perspectives on Research on Effective Mathematics Teaching*, Reston, VA: National Council of Teachers of Mathematics, pp. 27–46.

Bibby, T. (2002) 'Shame: an emotional response to doing Mathematics as an adult and a teacher', *British Educational Research Journal*, 28(5): 705–21.

Bloom, B.S. (1956) *Taxonomy of Educational Objectives: The classification of educational goals: Handbook I, Cognitive domain*, New York: Longmans.

Brown, T. (1998) *Coordinating Mathematics in the Primary School*, London: Falmer Press.

Carvel, J. (1999) 'Teachers "too ashamed" to admit inability in mathematics', *The Guardian*, 2 September.

Cockcroft, W.H. (1982) *Mathematics Counts*, London: HMSO.

Department for Children, Schools and Families (DCSF) (2008) *Mathematics Framework*. Available online at http://nationalstrategies.standards.dcsf.gov.uk/secondary/secondaryframeworks/mathematicsframework (accessed 12 February 2011).

Department for Children, Schools and Families (DCSF) (2009) *Assessing Pupils' Progress: Secondary mathematics guidance – day to day assessment in mathematics*, London: DCSF.

Department for Education and Employment (DfEE) (1999) *The National Numeracy Strategy: Framework for teaching mathematics from YR to Y6*, Cambridge: Cambridge University Press.

Department for Education and Skills (DfES) (2000) *The National Numeracy Strategy: Framework for teaching mathematics Years 7, 8 and 9*, Cambridge: Cambridge University Press.

Dowker, A. (2009) *What Works for Children with Mathematical Difficulties? The effectiveness of intervention schemes*, London: DCSF.

Fraser, H. and Honeyford, G. (2000) *Children, Parents and Teachers Enjoying Numeracy*, London: David Fulton.

Haylock, D. (1991) *Teaching Mathematics to Low Attainers, 8–12*, London: Paul Chapman Publishing.

Haylock, D. (2001) *Mathematics Explained for Primary Teachers*, London: Paul Chapman Publishing.

Lee, C. (2006) *Language for Learning Mathematics*, Maidenhead: Open University Press, McGraw-Hill Education.

Lim, C.S. and Ernest, P. (1999) 'Public images of mathematics', *Philosophy of Mathematics Education Journal*, 11. Available online at www.ex.ac.uk/~PErnest/pome11/contents.htm (accessed 12 February 2011).

Mujis, D. and Reynolds, D. (1999) 'Numeracy matters: contemporary policy issues in the teaching of mathematics', in Thompson, I. (ed.) *Issues in Teaching Numeracy in Primary Schools*, Buckingham: Open University Press, pp. 17–26.

Rose, J. (2009) *Independent Review of the Primary Curriculum: Final report*, London: DCSF.

Skemp, R.R. (1986) *The Psychology of Learning Mathematics*, Harmondsworth: Penguin.

Smith, J. (1999) 'Virtual mathematics', *Maths Teaching*, 166, March: 14–15.

Tanner, H., Jones, S. and Davies, A. (2002) *Developing Numeracy in the Secondary School*, London: David Fulton.

Vygotsky, L.S. (1978) *Mind in Society: The development of higher psychological processes*, Cambridge, MA: Harvard University Press.

Wood, T. (1994) 'Patterns of interaction and the culture of mathematical classrooms', in Lerman, S. (ed.) *Cultural Perspectives on the Mathematics Classroom*, Dordrecht: Kluwer Academic, pp. 148–68.

7

Supporting Science in the Primary School

Lois Kelly

My experiences, values and beliefs about science education

Science education has been a particular interest throughout my teaching career. My focus has been to develop children's understanding of science through science enquiry. More recently, I have worked as a lecturer in primary science supporting students to become confident to teach science. Working with primary teachers in both India and Uganda to promote effective science education has given me further insights into science education.

Introduction

Before thinking about how to support learning in science, take a few minutes to think about your own perception of science. Is science as a body of knowledge to be learnt or is it a way of understanding the world in which we live? How did you develop your view of science? Was it from learning science facts, which were tested in exams in school? Was it because you found science an interesting subject to study? Is school science different and separate from the science that society debates?

Examine Box 7.1, containing different beliefs about science. Read the opposing pairs of statements and consider where you would place your thoughts on the continuum.

Being clear in your own beliefs about science is important because it will affect the way you support children's learning.

Traditionally, many children experienced learning science as an objective body of knowledge that is value free and with little relevance to their lives and the world in which they live. A modern view of science is that understanding the natural and made world is more important than mere factual knowledge. Science is human endeavour that depends on making sense of our observations about the world in which we live; it is about learning a set of skills or a way of working that helps us to reason about the evidence and draw conclusions (Harlen, 2006). For example, when a group of ten to eleven year olds investigated the effect of putting different components in an electrical circuit, some noticed that in a circuit with just one 1.5v cell they could not

BOX 7.1 Contrasting beliefs about science. Adapted from Scitutors
(www.scitutors.org.uk/article.php?id=80)

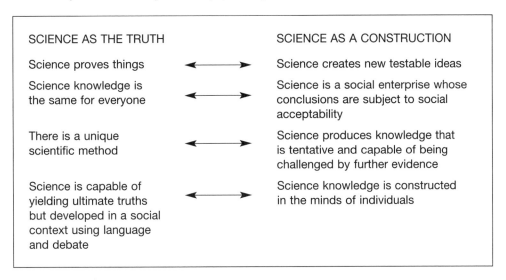

SCIENCE AS THE TRUTH		SCIENCE AS A CONSTRUCTION
Science proves things	← →	Science creates new testable ideas
Science knowledge is the same for everyone	← →	Science is a social enterprise whose conclusions are subject to social acceptability
There is a unique scientific method	← →	Science produces knowledge that is tentative and capable of being challenged by further evidence
Science is capable of yielding ultimate truths but developed in a social context using language and debate	← →	Science knowledge is constructed in the minds of individuals

make both a buzzer sound and the light bulb light brightly. Their teacher asked the children to explain this so that the children were using their knowledge of electricity to explain their observations and so further develop their understanding of electrical circuits.

Accepting that science is a human endeavour means that children need to be aware that science knowledge has developed over time and that it has a story to tell. Ward *et al.* (2008) argue that ignoring the historical aspect of science reduces science learning to learning about a body of knowledge and makes science sterile. When learning science children are learning to know the world in which they live, through observing, asking questions, testing out ideas to see if they are consistent with the evidence and explaining these ideas.

Reflect on your perceptions of science by looking back at your responses to the statements in Box 7.1. Your response is unlikely to be at either extreme of the continuum. While you might acknowledge that science does create new testable ideas when carried out by research scientists, in the primary school it is more likely to 'prove' something, for example that ice melts when in a warm environment or that salt dissolves in water. Similarly, we are developing knowledge about the science of global warming in a social context through media debate among scientists working on the issues, but, alternatively, a candle flame will need oxygen to burn wherever you are living on this planet. When supporting children's learning in science we need to recognise that school science is for all children, not just those who may follow a science career.

Learning and teaching

Before thinking specifically about supporting children's learning in science, let us take a sideways step and think about what we know about science learning. Learning is viewed as a process in which the learner's knowledge, for a particular topic, develops or is constructed when new information is built into and added on to existing knowledge, skills and understanding. We describe this as the constructivist view of learning, which draws on the learning theories of Piaget (1929), Bruner (1977), Vygotsky (1978) and Ausubel (1968), who describe how children construct their knowledge through their experiences and interactions with others. In science, children develop their knowledge and understanding by trying to link a new idea or experience with their existing knowledge. They test out their new ideas both practically, by carrying out an investigation, and by talking about their developing understanding. The role of talk to support learning needs to have a high priority in science lessons because, as Kibble (2008) points out, it is only when children talk about the practical investigations and their experiences that they develop their understanding. Talk also helps to clarify the specific meaning of the language of science. In this respect, small group discussions are more effective than whole-class discussions to help children develop their ideas (Alexander, 2006). If, as a consequence of their learning, children are able to make sense of the new ideas in terms of their existing knowledge, they will have strengthened their knowledge and understanding of the science topic. Alternatively, the teaching team may question children's ideas so they learn to consider other factors that help to explain the new idea. This explanation of learning is termed *constructivism*. An important first step, to support children's learning in science, is to find out their current understanding of the new science topic and then to help children develop, or construct, their understanding of the topic, which takes account of the established science explanation.

Wellington and Ireson (2008) reckon that science is probably the most difficult subject to teach because of the different factors to account for during lessons. First, there is a body of science knowledge relating to the different areas of science: life processes and living things (biology), materials and their properties (chemistry and some geology) and physical processes (physics). Second, science education develops children's knowledge of the procedural aspects of science: planning investigations, making observations, using science equipment, analysing and interpreting results, checking for reliability and drawing conclusions. Third, there is knowledge about the nature of science, which helps us understand how science ideas develop through interrogating and challenging the evidence to answer questions about how the world works. Although we are able to identify these different aspects of science, they are interrelated and learning in science combines them all. For example, children may learn a particular piece of subject knowledge, for example, that metals conduct electricity, but if they are to 'construct' their own understanding of this they need to test out this idea for themselves, observe whether or not metals do conduct electricity and debate why. Developing this understanding takes time and is developmental. The development of children's understanding of why metals conduct electricity may follow in this sequence:

- Children observe that metals conduct electricity by testing metal and non-metal objects in a circuit.
- At a later stage, the children learn how electrons move in an electrical circuit causing an electrical current.

- Children learn about the properties of metals and that electrons in metals 'move' more easily than electrons in non-metals.

- Children combine these ideas to develop an explanation for why metals are conductors of electricity.

Remembering that learning is assimilating new information into existing knowledge, understanding and skills, it is important to think about the following questions:

- What prior knowledge, experience and skills do the children have about the science topic?

- What is the next logical step in their learning?

- What do they need to do to develop their knowledge and understanding?

Planning for children's learning will involve children in practical activities, at the same time developing their thinking and reasoning about the science topic being taught by being encouraged to talk about the ideas, and learning about how these ideas have been developed over time.

Developing science skills with practicals and investigations

Practical work and investigations are key features of science education at any stage of learning but, to be effective in children's learning, practical activities need to be planned by teaching teams as an integral part of that learning. Ofsted (2008) notes that, where there is a focus on investigations and practical work, children's enjoyment and achievement in science is high. Practical work in science motivates and engages children in their learning. When children are interested and engaged they are more likely to learn. The 'hands on' nature of science sometimes sparks an interest in science, leading some children to study it at higher levels. The purpose of a science investigation or a science practical is to help children make links between their observations and the related scientific ideas (Millar and Abraham, 2009). Any book about science education, for both primary and secondary science, will have a chapter, or several chapters, about the role of practical work and science investigations in children's learning in science (e.g. De Boo, 1999; Harlen and Qualter, 2009; Ward *et al.*, 2008; Wellington and Ireson, 2008).

Science investigations help children develop their procedural understanding of science. Having an understanding of how scientists obtain and interrogate evidence means that children are better able to understand how scientific theories and laws are developed. The aim is that they will also be better able to appreciate that science evidence is always open to debate. Investigations also help develop children's understanding of science ideas and theories. Providing children with the opportunity to practice the skills associated with the procedural aspect of science helps children to learn how scientists develop the narrative of their research. To achieve this, children require opportunities to carry out science investigations that are relevant to them and support the development of their science skills.

A key skill in science is observation as this leads to focused questions from which science knowledge and scientific theories develop. It was observations of objects falling to Earth and of the movement of the planets that lead Newton to develop the laws of gravity. Similarly, it was observing that cowgirls who had had cowpox did not catch smallpox that led Edward Jenner to develop vaccinations to protect against this disease. A more familiar example of how detailed and accurate observations lead to the development of a scientific theory is the theory of evolution proposed by Darwin in *On the Origin of Species* (1859). It was through observing and noting small changes between different species and the changes that occurred in the flora and fauna over a number of years around his own home that provided the evidence on which to base his theory. (See examples of the notes kept by Darwin at http://darwin-online.org.uk/.)

From the earliest stages, children should be encouraged to make careful observations of objects and events in the natural world. When observing objects and events, children should be encouraged to use all appropriate senses. How things feel and smell, and how they look, gives valuable information about that object. By using equipment such as hand-lenses and microscopes, children can gain even more information about a living organism or an inanimate object. Unlike traditional microscopes, digital microscopes that display images on the computer screen are relatively easy for young children to use. Adults can help children to become more observant by focusing children's attention on specific features and by encouraging them to talk about and describe what they are observing. Discussion with other children as well as with adults makes them aware of features they may have overlooked. Careful observations help children develop two other science skills: classification and raising questions.

Classification helps children and adults to make sense of the world in which they live by organising the large range of objects or events into manageable sets. Although classification is most readily associated with living things through the Linnaean system of classification, it also applies to materials such as rocks. When learning to classify either objects or living things, children have to be encouraged to use their observation skills to note both similarities and differences. In the early stages of primary education, children will use readily observable features to discriminate between the different groups. As they progress through primary and secondary school, we should extend children's knowledge and understanding of the different systems of classification by providing them with a rich variety of specimens so that they not only take note of external features but also become aware of similarities and differences in the structures of the objects or living things.

Another important skill that is a prerequisite for any science investigation is asking questions and learning to recognise those that can be answered scientifically. Giving children the opportunity to explore, observe and 'play' with objects and materials is an effective strategy for encouraging children to ask questions. Inviting children to ask questions shows that they are valued as part of learning science, as does discussing the questions they raise. Not all the questions raised will lead to a science investigation, and identifying those that can productively be answered by an investigation and those that are answered more effectively by researching in books or on the internet helps develop an understanding of the scientific process.

A further step in helping children to develop their science skills is to support their ability to plan a test for those questions that can most usefully be answered by obtaining the evidence first hand. To answer questions such as 'Which of these paper towels absorbs the most water?' or 'Which foam lasts the longest?', children may need the support of an adult in identifying what may change and what to measure. With practice and experience, children become adept at asking these types of questions. Predicting what will happen in an investigation is another step in developing children's understanding of science. From their initial observations and from previous experience children will have some idea about which type of paper towel is more absorbent or whether shaving foam is more stable than bubble bath or washing-up liquid. However, a prediction is more that a simple statement of what might happen; a reason should be given based on this knowledge and experience. To help children understand that a prediction can only state what might happen, a useful strategy is to ask groups of children to think of more than one possible outcome. Once the children have obtained the evidence, they can then be asked which of their predictions was best supported by the evidence.

As children carry out their investigation, they will need to observe carefully to obtain the evidence they need to help them answer their question. Children should learn to record their evidence in the most appropriate way for their investigation. This could be by taking photographs, making a careful observational drawing, or recording a set of measurements on a table. For some investigations, for example when finding out how quickly water will cool to room temperature, it will be appropriate to use a data logger to record the temperature change and draw the graph.

Looking back at the story of scientific discoveries, understanding has developed not simply by observing what happens but because scientists have then looked for explanations about why. Darwin's theory of evolution developed not simply because he observed the variations in species and between species, but because he then wanted to solve the puzzle and explain why this happened. To support children's learning the teaching team should encourage them to interpret the results of their investigation. When dissolving different types of sugar in water they will observe that sugar that has larger crystals dissolves more slowly than sugar that has small crystals or is a powder. To develop children's scientific thinking, they need to be challenged not simply to record their observation, but to explain their findings. This requires higher-order thinking as their explanations link their observations with their existing science knowledge.

Although presented as a linear process, a science investigation should more properly be thought of as a cyclical or spiral process. Scientists make observations, ask questions and collect evidence to answer their question, which they then refine as the result of their observations. This may be repeated several times before sufficient evidence has been collected to support a conclusion or statement. It is at the early stages of experiments and investigations that science knowledge is most tentative. Unfortunately, it is difficult to replicate this aspect of science in schools, which can lead to children developing the idea that science proves things.

To support children's learning about science, not only do they need to conduct a science investigation, but they also need to review and discuss the process. Giving pupils time to explain what they were investigating and why, to present their results and to communicate their findings supports the development of their scientific thinking. Using a series of photos showing the different stages of an investigation supports children as they tell the story of their investigation. Questions such as 'What were we trying to find out?', 'Why?', 'What do the results show?' and 'What is the evidence for . . .?' encourage their scientific thinking. Once again, it is by talking that children's understanding develops. These questions also model for children ways in which they can challenge the science presented in the media, whether on the internet, through television programmes or in advertisements.

Children's experience of science should not be limited to 'fair test' investigations. The type of science investigations or experiments carried out will vary according to the question that has been asked and the science discipline. One type of investigation already mentioned is a classification investigation – a typical one would be to classify materials by a given property, such as whether they dissolve in water or whether they conduct electricity. In biology, concerning life processes and living things, when children investigate which types of plants, fungi or animals live in particular habitats they are carrying out a survey. Pattern-seeking investigations are used where the focus of the investigation is one particular attribute of a living thing but other factors also affect the results. An example of this might be how effective different types of fertiliser are because, although soil types can be controlled, it is difficult to ensure that all the seeds are identical. The results of this type of investigation are usually given as a trend.

Science enquiry also includes more focused practical activities that help children to gain first-hand experience of particular science concepts. 'Seeing it for yourself' is more memorable than just being told what happens. For example, being told that sound does not travel in a vacuum is not as effective as listening to a ringing alarm clock placed inside a bell jar, and then hearing the volume of the alarm decreasing as a vacuum is created inside the bell jar. As with all science investigations and practical work, simply observing what happens does not always lead to developing understanding. There also needs to be a discussion about the science ideas and the event that was observed. One way to encourage children to think about the science idea being illustrated by a practical activity is to present it as a puzzle and to encourage children to work collaboratively to solve it. Working collaboratively encourages children to talk about the ideas and, in doing so, they test out their ideas with each other and develop their thinking. Through talking in small groups about a practical activity, children develop their understanding of science topics (Loxley *et al.*, 2010: 36–44).

For example, a group of students were asked whether transparent objects made a shadow and whether a shadow could be coloured. Some of the students in the groups were sure that only opaque materials could make a shadow, because a shadow was black and did not show any features of the object making the shadow. They were given a torch and a clear transparent bottle, a coloured transparent bottle and an opaque mug. They shone the torch on the objects and made shadows. This led to a discussion about the shadows made by each of the objects. Those who initially thought that all shadows were black were surprised to find that transparent objects also formed shadows and that the coloured transparent bottle formed a coloured shadow. In this activity the students were being asked to link what they observed about the shadows with a scientific explanation that shadows are formed when *some* (not all) light from a source is blocked.

Using questions to support learning

Questions are an important feature of any science activity if we are to encourage children to think scientifically. De Boo (1999) notes that learning to ask questions is an important part of education and helps pupils to become self-motivated learners.

TABLE 7.1 Identifying two different investigations

	SAME *i.e. controlled variable*	DIFFERENT *i.e. independent variable*
Investigation 1	Food	Temperatures and conditions
Investigation 2	Temperature and conditions	Foods

When children undertake any form of investigation they should be encouraged to think about a range of different questions. At the start of an investigation, children need to learn how to phrase the question that they are investigating, for example 'How does the type of sugar affect the rate at which sugar dissolves in water?' Linked to this question are questions about what is being measured, which variable is being changed (independent variable) and therefore which variables are being kept the same (control variables). Table 7.1 shows how experiments with the same sets of variables can be set up in different ways.

To develop scientific thinking children also need to learn to ask questions about other aspects of their investigation. What is going to be the most appropriate way to find out the answer to my question? How reliable are the results? Do I trust this set of results? Why? How could I check these results? What have I learnt about sugar dissolving by carrying out this activity? How do I explain these results using the knowledge I already have about dissolving? Children who become accustomed to asking questions about the evidence they obtain from their investigations can apply these to claims made in the media about science. What is the evidence for this claim? How reliable is the research on which the article is based? Do other sources give me similar information? This is part of developing scientific literacy.

Other questions children need to learn to ask are those that help in classification and identification investigations. This type of investigation is common to a number of different science disciplines. The most familiar is when identifying any form of wildlife, and there are many guides available for this purpose. It is also one of the skills used in geology to identify different types of rocks. For this type of investigation children need to learn to ask very specific and closed questions, those to which the answer is either Yes or No. Learning to use these questions in a logical sequence helps children to develop their knowledge of, and ability to use, classification systems. The game in Box 7.2 is fun and very useful for developing classifications skills.

BOX 7.2 The Identification Game

Work in pairs.

For this activity, children are given an identification key and then the name of the rock, plant or animal is pinned on their back or on their forehead where they cannot see it. By asking questions of their partner, which may only be answered with a 'Yes' or a 'No', children work through the identification key to find the name of their particular item.

Thinking about what is a good science question is another skill children can learn that supports their learning in science. We can do this by thinking about what sort of questions are asked by other subject disciplines. Give children a selection of bags and ask them to think about the questions different groups of people might ask about the bags. Asking children to think about the questions a designer, a historian, a geographer and a scientist might ask about the bags is one way to help them develop their knowledge of questions that focus on science. Children can then discuss the features of a science question and compare those with the features of a question about the design of the bag.

The questions adults ask in a science lesson are also important in supporting children's learning. For questioning to be effective in supporting children's learning, it is important to have thought clearly about the purpose of the questions that are asked. Sometimes questions will be asked to help children recall their knowledge of a particular science topic, while at other times a question may be asked to focus children's attention and help them observe carefully. To ensure that questions are effective, it is not necessary only to think about what to ask; we also need to be sensitive about when to ask questions. A question asked at an inappropriate point in a lesson can disrupt a child's learning; conversely, a well-timed question can challenge children's thinking.

To support children's learning in science, teaching teams need to learn how to ask questions that help children at different stages of their investigation. De Boo notes that 'at their best and most productive teachers' questions can guide and stimulate thinking' (1999: 112). This places quite a responsibility on the teacher to think carefully about the types of questions to ask. When thinking about questions to help children develop the different science skills, we need to think how the child is likely to respond to the question. To help children observe a particular feature the question may be a closed question, such as 'How many pairs of legs are there on that woodlouse?' On a different occasion, a more open question will be appropriate, for example 'How does the worm move?' Questions that encourage children to make careful observations also encourage them to ask questions that can be investigated. 'What do you think might happen if . . .?' shows children that you are expecting them to make some predictions.

When considering how to support children's learning, we also need to think about how we respond to the answers to our questions. Harrison and Howard (2010) found that, when teachers encouraged other children in the class to add to the initial answer to a question, children became more thoughtful, which developed their thinking skills.

Developing a positive attitude to science

Common sense and our own experience tells us that children who are interested in a subject are more likely to be motivated to learn and will persist with activities even when they find such activities challenging (Harlen, 2006: 73). A concern for many in the science community is that, over the past decade or two, the number of students choosing to study science at degree level has been falling. Research studies have shown that this disaffection with science occurs towards the age of eleven, as children perceive it as a difficult subject that lacks relevance to them (Murphy and Beggs, 2005; Porter and Parvin, 2008). Many children will have decided before they leave primary school not to follow a career in science. This raises the question as to how best to develop positive attitudes to learning science.

Children's experiences influence their attitudes to science and they are more likely to develop positive attitudes when their peers and other adults show an enthusiasm for science and for developing their own science knowledge (Bricheno *et al.*, 2000). We can therefore support children's learning by showing a genuine interest and paying attention to new ideas in the media and things the children themselves are interested in. When discussing these ideas with children, we can talk about how the evidence has influenced our own thinking about the science idea. Both teachers and teaching assistants have the responsibility to provide positive role models for science education. One local primary school employs a teaching assistant, Claire, a former research scientist, who is responsible for supporting science throughout Key Stage 2 (ages 7–11). The high school, a science specialist college, funds the position to raise the status of science. Claire uses her enthusiasm for science and science enquiry to support children who have been identified as needing support and encouragement in the subject. The children benefit from the more personal interest Claire shows in the investigations they are undertaking. With Claire's support the school has been able to broaden children's science learning, as there are more opportunities to work collaboratively, which has been shown to improve children's attitudes to science (Bricheno *et al.*, 2000). One of the benefits of working collaboratively for developing positive attitudes to science is that children become more aware that scientific data do not necessarily provide a 'right answer' and that it is important to consider different views before coming to a conclusion. This challenges the perception that science has little relevance to them.

Another reason children lose interest in science is that they find science boring. Towards the end of primary school, this sense of boredom can be a result of repeating the same or similar science investigations throughout primary school. A key principle that underpins science teaching and learning is constructivism, the idea that children learn new knowledge about science by making links to their current knowledge, thus building on their previous learning. This means that children are learning about a particular science topic a number of times in their primary school careers. For example, the popular Qualifications and Curriculum Authority (QCA) Schemes of Work for Science (1999) include a unit on plants and plant growth at four different ages. One of the drawbacks of such schemes in schools is that children repeat the same activities each year instead of building on children's previous knowledge. An example of this can be that children carry out an investigation into the effects of light, temperature and water on plant growth each time they learn about plants in science. As one teacher said, 'You can become so focused on what your class have to learn that you do not always take note of the science that is taught in other year groups.' Repetition becomes a barrier to learning. By the age of ten children 'know' what the outcome of the investigation will be and consequently do not feel they have learnt anything.

Developing your own subject knowledge and consequently your own confidence to support children's learning in science is also an important factor in developing positive attitudes to science. Ofsted (2008) noted that, where teachers were confident in their subject knowledge, they were more likely to enjoy science because they were able to follow children's interests. Teachers who were less confident tended to follow schemes of work and were less likely to integrate science enquiry into their teaching. A recent report from the Royal Society (2010) also expressed concern that children were being 'turned off' science because teachers lacked subject knowledge and consequently the confidence to teach science.

Conclusion

In this chapter we have considered how to support children's learning in science. Not only do children need support to carry out the practical work associated with learning science, they also need support to think about the science they are learning and to think about how they are 'doing' science. To support children's learning we need to give them opportunities to talk about the science ideas they are learning. Such talk will help them link new ideas about the science topic with existing knowledge of that topic, so that they develop more scientifically accurate explanations and understanding. Just as important is developing positive attitudes to science. When children lose interest in science, they lack the intrinsic motivation that makes learning science enjoyable and rewarding.

Discussion starters

1   Why is first-hand active learning necessary when we can deliver the curriculum content easily in the form of a set of facts?
2   Why is it important that children make their own decisions about the processes involved in an investigation?
3   Why is it important that children are encouraged to reflect upon the impact of new scientific developments?
4   What constitutes a scientifically literate person?

Reflecting on practice

1   Work with a group of children, or observe your peers, engaged in a practical science activity. Note the language they use and the type of questions they pose (if any). Consider how you might develop their language skills during a science lesson and identify any areas for further development.
2   Create an interesting method of helping children describe their journey through a scientific investigation. The method must be appropriate to the age and aptitude of the children, for example oral reporting for younger children or those who have difficulty expressing themselves in writing.

Useful resources

www.aft.org/newspubs/periodicals/ae/subject.cfm: online articles available in science and other subjects.

www.ase.org.uk: the Association for Science Education.

www.cognitiveacceleration.co.uk: find a case study of Cognitive Acceleration through Science Education (CASE).

www.nsf.gov/publications: the National Science Foundation publications page.

References

Alexander, R. (2006) *Towards Dialogic Teaching: Rethinking classroom talk* (3rd edn), York: Dialogos.

Ausubel, D. (1968) *Educational Psychology: A cognitive view*, New York: Holt, Rinehart and Winston.

Bricheno, P., Johnston, J. and Sears, J. (2000) 'Children's attitudes to science', in Sears, J. and Sprenson, P. (eds) *Issues in Science Teaching*, London: RoutledgeFalmer, pp. 143–53.

Bruner, J.S. (1977) *The Process of Education*, Cambridge, MA: Harvard University Press.

Darwin, C. (1859) *On the Origin of Species*, London: John Murray.

De Boo, M. (1999) *Enquiring Children, Challenging Teaching*, Buckingham: Open University Press.

Harlen, W. (2006) *Teaching, Learning and Assessing Science 5–12*, London: Sage.

Harlen, W. and Qualter, A. (2009) *The Teaching of Science in Primary Schools* (5th edn), London: David Fulton.

Harrison, C. and Howard, S. (2010) 'Issues in primary assessment', *Primary Science*, 115: 5–7. Available online at www.ase.org.uk (accessed 12 February 2011).

Kibble, B. (2008) 'Becoming a good forces teacher', *School Science Review*, 88(328): 77–83.

Loxley, P., Dawes, L., Nicholls, L. and Dore, B. (2010) *Teaching Primary Science: Promoting enjoyment and developing understanding*, Harlow: Pearson.

Millar, R. and Abraham, I. (2009) 'Practical work: making it effective', *School Science Review*, 91: 59–64.

Murphy, C. and Beggs, J. (2005) *Primary Horizons: Starting out in science*, London: Wellcome Trust.

Ofsted (2008) *Success in Science*. Available online at www.ofsted.gov.uk (accessed 12 February 2011).

Piaget, J. (1929) *The Child's Conception of the World*, New York: Harcourt Brace.

Porter, C. and Parvin, J. (2008) *Learning to Love Science: Harnessing children's scientific imagination*, Huntington Beach, CA: Shell Education.

Qualifications and Curriculum Authority (QCA) (1999) *Schemes of Work for Science*. Available online at www.thegrid.org.uk/learning/science/ks1-2/resources/index.shtml (accessed 12 February 2011).

Royal Society (2010) *Primary Science and Mathematics Education: Getting the basics right*. Available online at http://royalsociety.org/State-of-the-Nation-Science-and-Mathematics-Education-5-14/ (accessed 13 August 2010).

Vygotsky, L.S. (1978) *Mind in Society*, Cambridge, MA: Harvard University Press.

Ward, H., Roden, J., Hewlett, C. and Foreman, J. (2008) *Teaching Science in the Primary Classroom: A practical guide* (2nd edn), London: Sage.

Wellington, J. and Ireson, G. (2008) *Science Learning and Science Teaching*, London: Routledge.

The Challenges in Teaching Culturally and Linguistically Diverse Learners

Roshan Ahmed

My values and beliefs about diversity

I share a personal, poignant challenge as a teacher, a learner and as a culturally and linguistically diverse member of a wider global community to affirm the experiences, cultures and languages of the many students we educate. If we consider educational equality of opportunity, education should incorporate rich linguistic and cultural backgrounds allowing all learners to gain full access to the curriculum to which they have entitlement. Therefore, it is unacceptable that low levels of attainment in education associated with minority ethnic groups continue to exist today. Many visions and commitments for cohesion within communities in society are visible within current government policy frameworks. I believe it is possible to bring small changes to our world from our classrooms when we focus on transforming the social future towards which children are moving. By taking these small steps, I believe we can erase racism and intolerance towards societies. Through education, rather than reproducing the past, there are means of transforming the future, but we need to challenge and change the patterns from the past towards a peaceful future. It is our duty to educate every child as tolerant and respectful global citizens, to instil and develop a sense of pride as to who they are. In times of rapid social change, through immigration for example, redefining one's relationship with the environment is crucial to teaching in increasingly diverse classrooms.

Introduction

There has been a 50 per cent rise in learners with English as an additional language (EAL) in schools in Britain since 1997 (NALDIC/TDA, 2009). By 2007, 12 per cent of the whole school population was learning English as an additional language. Teaching in linguistic and culturally diverse classrooms is not a passing phenomenon, but is becoming the norm in English society. In Manchester schools, there are 130 different languages. As more children enter schools from families where English is not the home language, all teachers need to know something about how these children learn English as an additional language. Moreover, since language proficiency is important to nearly everything that takes place in education, it leads us to the challenges faced by teachers in meeting the needs of the EAL child. Genesee (1994) reminds us that all teachers are teachers of language. They serve as models of language, learning and culture. Wood (2007) concludes that strategies are necessary for the learner whose culture, language and social skills require a different curricular model, linking to diverse background experiences rather than the traditional models of teaching towards a specific monolingual, monocultural learner.

There is no separate syllabus for teaching EAL in English schools and neither is it a subject specialism in teacher training. Thus, we need to address the most effective approaches to developing language skills of learners. In mainstream teaching, the approach to teaching EAL is primarily about teaching and learning language through the content of the whole curriculum. However, the issues are not only those of language and pedagogy. Schools need to develop a holistic approach that encompasses social, cognitive and academic, as well as linguistic, development (Genesee, 1994), since a language is not learnt in isolation. As far back as the Bullock Report, *A Language for Life* (DES, 1975), there was recognition that a child's language and culture should be embraced by the school.

The Children Act 2004 and the *Every Child Matters* agenda (DCSF, 2003) specifically outline the need to overcome barriers to learning and achievement and imply the need for a holistic approach to education in recognition of the fine balances of experiences overlapping in a child's life, which need to be taken into account through a 'personalised learning' approach. Considering its identity and pupil constituency, EAL should be a well-founded specialism within schools. However, initial teacher training does not usually offer it as a specialism, so it appears as a marginal, diffused curricular concern.

In a class where all the children are EAL learners, teaching teams have a serious challenge to provide an education that is inclusive, holistic, personalised and responsive to the diverse needs of their learners, since national statistics point to relatively poor educational performance of some ethnically defined groups of EAL children (Kotler *et al.*, 2002, cited in Flynn, 2007). For example, the underachievement of Bangladeshi boys and girls at GCSE is well documented (Lais, 2003). Significantly, the group are also under-represented in employment. We need to ask ourselves why. Genesee (1994) identifies that trouble understanding the nature of children's backgrounds is the cause of academic difficulties and the disproportionate failure of children from minority sociocultural groups.

Another view is that the minority language is perceived as cause for social, economic and educational problems – an example of blaming the victim. Black, Bangladeshi and Pakistani pupils have the lowest level of attainment across all ages in school. People commonly interpret this consistent and disproportionate failure in educational achievement of children from minority groups as language deficits, associated with low cognitive ability and deficit background knowledge (Genesee, 1994). Baker (1993) observes that people with a minority language often have problems of poverty, underachievement in school, minimum social and vocational mobility, and lack of integration with the majority culture. Statistics from 2007 show the poverty rate for Britain's minority ethnic groups at 40 per cent, twice that found among white British people (Joseph Rowntree Foundation, 2007). Such data lead us to analyse the broader societal features such as living conditions, and psychological and social features such as discrimination, racial prejudice and inferiority, not language as a sole factor for underachievement.

The broad range of complex factors connected with learning EAL highlight the issue that the underachievement of pupils learning English as an additional language is not simply one of acquiring English language skills. Commonly, schools report deficiencies hampering achievement that are attributed to certain home practices, such as parents not supporting specific academic areas – counting, reading or visiting galleries and so on. Unfortunately, the values underlying these reports are the middle-class, dominant-culture values that permeate school communities. It is important for teachers to understand a sociocultural view that provides an insight into diverse learners' background knowledge and ultimately the language learning experiences for EAL children, since social structures and dominant social values affect childhood development and shape the language experiences that children bring to school. Lindon (2005) cites Brofenbrenner's (1994) model of interrelationships between different contexts of a child's life.

The core experience is socialisation within the home, the school and places of worship and between friends. This is affected by local neighbourhood experiences and the world-views filtered by parents. In turn, the local experience is influenced by the broader social, educational and economic systems and the interrelationships between the ethnic identity and the dominant culture. The model implies a multi-faceted context where few children learn the same thing at the same time, and support for learning a language and ultimately access to the curriculum cannot proceed as if all children have an identical sequence of experiences; or indeed the experience of a western culture. Research by Boushel *et al.* (2002) found that, in a stratified society, 'school ways' are not necessarily those of the community, and classroom experience is exclusively based on western perspectives of childhood learning. Practitioners need to understand individual children's backgrounds and their learning approaches to promote additional language development effectively and efficiently in context.

Depending on the knowledge and expertise of the teacher, the curriculum can provide some opportunity and scope to reflect the children's cultural backgrounds. In addition, the diverse linguistic backgrounds are equally important, since the processes involved in learning another language (English) cannot be altered (VanPatten and Benati, 2010). Knowing how to affect the rate and ultimately the proficiency of language development is of value to teaching practice. Teaching teams need to know:

- how an additional language is learnt compared to a first language;
- the language development sequence;
- the correlation between cognition and age affecting the rate of learning an additional language;
- the impact of learning two languages on cognitive development;
- the relationship between oral, social communication and academic language skills, encompassing the social and cultural diversity that affects language learning styles.

Expectations must be realistic, based on accurate understanding of the sequence in additional language development. Teaching teams need to know how it links closely to, and reflects, the acquisition of academic skills and knowledge. We cannot postpone academic learning until children reach the expected level of language proficiency. It is equally important to examine assumptions or misconceptions about language learning and bilingualism that might exclude children from educational opportunities.

My reflexive practice has guided my teaching immensely and I refer to wider reading that informed my EAL knowledge base from theory and research, as part of my professional development practice. Cummins (1991) emphasises the continuous spiral action of how theory integrates our observations and practices into coherent perspectives, and that it is these perspectives that feed back into practice and from practice into theory again. I would hope that readers share my perspectives on EAL matters and relate their thoughts and practices to the chapter, which may lead to developments in their own teaching practices to address barriers to achievement for all learners.

My bilingual influence

The challenge of teaching large cohorts of EAL pupils has given me a passion to build on previous knowledge gained in ten years' experience as a teaching assistant with the Ethnic Minority Achievement Service (EMAS) in Manchester. The service provided continuous professional development and training in areas specific to EAL issues, which linked directly to my role. The National Association for Language Development in the Curriculum indicates that EAL pupil numbers have grown significantly since 2004 (NALDIC, 2009), while a disproportionate number of specialist EAL teachers exist. All teaching teams require some knowledge and expertise in this specialism.

While addressing the challenge of meeting the needs of thirty pupils at various stages in developing EAL, there has been opportunity to explore issues in my practice. I researched the local Bangladeshi community, which illustrated a mismatch in personal, social, cultural and family expectations for the children. These young EAL learners actively negotiate the different language usages to interact within the school, and with their families and the community in their daily lives, which are in contrast with one another. I have collated common questions from colleagues and families that readers may identify with:

- If two languages are learnt, is there a difference in the sequence of language development compared to a monolingual child?
- Will learning two languages simultaneously confuse or delay a child's language acquisition?
- Is there interference in cognitive development when learning in two languages?
- How can I support a child who needs to learn English but has a different home language?
- What strategies can we use in our teaching, considering the child has knowledge that is different from the language and culture in school?

■ Should we encourage parents to use the majority language, under the assumption that the sooner we expose children to English, the faster they will learn and the more they will achieve academically?

The answers to these questions, and others, ought to become clear throughout the chapter.

In England, we expect children to follow the National Curriculum and achieve age-related targets. For schools having children with limited language proficiency in English, achieving the same goals in an additional language is often a challenge beyond the academic development of such learners. Researchers and educators (Genesee, 1994) have argued that academic success is influenced by cultural and social, as well as linguistic, backgrounds, so what are the implications in teaching the 'whole child'? It is evident that teaching teams need to view learners beyond the deficit language and cultural model, to recognise the influences of different cultures and languages, which can transform classrooms into a multicultural hub of languages, diverse cultures and global perspectives. Linking with the diverse communities residing in the school's vicinity is an exciting way to explore and extend the learning and teaching of pupils beyond the classroom. Good knowledge of prior learning is a precondition of good teaching (Genesee, 1994; Heath, 1983). Teaching teams may use such knowledge as a starting point for developing curriculum models of local knowledge. Using these rich resources to assist in designing the curriculum simultaneously validates and values children's backgrounds and languages. We should not ignore the multiple benefits of bilingualism and a multicultural heritage. This contrasts with a common view that everyone should speak English, marginalising and devaluing the learning and speaking of other languages.

As a school pupil in another country, I experienced frustration trying to comprehend a new language, alongside the culture shock. I also observed my son, bilingual through exposure to two languages from birth living in England. I therefore share circumstances involving additional language learning that some learners entering our schools are now experiencing. Some EAL learners have experienced horrific events – wars, seeking asylum, living as refugees – which I can never comprehend. My experience as bilingual differentiates my professional position, to a certain extent, as an 'insider' as opposed to an 'outsider' when understanding aspects of EAL issues. This chapter aims to address the barriers to the acquisition of an additional language through reflection on aspects related to my practice.

Categorising the additional language learner

To categorise language learners as bilingual, additional language learners or monolingual leads to assimilating speakers within a rigid set of commonalities. Martin-Jones and Bhatti (2003) conclude that terms such as 'native speaker' and 'mother tongue' are inadequate labels and evoke notions of proficiency in a language, cultural inheritance and language loyalty. Social change is widespread and identity is fluid, so personal identity cannot be summarised accurately in large language groupings. One person could have a multiplicity of identities and language use.

I can illustrate the complex factors though describing my language learning experiences. I was a monolingual, monocultural student in an English primary school until I was seven, when my identity changed dramatically after the divorce of my parents. I became bilingual within a year of immersion into a new language, Bengali, in Bangladesh. In addition to learning a new language, I acquired some knowledge of the written system and contrasting cultural values. On return to England, my bilingualism was never recognised or used beyond my home life, in school. My bilingualism and diverse cultural background was not the norm. I certainly had no perception that I had entered a global majority group of speakers of more than one language.

I also learnt the phonetic approach to reading Arabic through a strict rote teaching style – the teaching methods adopted by many minority ethnic groups. I learnt during evenings as part of my religious Islamic teaching, without any comprehension of Arabic. At secondary school, French was compulsory for the first three years. This was a discrete subject area with a specialist subject teacher. I did not study French after the third year because my family considered it irrelevant to the Bengali culture and my life. However, I was aware that the French language was, at that time, given high status, utilitarian value and recognition, while Bengali as a minority language was considered a low-status community language, not promoted at school.

Perpetuating language minority and diversity has the potential to cause less integration and less cohesiveness, and to increase social conflict in society. Only now, as a confident adult, can I appreciate and reflect upon the rich knowledge and contrasting dimensions of the cultures and diversity that have existed in my life through language learning. Every day, it influences every aspect of my life. I conclude that my diversity enables me to integrate in two societies with a broad understanding of cultural expectations and the ability to communicate with a wider range of people. My background is a fantastic resource in teaching and in facilitating community links with school and parents.

My points illustrate the fact that additional language learning is a very complex topic within which conflicting arenas exist that represent family values, cultures and religions alongside broader societal contexts that mould a child's existence. These complex individual experiences of EAL learners affect the extent, competency and fluency in languages learnt. I hope to portray language learning as it overlaps with the social and emotional, as well as the cultural, arenas of development, affected by the changing identity and self-esteem of learners.

The development of a first and an additional language

We will reflect briefly on how children develop their first words as a backdrop to contrasting this with the development of an additional language. During early cognitive development, children's first words emerge because they symbolise concrete objects or emotions, facts of life that children know: people, foods, feelings. They communicate in the present because there is a reason to do so in relation to their current level of cognitive and physical development. The child's emerging words connect with what the child is already thinking and doing, known as concrete or embedded language skills. These words represent rather than introduce new meaning. Later, the language precedes the actions and functions for processes beyond immediate experiences, known as abstract or disembedded language skills. Genesee (1994) notes that Chomsky concluded that children actively construct their own principles to learn a language. Saying 'foots' and 'goed' indicates the use of principles, but not what they have heard. Children naturally pass through this phase of language development and gradually modify the rules.

As the developing language emerges through interactions and shared activities, the parent usually adapts their language to the level of the developing language. Typically, parents use simpler sentences, repeat keywords, and keep language to the present time with familiar objects and activities that children can understand. Language develops further through culturally influenced conversations children have with members of their family. Additionally, children adapt socially by observing and learning the customs and ways associated with family interactions and shared activities. They learn the family's value system, often shared by its community. The content of the developing language also provides an understanding of the world, assisting children's rapidly developing cognitive abilities. The close relationship between cognitive development, language, and cultural and social conditions is therefore clear.

Additional language learning occurs in a similar pattern, but more likely within social and cultural contexts not associated with the language. However, using similar strategies to those that parents use for infants developing their first language assists additional language learning, for example:

- using a high-pitched voice and more expression and gestures than in an adult conversation;
- speaking at a slower pace and with more pauses;
- using simple short sentences and repetition of keywords;
- speaking in the present tense through shared activities with two-way verbal interactions extending the child's language.

Thus, there are parallels in the process that teaching teams may use in the classroom.

Simultaneous and sequential or successive bilingualism

What are the implications for language learning if a child is learning two languages from birth? This is *simultaneous* bilingualism, when a child learns two or more languages from birth, or is introduced to a second language before the age of three. There are many common myths about language development associated with simultaneous bilingualism, for example the belief that the infant does not have a sufficiently developed cognitive ability to handle two language systems at this stage and can have delayed speech problems or intermix languages due to confusion. Many believe that using only English at home would ensure rapid development. Neurolinguistic research has found that bilingual infants can differentiate two languages, since they can differentiate sounds associated with each language. There is no delay either in the appearance of a bilingual infant's first word or with the subsequent development sequence rate of language compared to a monolingual infant. However, a child is usually stronger in one language and can use words 'borrowed' from either language, which is due to a limited vocabulary competency rather than confusion between languages. Evidence has indicated that infants are aware of the two systems and can use the knowledge of 'languages' to switch between them from a young age. I have observed my neighbour's successful bilingual two-year-old daughter who attempts to converse with me in her developing English while instantaneously and effortlessly functioning in Urdu with her siblings. My conversations with my son also include code-switching effortlessly, by choice, between two languages, which supports Krashen's view (1987, cited in VanPatten and Benati, 2010) that the optimum way to learn two languages is simultaneously from birth, which allows a longer time span for languages to develop with a more native-like accent, which alters as we get older.

Many children entering English classrooms fall into the category of 'sequential or successive bilingualism', when a child is exposed to an additional language after the age of three and the first language is already sufficiently developed for communication. They are sophisticated language learners and are already adept at learning a first language and their brains can foster new language patterns based on this. This pinpoints the issue central in this chapter and my profession, since first language development is crucial to ensure progression in the academic and social development of all learners while addressing their language needs.

Another common misconception is that the development of the English language should be reinforced as quickly as possible without acknowledgement of, or relevance to, the first language. This is possibly the worst-case scenario in the development of EAL learners, not just academically; there are broad implications if such misconceptions are accepted. Fillmore (1991, cited in Genesee, 1994) states that the loss of a first language results in communication difficulties and significant alienation from parents. Teaching teams need to be aware of both personal and academic consequences caused by replacing the student's first language with English. It may undermine the personal and cultural confidence that is essential to a student's academic progress. Moreover, promoting home language literacy correlates well with academic development across languages, since it is transferable, as demonstrated by English-speaking Canadian children who developed high proficiency in French (Lambert and Tucker, 1972, cited in Genesee, 1994). Therefore, it is not beneficial to encourage parents in using a developing new language with their children where a stronger foundation in a home language is intact and is in use. We should encourage parents to continue the growth of a home language and, if possible, develop it further through out-of-school clubs. Hall (1995) notes that research has shown that minority language children who develop their first language skills fully during the preschool years often make transition to schooling in English more easily and effectively than children who do not maintain their first language. Young children aged four to five learn new languages at a faster rate than older children or adults. The amount of language and cognitive and experiential experiences necessary to be on a par with their monolingual counterparts is comparatively small when considering that older children and adults require more sophisticated and broader language use due to greater cognitive demands. This leads us to the next question.

Is there a pattern of sequential development in an additional language?

When children use fluent, native-like, social forms of English language skills, we might assume they are accomplished speakers in the new language. In fact, such oral fluency, known as basic interpersonal communication skills (BICS), relies on contextualised language and language commonly used by peers or on television. Cummins (1984) has indicated that a further five to seven years is required to develop disembedded, decontextualised cognitive academic language proficiency (CALP). This enables learners to articulate higher-order abstract thought beyond the present and without reliance on concrete materials to support language development or cognition. A brief overview of the second language acquisition sequence shows how a child will follow some of the same steps they followed when acquiring their first language (Hall, 1995): (1) silence, (2) ease of communication, (3) grammatical or syntactic accuracy and (4) age-appropriate academic English.

It is common for children to pass through a silent phase as they internalise language they hear and seek verbal patterns to derive meaning from the environment before they start to experiment with a new language. Research from the 1970s identified that learners must pass through a hierarchical development. At an early stage a child might say 'No eat apple.' Progress is indicated when the child says 'I no eat apple.' The stages indicate the process of language being organised over time and can be used to assess the point of development the learner has acquired. If a child starts nursery as an early stage EAL learner, a long-term effective teaching programme is necessary to reach the same fluency level of their English-speaking peers. Time on task is not an important factor when learning English. In classes where children use their home language and English, children acquired English language skills at the same rate as those in English-only classrooms. There is much more involved in learning an additional language than time spent learning how to speak it.

The relationship between a first and an additional language

If we consider the development of a first language from birth, it is evident that there is a link between the cognitive, social and linguistic domains. All interplay in the child's development but in different ways according to the stage of development. Early cognitive development contributes to first words in a social world. Later in life, language, in various social contexts, facilitates the development of higher-order cognitive ability.

For EAL learners we must recognise that knowledge is generated during and through first language acquisition, and cognitive development through their social interactions with others (Genesee, 1994). Teaching teams must not dismiss the importance of the first language skills because they are a vital key to the child's knowledge of the world and further language learning skills, and are where the child's self-identity and values in that language group are entrusted. Cordier (1967, cited in VanPatten and Benati, 2010) noted that advances in language instruction would not occur until we understand what language learners bring to the task of acquisition.

To reach the end of the language continuum, first steps must be built from the familiar contexts in which a first language meaning has been built upon as a basis for any additional language development programme.

Home–school links

Schools socialise children to the goals, values and beliefs of the dominant society and the communicative interpersonal context for language learning. Homes that match 'school ways' help children adapt, while homes that have different socialisation may cause conflict for the child and the family. Some children, and their families, take longer to accommodate and develop two socialisation patterns in their developing dual cultural existence. However, those children and families who behave and adapt to a majority group language, socialisation and cultural expectations may be alienated from their peer groups (Lindon, 2005) in the wider community. Children in my research are giving greater precedence to their acquired language and reinforcing their power and status at home as bilinguals: a new identity acquired from school, which involves new values and beliefs. Parents find it threatening. Schools must find ways of reducing these anxieties and enabling confidence in both language and cultural change. The recent introduction of multi-agency teams, providing specialist services and support to children and their families, illustrates the recognition of the necessary holistic approach.

Parents as educators

Many parents have been educated in their home countries. Many give high status to education but believe it is the teacher's duty to educate and therefore do not always support homework activities or home-school initiatives. Despite this, some projects, such as that by Tizard *et al.* (1982), to involve ethnic minority parents in education have been very successful over the past twenty-five years, leading to increased attainment of their children. Problems may arise when staff make suggestions as to how parents can assist (Genesee, 1994), such as with homework reading materials depicting middle-class values in the dominant language, with an expectation that this parental interaction with their children will mirror school practices, without considering carefully family situation or culturally preferred ways of interacting. My own research revealed that, usually, older siblings or family members who had attended school in Britain read to the children in my class, not other members of the family. We might argue that parent–school partnerships threaten patterns of the socialisation environment of children at home by not recognising cultural/social norms, thereby marginalising families and creating further rifts between school and home, which affects the self-esteem of children and, consequently, their experience of learning.

Influences on the learning of a second language

There are barriers affecting the progression to language proficiency. Genesee (1994) discusses sets of internal and external conditions affecting children. The 'internal' conditions include age, gender, cognitive and linguistic abilities, and physical and emotional well-being. External conditions include many of those previously discussed – the social context, family, neighbours, friends, school, home and community languages, political issues such as asylum seeking, and religion. An example of a specific internal condition is that of marriage between blood relations in Pakistani families, which has caused over-representation of this ethnic group as having special educational needs (SEN). Some external conditions are far-reaching and beyond the scope of this chapter, but an important one is the teaching team's expertise, which clearly influences the quality of instruction.

EAL and the education system

Every lesson is a language lesson. Current government schemes of work and guidance provide the vocabulary relevant for conceptual development and to assist assessment. Additional language learning has not always been integral with all aspects of education. Historically, teaching bilingual learners has reflected two different perspectives of effective language teaching. In 1970s' English schools, children were usually withdrawn from mainstream classrooms to learn language separately from subject learning, some children travelling to a different building for this. An advantage of separate classes, with a specialist teacher, was space and time to develop language with similar peers without feeling too intimidated to speak. The repetition of language in decontextualised contexts was a common strategy. This was before the pressures of national testing.

Nowadays, all children need to achieve age-related subject attainment targets; we cannot postpone subject learning until children reach the expected level of language proficiency. Moreover, learners need to use language in many different contexts. Language is not just for education, but also for social integration and future economic success. New practices for EAL provision within mainstream classrooms began to emerge in the later 1970s with specialist teachers supporting the curriculum within the classroom. Levine (1990) reports the specialist teacher adjusting and mediating materials, tasks and processes for EAL learners to complete the same as their peers in a staged and defined way for progressive development in English. A teaching certificate from the Royal Society of Arts was recognised for EAL teaching – the Certificate in the Teaching of Language as a Second Language in Multicultural Schools. By the end of the 1970s there were funded Ethnic Minority Achievement Services (EMAS). During the 1980s a new mainstream partnership between local education authority (LEA) support services and specialist English teachers influenced whole-school curriculum development as inclusive practice. Over a twenty-year period the services evolved according to local and national influences. The Children Act 2004 gave schools more autonomy and, with it, the responsibility to employ and train bilingual support staff and teachers as part of whole-school development. Thus, there has been a significant change over the last forty years, from externally provided, isolated language learning to fully integrated, locally provided education within each school.

There are noticeable differences in the acquisition rates and proficiency levels among EAL learners. This is not surprising, since learners are trying to comprehend the meaning from a new language while their brains are acquiring the linguistic system. Krashen (1987) identifies that 'unconscious acquisition' occurs as an alternative to 'conscious learning'. He emphasises that formal instruction does not influence acquisition, nor alter the sequence or rate of acquisition up to adolescence. So what does affect acquisition? Teaching teams might focus on how learners internalise the linguistic system:

- by making use of the linguistic system during comprehension tasks (input);
- by constructing language for speech production (output).

Krashen claims that his theory of *Comprehensible Input* is the most important variable central to language acquisition. Conversely, Swain (1985) advocates the theory of *Output Hypothesis* as the most influential, where the oral use of language in broad contexts supports acquisition. Both theories are widely promoted as beneficial to EAL practice.

In the 1950s researchers found that aptitude was linked to cognitive abilities; more capable children were more likely to be motivated and learn quickly. Motivation links with psychological and emotional elements, and to perceptions of self-identity and self-esteem, which influence the pace of children's additional language acquisition. Culture is therefore important and there is much research into learners' perceptions of the relevance of language to their identity and culture. Differences in culture also affect learners' perceptions of themselves within the class group measured by social class, skin colour, dress etc. Research reveals that there is an inverse relationship between social distance and language proficiency; the greater the social distance, the lesser the proficiency (VanPatten and Benati, 2010). Language learning is not just about language at all; as Heath (1986) states, 'Language learning is cultural learning.' Acculturation, the process of adapting to a new culture, is directly linked to language acquisition. It is vital that learners integrate into the dominant cultural group where all learners develop positive attitudes to each other's languages, cultures and differences, since anxiety, low self-esteem and confidence lead to a decrease in motivation to acquire a language with its cultural expectations.

Moore and Gilliard (2007) concluded that teachers who come from cultural backgrounds different from those of their students may experience difficulties in understanding the basic communication and behaviour tenets associated with their learners. Teaching teams, therefore, must learn about their students' cultures. Moreover, Armstrong and Barton (1999) have also identified correlation between behaviour problems and culture. From the age of eight, my neighbour, of Afro-Caribbean background, recalls being teased by his teacher and peers for his different English accent and Jamaican Patois language. His Jamaican peers became disillusioned by, and aloof from, the British schooling system and society. Some minority groups feel unable to adopt the cultural beliefs of the dominant group portrayed by schools, leading them to emphasise their distinctive cultural beliefs even more. My neighbour's peers exhibited negative behaviour resulting in school exclusions due to their inability to feel accepted and to integrate.

Pupils often react badly when teaching teams lack respect for or interest in them (Ofsted, 2005). Even if school practices and policies for inclusion have changed, some historical effects may pass from first-generation migrants' experience, affecting the behaviour and social patterns of second-generation groups. Maybe this accounts for reported statistics (DfES, 2005) of Black Caribbean, White Caribbean and other black pupils as being most likely to be excluded from schools.

Positively promoting diversity and difference

The current National Curriculum encourages the use of culturally diverse resources and promotes inclusion for minority ethnic pupils. Teaching teams must ensure that all learners are recognised and valued in lessons, using resources that positively depict the cultural values of the learners. Learning is best when teaching teams know pupils well and plan lessons that take account of their different abilities, interests and backgrounds (Ofsted, 2005). In my experience, introducing Somali artefacts or learning about Black history does not suit all children in a school with diverse cultures. Such activities might clash with another culture's values and beliefs. To improve my own practice, I reflected how I could identify and incorporate experiences relevant to the learners' diverse backgrounds within my teaching.

I teach five- to six-year-old children. All have diverse backgrounds. I have faced many challenging experiences where learners are at different stages in language acquisition. In addition, these minority ethnic learners are of an age where they are forming their identities, and I have witnessed many negative conversations between learners about their different identities and those of others. Interestingly, by the age of seven, not only are children aware of gender and skin colour, but they can understand that they can be a member of several groups, for example a family, a classroom, an ethnic group and a religion. Klein (2001) stated that teachers have a responsibility to limit negative influences from family and media that affect children's attitudes. Therefore, I need ways in which I can promote human diversity without prejudice, to ensure that all learners feel valued and accepted for who they are. If the learners value each other, negative emotional reactions to anything different from the child's customs and beliefs are reduced and prejudice discouraged.

I challenged myself to deliver a session that emphasised the uniqueness of each child, as well as developing the language and cognitive development of children. Derman-Sparks (1979, cited in Klein, 2001) states that such activities, exploiting children's uniqueness, help them deal with issues of ethnic and racial identity and bias. The activity for a personal, social and health education session promoted the development of social skills. A focus on social skills is important, since the challenging behaviour of many younger pupils arises mainly as a result of poor language and social skills (Ofsted, 2005). The focus was 'We are all alike and we are all different.' Children taped their voices, followed by discussion of the similarities and differences between voices. The topic shifted sensitively from voices to physical appearance. I observed that they enjoyed discussing their skin and hair colour and the different foods and clothes in their cultures. All the children completed a mini-book called 'I Am Special', where they drew themselves and identified different foods and clothes. The children reviewed and assessed each other's work during the plenary.

The children developed respect for each other within a positive classroom climate. I noticed children listening attentively to each other and revealing personal information. One boy remarked that he ate rice with his fingers, but at school he used a knife and fork to eat his dinner. I mentioned that I also occasionally ate rice with my fingers. Consequently, other children felt confident to raise the fact that they ate chapattis with their fingers. I observed that the children were motivated and curious about each other and had not made any derogatory or negative remarks.

Curriculum development and planning for EAL

Differentiation enables equal access to a learning experience. The teaching team's challenge is to provide common experiences for children with diverse linguistic and cultural backgrounds. Doddington (1996) raises the point that the language of the National Curriculum suggests a preformed set of constructed vocabularies. This notion contrasts with the idea of accepting diversity. Having a fixed curriculum that scaffolds publicly accepted knowledge, mainly relevant to children with English as their mother tongue, goes against the idea of understanding the broader world of mother tongue knowledge. The concept of standardised knowledge confines human understanding to a fixed reality. Knowledge is actually embedded in different cultures and traditions, evolving with time. Transmitting knowledge through a different cultural frame will not encourage learning. Information is analysed in the light of one's experiences and emotions, providing an authentic context in which additional language acquisition can be supported.

Accessing the diverse knowledge and backgrounds of learners

Some activities developed to extend children's concepts and understanding may be incongruent with children's experience, and my research concluded that many EAL children cannot extend their views, or choose to remain silent, during activities. Figure 8.1 illustrates the connections and challenges involved.

I explored the geography topic 'Where in the world is Barnaby Bear?' for links with the background knowledge of my diverse learners. Links with the children's background knowledge of their countries and communities enabled a meaningful context in which to decipher words and further develop language acquisition skills. Over the next few weeks, children and parents were encouraged to contribute items from their homes and community. Saris, Somali cowbells, rolling pins and flour, traditional African hats and photos from New York appeared. The class invited staff and parents to talk about their backgrounds, countries and languages. The context reflected a pluralistic society linking a diverse view of the world beyond our

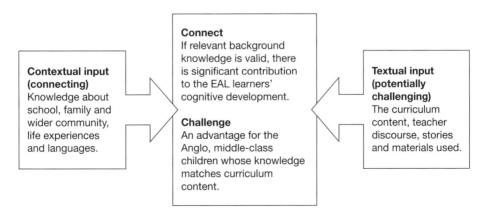

FIGURE 8.1 Connections and challenges

communities; in fact, we were a community of learners. The sense of community enhanced the feeling of belonging as individuals in school, forging genuine home–school partnerships and community cohesion. It promoted equality, reflecting the requirements of the Race Relations (Amended) Act (2000) to:

- provide equality of opportunity;
- tackle unlawful racial discrimination;
- promote good relations between members of different ethnic communities.

The experience enhanced my understanding of many backgrounds and cultures in the class. By establishing good communication with parents, I too can learn about the different cultural views and recognise and address any conflicts sensitively.

Some commercial resources are culturally rich, but teaching teams must consider the impact on each individual child, since providing an incomprehensible context could be overwhelming. Teaching teams should adapt materials or texts. For example, in the story called 'The Tiger Who came to Tea', my learners could not comprehend the foods eaten in the story. The high cognitive and linguistic demand led to distraction and tiredness. Another example in maths is the use of appropriate everyday contexts. Using chickpeas or rice in shopping activities is more real than going to the cinema, for example. This illustrates the importance of infusing culture into curriculum topics in a way that enhances self-identity and comprehension of language.

Promoting language and academic development in EAL learners

I emphasise language development though curriculum subject planning. I aim to address age-appropriate intellectual skills, alongside social and emotional development. Hence, there is a match between the level of language learning needs and conceptual ability. It is important to adapt the level of instruction, support comprehension and build up language through a variety of teaching strategies. Cummins (1984, cited in Hall, 1995) devised a simple matrix that assists differentiation in planning (Figure 8.2). It ensures that teaching teams assess EAL learners' levels of language and provide contextual support to enhance cognitive development. Gradually, the high demand for context cues to support language reduces as the language develops; the two-dimensional matrix also reminds teachers about the need to plan cognitively demanding activities.

Initially, I grouped learners according to literacy attainment levels. There was little transition or interaction between groups. Both children and their families were aware of the status of the ability groups, as I was. However, the groups did not facilitate language necessary for social integration alongside opportunities to develop academic language. Neither did the classroom organisation enhance the self-esteem and identity of some groups. The segregation of learners in lessons provided those with the most need the least opportunities to hear language at an advanced stage of proficiency. I considered how to adjust my grouping strategies to maximise the learning potential of my diverse learners within a sensitive interpersonal learning environment.

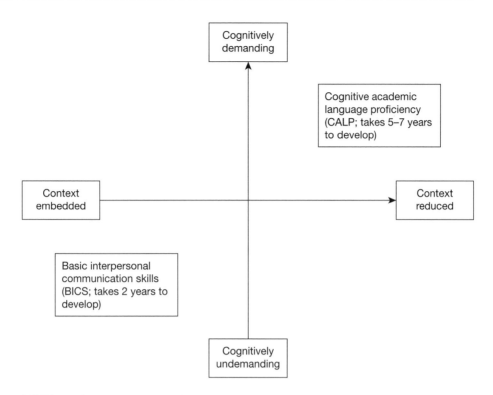

FIGURE 8.2 Cummins' planning model

Grouping strategies

Mixed-ability groups or talk partners manipulate the social dynamics in classrooms, increasing the interaction between more proficient speakers and less proficient speakers. Children can and do modify their speech and are aware of the need to do so. EAL children can answer questions because their peers assist them in formulating sentences in order to enable them to answer questions, and they do not mind doing so. In fact, building new friendships with others is one of the most powerful motivators for language learning.

Literacy groups

I retained the literacy groups as a means of providing effective intense target language input and differentiated tasks to provide challenge at their level, suitable for guided reading, guided talk and guided writing tasks. There is opportunity to provide useful language input for language acquisition using props and visuals to suit the need. A variety of language strategies can be used, such as repetition and rephrasing, with the teacher or peers. Teaching teams extend conversation and thinking by supporting conversational interaction in a similar way to parents supporting children's language acquisition at home. An interpersonal context is created where the learners can experience, test and interpret meaning at a comprehensible level. Research also suggests that a teacher or teaching assistant working with a small group can be one of the most valuable participation structures for EAL learning. Wong (1985, in Genesee, 1994) has noted that small group work with teachers enables the use of appropriate strategies to make language comprehensible and tailor it to learners' specific needs.

First language groups

Learners with a shared first language can support learning and confirm additional language meaning. Hall (1995) discusses the theory that there is an underlying conceptual and linguistic proficiency that is transferable between languages as the new language develops. Because the additional language acquisition takes time, children will need support with the home language, to avoid falling behind with academic learning. Trained bilingual staff may provide additional support in the home language, enabling children to participate alongside their peers in school activities.

Collaborative learning groups

These are mixed-ability groups. The opportunity makes learners responsible for their own learning. They share skills and support each other using social and academic language. This provides an interpersonal context in which to use authentic meaningful communication and develop conceptual understanding. I had previously used this approach during talk partner grouping, to enable collaboration between learners before sharing their views with the class.

Using curriculum content to support language acquisition

I was aware that I was transmitting knowledge and skills that I identified with, which disempowered the shared experiences and voices of my learners. I wanted to deviate from my teacher talk and the concept of children as passive learners. I was propelled by Vygotsky's (1978) proposal that 'conceptual thought is derived from dialogue'. Reading about a classroom where the ethos evolved around the class as a whole community engaged in dialogue to share knowledge (Doddington, 1996) inspired me. It followed Vygotsky's theory that learning occurs first in the social context and then as individual thought; thought occurs when talk is internalised.

The topic of Ancient Egypt, historical and geographical knowledge, was linked to language and mathematical learning activities. Opportunities to use oral language were organised in a social situation linked to learning outcomes. The children worked as a community where understanding and knowledge were promoted through role-play, engaging the class in a common experience. Gaps in individual learning were filled by other learners. There were cognitive challenges in thinking, language interactions, meaningful contexts for language development and a supportive social context where all individuals had an active role.

Through a stepped, interactive literacy process, the children have the possibility of acting out their own realities and analysis of issues, rather than accepting the truths implied in the given curriculum. The steps are:

1   *Descriptive phase*: Learners' comprehension is limited to acting on the text only; knowledge remains inert rather than becoming a catalyst for further exploration (transmitting knowledge).

2   *Personal interpretive and critical stage*: Delve into the personal thoughts of the learners as they relate to the experience – What is happening? When did this happen in the text? Best as a collaborative activity.

3   *Personal interactive phase*: Interpretation depends on individuals' comprehension by grounding knowledge in the personal and collective narratives that make up our experience and history.

4   *Critical analysis phase*: This stage further extends the comprehension process by examining the internal logic of information and how it fits with other knowledge.

5   *Creative action phase*: This constitutes concrete action from the learner as a transformation of social reality (Genesee, 1994).

This process coincides with Vygotsky's 'zone of proximal development', as discussed by Pat Hughes in Chapter 3. Swain (1985, cited in VanPatten and Benati, 2010) also emphasises the need for frequent and sustained opportunities to produce language through collaborative group learning in order to promote language acquisition.

Collaborative learning in science

In one science lesson, I aimed to develop knowledge through a discovery process within my role as a scaffolder of language, in order to promote learners to the next level of conceptual understanding through talk. The topic of waterproof materials was a recent introduction. I used a traditional tale – baby bear got caught in the rain in the woods. Water poured over a teddy bear created a context to demonstrate the meaning of wet and dry. Children had a selection of materials available, a small bear and a cup of water. I asked them to collaborate to find out how teddy could be kept dry. The children knew about materials from a previous topic, so I emphasised the notion of being 'waterproof'. Children negotiated to find an effective waterproof material. I did not intervene in the process. These active learners had their own ideas, language and concepts from their own backgrounds and experiences. The children thought aloud and used a range of language opportunities:

■   they heard the target language from other pupils;

■   they used academic and social styles of language;

■   there were interactions between a broad range of speakers;

■   words were rephrased, repeated, spoken and heard;

■   they used various sentence structures such as questions and answers;

■   there were different uses of intonation;

■   talk was used as a learning tool;

■   there were numerous opportunities to support language acquisition.

The process encompassed the idea of comprehensible input and constructing language for output. Less experienced or less confident children observed and listened to others but were still part of a group. A record sheet allowed children to stick on or write about the materials they sorted as waterproof or not waterproof, which provided assessment without the need of language proficiency or writing skills. The plenary enabled children to discuss the task and findings. My role in the plenary was to extend thinking by asking questions and probing into conceptual understanding.

The quality of the teaching team is unquestionably the most important factor in determining the success of an EAL learner's language acquisition alongside academic development in curriculum subjects. I hope that my examples and discussions have provided some insight into the research and preparation needed to provide suitable learning experiences for a diverse community of children.

Conclusion

Within the shifting current context among the global population, it is vital that teaching teams reflect inwardly on the values and beliefs we bring to our classrooms, for example the awareness of, and orientation to, issues around equity and power in the wider society. We are all affected by biased views through the media's portrayal of racial or ethnic communities, locally and globally. It could be argued that such influences directly impact on our views and relationships towards different communities, which may, to some extent, alter our relationships, positively or negatively, towards learners and affect the 'climate' in our classrooms. These potential repercussions affect classroom interaction between educators and students, which, according to Cummins (1991), is the most direct determinant of educational success or failure for culturally and linguistically diverse students.

Discussion starters

1   What external agencies and services are you aware of in your locality that link with families and enable schools to provide for the holistic needs of a child from an ethnic minority group?
2   How does a school promote community cohesion?
3   How is the importance of the development of a home language as a vital factor supporting the acquisition of English language skills communicated to children's families?

Reflecting on practice

1   Look at a selection of local and national assessment data. Are there variations in the attainment of minority ethnic groups? Discuss possible reasons for the variations.

2   I currently scribe children's use of language alongside pieces of work as a form of summative language assessment. I am considering taping children's use of language to use for assessment and evidence of the language acquisition process and to target language support in planning. What are the implications for my planning, preparation, assessment and time management?

Useful resources

Websites

www.globalgateway.org/Default.aspx?page=4073: a website that links schools.

www.iteachilearn.com/cummins: Jim Cummins' home page, with links to various articles.

www.jrf.org.uk: Joseph Rowntree Foundation; carries various research reports and other materials related to social issues, including ethnicity, faith and education.

www.naldic.org.uk: National Association for Language Development in the Curriculum – various resources and links.

www.sdkrashen.com: Stephen Krashen's website, which includes texts on literacy and bilingual education.

Interesting fiction books

Ali, S. (2008) *Belonging*, London: John Murray (a true story set in England and Pakistan, providing a very moving insight into what it means to belong to a culture, family and language).

Hosseini, K. (2007) *A Thousand Splendid Suns*, London: Bloomsbury (a story reflecting life, culture and traditions in Afganistan).

References

Armstrong, F. and Barton, L. (1999) 'Is there anyone there concerned with human rights? Cross cultural connections, disability and the struggle for change in England', in Armstrong, F. and Barton, F. (eds) *Disability, Education and Cross Cultural Perspectives*, London: Open University Press.

Baker, C. (1993) *Foundations of Bilingual Education and Bilingualism*, Clevedon: Multilingual Matters.

Boushel, M., Fawcett, M. and Selwyn, J. (2002) *Focus on Early Childhood: Principles and realities*, Malden, MA: Blackwell Science.

Cummins, J. (1984) *Bilingualism and Special Education: Issues in assessment and pedagogy*, Clevedon: Multicultural Matters.

Cummins, J. (1991) *Language, Power and Pedagogy: Bilingual children in the crossfire*, Clevedon: Multilingual Matters.

Department for Children, Schools and Families (DCSF) (2003) *Every Child Matters*, London: DCSF.

Department for Education and Skills (DfES) (2005) *Ethnicity and Education: The evidence on minority ethnic pupils aged 5–16*, London: DfES.

Department of Education and Science (DES) (1975) *Language for Life* (Bullock Report). Available online at www.educationengland.org.uk/documents/bullock/bullock01.html (accessed 31 August 2010).

Doddington, C. (1996) 'Grounds for differentiation: some values and principles in primary education considered', in Bearne, E. (ed.) *Differentiation and Diversity in Primary Schools*, London: Routledge.

Flynn, N. (2007) 'Good practice for pupils learning English as an additional language: lessons from effective literacy teachers in inner-city primary schools', *Journal of Early Childhood Literacy*, 7: 177–98.

Genesee, F. (1994) *Educating Second Language Children: The whole child, the whole curriculum, the whole community*, New York: Cambridge University Press.

Hall, D. (1995) *Assessing the Needs of Bilingual Children*, London: Fulton.

Heath, S.B. (1983) *Ways with Words, Language, Life and Work in Communities and Classrooms*, Cambridge: Cambridge University Press.

Heath, S.B. (1986) 'Sociocultural contexts of language development', in Bilingual Education Office (ed.) *Beyond Language: Social and cultural factors in schooling language minority children*, Sacramento, CA: California State Department of Education, pp. 143–86.

Joseph Rowntree Foundation (2007) *Poverty and Ethnicity in the UK*. Available online at www.jrf.org.uk/publications/poverty-and-ethnicity-uk (accessed 12 February 2011).

Klein, M.D. (2001) *Working with Children from Culturally Diverse Backgrounds*, New York: Thomas Demar.

Krashen, S.D. (1987) *Principles and Practice in Second Language Acquisition*, London: Prentice Hall International.

Lais, M.A. (2003) *Bangladeshi Children: Fight the decades of underachievement*, The Muslim Council of Britain. Available online at www.mcb.org.uk/features/features.php?ann_id=111 (accessed on 12 February 2011).

Levine, J. (1990) *Bilingual Learners and the Mainstream Curriculum: Approaches to teaching and learning*, Bristol: Falmer Press.

Lindon, J. (2005) *Understanding Child Development: Linking practice to theory*, London: Hodder.

Martin-Jones, M. and Bhatti, A. (1999) 'Literacies in the lives of bi-lingual learners in local communities in Britain', in South, H. (ed.) *Literacies in Schools and Communities*, York: York Publishing.

Moore, R. and Gilliard, J.L. (2007) 'Preservice teachers' perceptions of culture in early care and education programs on a native American Indian reservation', *Journal of Early Childhood Teacher Education*, 28: 17–30.

National Association for Language Development in the Curriculum (NALDIC) (2009) *New Inquiry into Teacher Training: Executive summary*. Available online at www.naldic.org.uk (accessed 1 February 2010).

National Association for Language Development in the Curriculum (NALDIC)/Training and Development Agency for Schools (TDA) (2009) *The National Audit of English as an Additional Language Training and Development Provision*, London: TDA.

Ofsted (2005) *Race Equality in Education: Good practice in schools and local education authorities*. Available online at www.ofsted.gov.uk/Ofsted-home/Publications-and-research/Browse-all-by/Documents-by-type/Thematic-reports/Race-equality-in-education (accessed 13 February 2011).

Swain, M. (1985) 'Communicative competence: some roles of comprehensible input and comprehensible output in its development', in Gass, S. and Madden, C. (eds) *Input in Second Language Acquisition*, New York: Newbury House, pp. 235–56.

Tizard, J., Schofield, W. and Hewison, J. (1982) 'Collaboration between teachers and parents in assisting children's reading', *British Journal of Educational Psychology*, 52: 1–15.

VanPatten, B. and Benati, A.G. (2010) *Key Terms in Second Language Acquisition*, London: Continuum.

Vygotsky, L.S. (1978) *Mind in Society*, Cambridge, MA: Harvard University Press.

Wood, E. (2007) 'Reconceptualising child-centred education: contemporary directions in policy, theory and practice in early childhood, *FORUM*, 49(1/2): 119–34. Available online at http://dx.doi.org/10.2304/forum (accessed 1 February 2010).

Counselling and Guidance in Education

Shirley Potts

My values and beliefs

When interviewing prospective trainee teachers, I have always been intrigued by their descriptions of those teachers who have inspired their career choice. They always contain phrases such as 'she was so enthusiastic', 'he really cared about his students', 'she understood me', 'she had a good sense of humour' or 'he really encouraged us'.

Note that there is no mention of academic prowess. Obviously, subject knowledge and pedagogical skills are a requirement in the educational process – but I have a fervent belief that the personal qualities of practitioners have the most profound impact upon their students. Emotional literacy is not an inherent quality of all human beings, and some are more naturally imbued with it than others are – largely due to upbringing and life experience. However, I do believe there are core skills that people can acquire through training, perseverance and reflective practice. The emotionally literate classroom is a flourishing environment that endorses positive relationships and tacitly discourages negative experiences such as bullying and rivalry. Teaching teams may adopt many of the core counselling skills explored in this chapter.

Introduction

Some of the vocabulary of enabling roles has gained increasing viability and credence in current educational environments: counselling, guidance, mentoring, behaviour management, coaching, advising, supporting and so on. There are those who would see very blurred lines between several of these functions, while other people might offer very clear delineation and differentiation between them. Nevertheless, there are also distinctions to draw – not only from the perspective of semantics, but also from ethical and professional angles. The evolution of teaching from a didactic, instructive role into a holistic appreciation of the individual student has been a welcome and progressive development. Subjects such as Physical, Social and Health Education (PSHE) have entered the curriculum and the language of psychotherapy has merged into common parlance. Hence, we consider the 'baggage' students or staff may bring with them, we are aware of 'unfinished business', we listen to our 'inner child', we endeavour to 'empathise' and we nod sagely and 'hear where someone is coming from'. There is, however, a yawning chasm between talking the talk and walking the walk. The Reggio Emilia pedagogy, originating in Italy, describes children as 'co-constructors in the process of learning' (James and James, 2008) and this description similarly befits the therapeutic encounter when offering counsel or guidance to a young person.

Defining terms

For the purpose of this chapter, it is necessary to clarify what I will and will not address. I believe counselling, guidance and behaviour management are three distinct specialist roles offering particular styles of support in specific situations.

Counselling is, largely, a one-to-one, confidential, client-centred relationship whereby the counsellor encourages, enables and empowers clients to find their own way to clarification or solution of a particular issue. There are various counselling approaches and theories but most will include the potency of a non-directive, sincere, listening relationship between counsellor and client. The professional, practising counsellor must be trained and qualified and in receipt of regular supervision. Additionally, most training courses recommend a period of personal therapy and this is compulsory for membership of the major professional bodies.

Guidance is more directive than counselling and – in an educational setting – bears more relevance to career or subject choices, academic development, decision-making and wider personal issues such as safe sex or financial independence. The guidance professional, then, is likely to have trained in a particular category of supportive intervention and might be a careers adviser or health professional.

Behaviour management relates most frequently to behavioural challenges that are difficult to tolerate or accommodate in an educational setting, for example the disenfranchised adolescent with poor attendance or the withdrawn eight-year-old victim of bullying. Behaviour management might then become the domain of other professionals through referrals to educational psychologists, social workers or family therapists.

Therefore, to clarify, this chapter will not be addressing the essential training requirements of the above professions. However, we will examine some of the core skills common to various helping professions that educationalists – from teaching assistant to head teacher, from university professor to nursery nurse – may incorporate in their interactions with children and young people.

Carl Rogers (1978), who initiated the person-centred counselling approach, spoke of a 'way of being', not only in the counselling relationship but also as a person of integrity beyond the counselling room. He suggested that the core conditions of a counselling relationship are empathy, unconditional positive regard and congruence – sometimes interpreted as non-possessive warmth, non-judgemental acceptance and honesty. Without oversimplifying the issue, are these not three basic characteristics that will inform, enrich and enhance relationships between educationalists and students? What better foundation is there for classroom rapport than to display warmth, acceptance and honesty to those in our care. This may sound too naive and idealistic for the unruly urban classroom or the nursery full of noisy, egocentric three year olds, but it is the quality of the teaching team, more than the variables of the situation, that is being addressed here.

In recent years the concept of 'emotional literacy' has rapidly gained ground and infiltrated the educational establishment through the works of authors such as Gardner (1983, 2008), Goleman (1996), Mortiboys (2002), Orbach (2001) and Weare (2005). Holistic approaches to student care have heralded approaches such as accelerated learning, educational kinesiology, neurolinguistic programming and the learning revolution. Smith (2003) suggests a continuum of facilitative input from presenting, through authenticating, directing, leading, training, facilitating, developing and mentoring, to coaching – the first being a large group activity and the last being a one-to-one process. Teaching teams may feel more comfortable with a specific style of interaction and it is relevant to remember that individual educationalists have differing skills and need not all practise in the same way. However, much of the current movement resonates with Rogers' (1969) earlier words:

> We know that the initiation of such learning rests not upon the teaching skills of the leader, not upon scholarly knowledge of the field, not upon curricular planning, not upon use of audiovisual aids, not upon the programmed learning used, not upon lectures and presentations, not upon an abundance of books, though each of these might at one time or another be utilized as an important resource. No, the facilitation of significant learning rests upon certain attitudinal qualities that exist in the personal *relationship* between the facilitator and the learner.
>
> (1969: 197)

Relationship is the potent tool that each teaching team brings to their interactions with young learners. With or without intention, a 'way of being' is communicated by teaching teams in such a way that the young learner will have formed an opinion of each member of the team that will colour all future interactions. For this reason, some basic communication and counselling skills are the surest foundation for teachers and teaching assistants who will inevitably be drawn into 'counselling' or guidance situations in the course of their career. The formal acquisition and application of skills is insufficient to guarantee a therapeutic encounter, but more on the personal qualities of the teaching team later. Suffice to say, most teaching teams have awareness that 'they inevitably fulfil a role as models for their students and they will try to promote responsible behaviour through demonstrating such behaviour and encouraging it' (Geldard and Geldard, 2009: 208).

Counselling skills

Three of the principle counselling theories are psychodynamic, cognitive-behavioural and person-centred, with many other approaches emerging over the past half century, for example transactional analysis, gestalt therapy, psychosynthesis, psychodrama and existential and transpersonal approaches. Some counselling practitioners would now favour an integrative approach in which they would not exclusively follow one theory, but appropriately integrate elements of several theories. The British Psychological Society's Division of Counselling Psychology has explicitly taken an integrative approach, insisting that students should have an understanding and working knowledge of at least two theoretical models (O'Brien and Houston, 2007: 7).

The micro-skills highlighted below are common to most counselling approaches but are also, significantly, applicable to the teaching team's repertoire of interpersonal skills.

Empathy

This is colloquially described as 'walking a mile in the other one's moccasins'. Essentially, empathy is the ability to see from the client's frame of reference. It is not to be confused with sympathy, or having experienced a similar situation – 'I know how you feel' is not an appropriate counselling response. Nobody knows precisely how another person feels. The skill of empathy actually requires concentration, perseverance and honest self-reflection. We may be confronted by a young person with a problem that would appear trivial in our own life, we might have chosen strategies very different to those adopted by the client, and we may be shocked or disgusted by what we hear – but the cornerstone of empathy is to remain fixed upon the client's viewpoint and circumstances. A deeper level of empathy can only operate subsequent to the formation of a trusting relationship. This may precipitate opportunities to identify hidden agendas, where there is perhaps a discrepancy between what a client is saying and their body language or manner. In these circumstances, a counsellor/teaching team may be able to gently and sensitively illuminate these discrepancies and suggest the unacknowledged feelings implied by them.

Congruence

This is colloquially described as 'being the same on the outside as on the inside'. Congruence has variously been translated as honesty, sincerity, transparency and being real. 'The counsellor should be herself [sic] in the relationship, putting up no professional front or personal façade' (Rogers, 1978: 9). All of these skills are interwoven and congruence can offer a profound link to empathy. Wosket (1999) describes how empathic responses have their limitations where the experience a client describes is far beyond the imagination capabilities of the counsellor striving for empathy. In such a situation, the congruent response from the counsellor – 'I cannot imagine what you feel . . .' – may prove effective in deepening trust and acceptance. Congruence must always be balanced with a compassion and understanding for the client. It is never the intention to brutalise with honesty or dismantle someone's self-constructed protective mechanisms with excruciatingly painful haste.

Positive regard/non-judgementalism

This skill entails valuing the other person, regardless of differences in moral stance, belief or opinion you may have. There is a power in honouring unconditionally another person's right to exist. Clearly, in educational settings there are limitations to 'unconditional positive regard' where certain conditions must be placed on behaviour and actions in order for the structure of the establishment or session to remain intact. This is where, again, honest self-reflection is required on the part of the teaching team to ensure decisions are made and conveyed in a non-judgemental way. It is possible to value a child or young person but dislike their actions. This may carry echoes for parents who have appreciated how it is possible to love their child while occasionally disliking the child's actions.

Active listening/attending

This is a deceptively complex skill. Many people pride themselves on being a 'good listener' without ever having truly evaluated their skill (see 'Personal qualities', pages 138–9). Helpful listening requires focus and concentration as well as an appropriate environment. There are various physical factors to consider, such as the seating arrangements, being at the same level physically – particularly if you are an adult addressing a child, privacy without intimidation, body language and time available. If a client is to be aware that they are being listened to sincerely, the teaching team's body language should be open and relaxed without appearing too unperturbed. Maintain adequate eye contact without staring intently. Try not to fiddle with pens or keys, or glance at your watch. These may seem obvious trivia but, until we have had the opportunity to observe ourselves, perhaps in a role-play situation, it is remarkable how many of our personal idiosyncrasies go unchecked. Most importantly, active listening requires a counsellor to become comfortable with silence. In everyday conversation there are few silences – there is a natural tendency to complete a sentence, fill a gap, prepare a response . . . but, in a helpful, counselling exchange, there must be a readiness to allow space for thought. Sitting in silence for just thirty seconds is difficult and can be a source of much discomfort to the novice counsellor. However, the developing ability to sit with someone while he or she pursues a train of thought, uninterrupted but supported, is a skill well worth acquiring.

Paraphrasing and summarising

These skills link very closely with active listening as they offer the client a positive demonstration of your attendance. Paraphrasing involves reiterating what has been said by the client, but in the counsellor's own words – it is a tool to ensure the client is aware of your level of understanding of the situation. Summarising is very similar but involves a précis of the client's story by the counsellor, with repetition of the client's own words. This can feel quite artificial during initial usage, yet can be a remarkably helpful tool when the clients hear their own words from another perspective.

Prompts, clarification and open-ended questions

These are also evidence of active listening. Prompts may simply be nods of the head or brief interjections (the 'mm-hms' of the much maligned archetypal counsellor!). Clarification may be sought by the congruent listener who needs to admit their confusion or uncertainty over what they are hearing. Thus, it would be quite acceptable for the counsellor to say 'I'm not sure I got that bit – can you explain it again to me?' Far better to let a client know that you are listening intently than to allow them to meander on when you lost the thread some time ago. Within the same context, any questions posed by the counsellor should be open-ended, that is, not able to be answered with a simple 'yes' or 'no'. For example, 'how do you feel at playtime?' invites a more full response than 'do you get lonely?' It is essential to avoid asking questions simply to satiate the curiosity of the counsellor. Also worth a mention here is the danger of collusion. It is possible to collude unwittingly with a client in our endeavour to sound empathic and supportive. For example, it is not unknown for a client (especially a child) to laugh inappropriately while recounting a serious issue – but it would not be fitting for a counsellor to share the laughter. Similarly, when a client recounts a liturgy of discontent it could be dangerously collusive for the counsellor to join in the 'ain't it awful' script.

Immediacy

This refers to the ability to stay with a client emotionally and intellectually. A common distraction is to be planning one's response while the other person is still speaking. This, again, is a popular format of everyday conversations, but the tempo must be slowed in a counselling exchange. Immediacy is another skill that will only evolve through practice and experience, as it is inevitable that the trainee counsellor will be ransacking their mind for the appropriate response, the correct body language, the wise word – while failing to give full attention to what the client is saying. Barker et al.'s discussion of mindfulness (2010: 167) gives helpful and practical illustrations for staying in the present moment.

Challenging

This combines with the deeper level of empathy mentioned earlier and is not a tool that can be introduced flippantly into an encounter. As its name suggests, challenging entails pointing out discrepancies in a client's language or actions. For example, a counsellor might say' 'you're telling me you weren't bothered by what they said, but it seems to me you're close to tears'. Clearly, this can be a demanding exchange for a client and must be introduced with sensitivity and caution.

The technical vocabulary of much counselling theory holds little relevance to the uninitiated and it is important that counsellors/teaching teams/listeners are able to communicate with their clients through a mutually relevant 'feelings language' (Hobson, 1985). No counselling or communication skills should be applied mechanically or superficially, but with humanity and integrity. These are skills that should become integral to a teaching team's way of being.

Counselling in educational settings

Within an educational setting, it is likely that staff will regularly encounter certain dilemmas among children and young people. Friendship difficulties will frequently arise, as will learning anxieties or pressures, personal embarrassments such as blushing or shyness, or isolation through cultural differences or through bullying. Many of these anxieties can be allayed through the reasoned support of a caring and skilful listener. Some issues, too, may be usefully addressed in a group or classroom situation. Generalised discussions around bullying, self-esteem, loss or friendship are standard ingredients of the PSHE curriculum and, from circle time with primary children to the heated debates of undergraduates, it is possible to confront some contentious or painful problems within the relative safety of a group encounter.

Occasionally, situations that are more complex will arise and it is the responsibility of the teaching team to be aware of the need to refer on to other professionals. Some situations will be beyond the remit of the school situation and require wider discussion or involvement. Examples of more complex situations might include bereavement, abuse concerns, disabilities or additional needs, health issues such as anorexia, drug abuse or sexual matters, bullying and the risk of suicide. While any of these areas might be approached within discussion topics, individual circumstances may also dictate the involvement of other agencies or professionals. This necessarily impinges upon issues of confidentiality, which always present a dilemma to the counsellor/teaching team supporting a child or young person. As far as possible, a child or young person is afforded the privacy of a confidential exchange with the person who is helping them. However, McLaughlin *et al.* (1996) remind us that:

> Legally teachers do not have to maintain or breach confidentiality. They must comply with school policy and the head teacher's instructions on this matter and use their professional judgement.
>
> It is desirable professional practice to maintain students' confidences and it is desirable always to tell the student first if confidentiality is to be broken. It is also important, especially in child protection matters, to reduce the number of times a student has to repeat a distressing disclosure.
>
> (1996: 70)

It is important that staff should understand the boundaries of their role and this should be made explicit through school policy. Schools may offer an integrated or differentiated model of counselling support or guidance. Within an integrated model, personal, emotional and social support is seen as a shared responsibility throughout a staff team and an inherent part of each staff member's role. On the other hand, a differentiated model would see specific professionals identified for a particular supporting role with staff obliged to encourage appropriate referrals.

On a practical note, it is wise to remain as transparent as possible in your actions. In this age of accountability, it is feasible to inform other staff of your supportive role without necessarily breaching a student's confidentiality. Similarly, it is sensible to avoid situations where extreme privacy leaves you open to allegation or accusation. Children are quite likely to ask if you can keep a secret. It is an ethical requirement for the counsellor to explain that should any topic raise concerns that have to be shared elsewhere, he or she will always inform and involve the child first. Confidentiality should always be taken seriously but, equally, there are ethical responsibilities where children are involved:

> If the educational establishment has responsibilities similar to those of parents, due to the age of the pupil, or granted to them by a court because the young person's family has broken down or the young person is considered 'at risk' for any reason, it is understandable that the management of the organization is

reluctant to have significant information withheld from them. Indeed, numerous enquiries following the deaths of young people subjected to physical or sexual abuse have emphasised the importance of professionals liaising with each other to ensure that they are not each individually aware of different aspects of a situation which, had these been communicated, could have been joined together like pieces in a jig-saw to provide a more complete picture of the young person's circumstances.

(Bond, 1998: 13)

Conversely, confidentiality and ethical issues may become a camouflage beneath which schools may conceal their reluctance to encounter personal issues in students' lives. This unwillingness and fear finds its worst manifestation in the cases of unidentified long-term child abuse, sometimes even resulting in the death of a child, where the media are quick to point the finger at non-collaborating professionals.

The school environment is likely to dictate the level of counselling support offered by staff. Some establishments adhere to a mission statement and policy that encourages the holistic support of students and an attendant interest in their social and emotional development. Other establishments are more academically focused, with a belief that emotional or social support is an extra-curricular activity beyond the remit of educationalists. Only one of the twenty-five recommendations of the Rose Review (2009) refers to personal development, despite the paper referring to personal development as 'this central aspect of the curriculum' (recommendation 13). The prevailing mood, however, is to regard students holistically in the understanding that it is virtually impossible to separate emotional or social contentment from academic progression. Links between home and school have been increasingly emphasised and encouraged in recent years with, particularly for younger children, strategies such as home–school diaries giving a clear message to children of cooperation and mutual care and concern.

Geldard and Geldard suggest that 'the desired attributes of a child-counsellor are that the counsellor must be:

1   congruent

2   in touch with their own inner child

3   accepting

4   emotionally detached (2002: 18).

Emotional detachment should not be confused with a distant or aloof manner. It only implies that a child can perceive their supporter to be sufficiently detached from a situation to receive the child's words without incurring personal distress.

It is impossible to avoid a power imbalance within counselling support and guidance in education. There is the clear contention between adult and young person, as well as the hierarchical roles intrinsic within the education system. James and James speak of:

the power relations that enable adults to maintain control over children, forcing them into positions of subordination and dependency. To explore the world from the standpoint of children entails acknowledging the importance that this generational position has for shaping children's everyday experiences and understandings of the social relationships with which they are involved.

(2008: 133)

Additionally, there is a language of deficit implicit in the teaching role. Patently, children arrive at school assured of the limitations of their knowledge, which they must enhance and enlarge through the assistance of those who are older and wiser. Children have a need – and the educational establishment can supply the solution. This may be an oversimplification, but it is a foundation that teaching teams must be aware of in their role. It is particularly difficult for young people to share intimate concerns or awkward fears with someone who holds a powerful role in the child's life.

Conversely, the paradox of supporting is that *too much* support can be equally debilitating. One of the primary outcomes of a holistic education is to enable young people towards independence and self-regulation. Rather like the withered muscles within a long-term plaster cast, excessive support can undermine the natural maturation processes of life. Obviously, the maintenance of balance requires insight and consideration on the part of the counsellor/teaching team, which brings us, finally, to the personal qualities of those who would counsel and support young people within educational settings.

Personal qualities

As mentioned earlier, clinical knowledge alone will not produce the required environment for a supportive encounter. Counselling, guidance, helping, emotional support – whatever term we use – requires a warmth and compassion that must be sincere. The word *sincere* takes its root from *sans cerre*, meaning 'without wax'. The linguistics evolved from the ancient Greek practice of pouring wax over marble statues or busts to conceal any cracks or flaws in the marble – thus enabling them to deceive prospective purchasers. A *sans cerre* piece of work, without wax, was therefore much to be prized – as, indeed, is the quality the word has come to represent. A teaching team must be genuine – caring without smothering, encouraging without patronising, friendly but professional, making reasoned assessment of a situation without judgementalism. One of the most desired attributes within counselling training is self-awareness. It is crucial to become aware of one's own flaws and weaknesses – the tendency to rescue someone who is struggling to find words or the inclination to breach boundaries in offering too much support. We have gender preconceptions that we are barely aware we hold, and racism or disablism that we do not even address, so convinced are we that we have no discriminations. This is the penetratingly honest self-awareness that the prospective counsellor or teaching team must tackle if they are to evolve into fully functioning practitioners. O'Brien and Houston endorse the imperative of self-awareness, coupled with personal support, for those in a helping role:

As ordinary human beings they will encounter pain and distress which needs to be faced and contained without personal bias or prejudice and some provision for personal support, and development of interpersonal sensitivity and self-awareness, is therefore vital.

(2007: 158)

These issues can only be attended to within a candid and encouraging environment. Some elements can only be addressed privately and individually, but others must be rehearsed and honed within a tolerant group of colleagues. All the discomfort and awkwardness of highlighting our inadequacies or deficiencies within the exercise of our evolving counselling skills should be appreciated as an opportunity to experience the hurdles a young person may encounter in revealing their problems to a listener.

In conclusion, there is a wealth of additional literature and training courses accessible via the websites or recommended reading below, but there are also personal qualities that can be refined through independent self-analysis and self-awareness in the discerning practitioner. Emotional support and guidance in schools must commence with the appropriate attitudinal stance of the teaching team, achieved through informed self-awareness, together with a practical and theoretical understanding of the appropriate skills.

Discussion starters

1   Based on your own experiences in classrooms, what are the most common emotional or social difficulties experienced by children and young people?
2   A child or friend is undergoing personality changes and expressing antisocial behaviour beyond the usual expectations of adolescence. How will you respond?

Reflecting on practice

Find references in school documentation that provide guidance for teachers or teaching assistants on counselling, guidance and managing pupils' behaviour. Discuss the effectiveness of this guidance in relation to your observations of school practice and discussions with others. If considered necessary, collaborate with others to make recommendations for change and justify your suggestions.

Useful resources

www.alite.co.uk: Alite provides learning and motivation programmes and resources for training.
www.angermanage.co.uk: the British Association of Anger Management.
www.antidote.org.uk: Antidote concentrates on emotional literacy to help schools develop more dynamic learning environments.
www.bacp.co.uk: the British Association for Counselling & Psychotherapy.
www.educationalists.co.uk: provides online resources for education specialists.

www.playtherapy.org.uk: provides information resources for play therapies to help children with emotional literacy, behaviour or mental health problems.

References

Barker, M., Vossler, A. and Langdridge, D. (2010) *Understanding Counselling and Psychotherapy*, London: Sage.

Bond, T. (1998) 'Ethical issues in counselling and education', in Crawford, M., Edwards, R. and Kidd, L. (eds) *Taking Issue*, London: Routledge.

Gardner, H. (1983) *Frames of Mind*, New York: Basic Books.

Gardner, H. (2008) *5 Minds for the Future*, Boston, MA: Harvard Business Press.

Geldard, K. and Geldard, D. (2002) *Counselling Children*, London: Sage.

Geldard, K. and Geldard, D. (2009) *Relationship Counselling for Children, Young People and Families*, London: Sage.

Goleman, D. (1996) *Emotional Intelligence*, London: Bloomsbury.

Hobson, R. (1985) *Forms of Feeling*, London: Routledge.

James, A. and James, A. (2008) *Key Concepts in Childhood Studies*, London: Sage.

McLaughlin, C., Clark, P. and Chisholm, M. (1996) *Counselling and Guidance in Schools*, London: David Fulton.

Mortiboys, A. (2002) *The Emotionally Intelligent Lecturer*, Birmingham: SEDA.

O'Brien, M. and Houston, G. (2007) *Integrative Therapy* (2nd edn), London: Sage.

Orbach, S. (2001) *Towards Emotional Literacy*, London: Virago Press.

Rogers, C. (1969) *Freedom to Learn*, Columbus, OH: Charles E. Merril.

Rogers, C. (1978) *On Personal Power*, London: Constable.

Rose, J. (2009) *Independent Review of the Primary Curriculum*, London: DCSF.

Smith, A. (2003) *Alite Train the Trainer Resource Pack*, Beaconsfield: Alite.

Weare, K. (2005) 'Taking a positive, holistic approach', in Newnes, C. and Radcliffe, N. (eds) *Making and Breaking Children's Lives*, Ross-on-Wye: PCCS Books.

Wosket, V. (1999) *The Therapeutic Use of Self*, London: Routledge.

10

Inclusion: Special Needs

Gareth Crossley

My values and beliefs about inclusion

Issues of inclusion and integration of children with special educational needs (SEN) are not rare within educational settings, and finding the best solution for all involved is seldom simple. As a Christian, I believe that all people are intrinsically valuable and I uphold the fundamental philosophy of inclusion: that we should give all children equal access to a broad and balanced curriculum, irrespective of their abilities, strengths, weaknesses and backgrounds. However, ensuring that practices are inclusive is never a black-and-white issue and must be viewed on a case-by-case basis to ensure that all children's needs are met, not only those with SEN. In my time as a teaching assistant, class teacher, Key Stage-leader and Special Educational Needs Co-ordinator (SENCO), I have made professional choices that have not appeared inclusive, but my motivation has always been to ensure the best approach for all of the children in my care. I do not believe that the government-led, top-down approach to inclusion has been able to consider all children's needs as its main priority, all of the time. There is a danger with all legislation related to education that it can prevent positive local interventions, in favour of a national, 'one size fits all' approach. I believe that inclusion should be implemented in a way that allows a degree of autonomy for education professionals and parents to develop interventions at a local level that take into account the uniqueness of the children involved, and their individual and corporate needs.

Introduction

The focus of this chapter is inclusion and special educational needs. Its aim is to provide a broad overview of the concept of inclusion since all educational practitioners will likely encounter children with SEN in their settings. It will also describe some of the more common difficulties that children face within the mainstream classroom, giving practical advice for teaching teams to ensure that provision is inclusive, appropriate and effective for every learner. The chapter is grounded in my experience rather than theoretical perspectives, since it cannot possibly provide detailed debates about each aspect of SEN. Further information and resources about specific conditions may be found on various websites, and there are theoretical debates and research in relevant academic journals (see 'Useful resources').

If we assert that all children are intrinsically valuable and unique, and all have the potential to achieve, then it follows that it is not acceptable to deny any child opportunities to develop their potential strengths or overcome their weaknesses. In our search for quality education that enables full participation of all learners, we see that an education system whose beliefs, policies and practices devalue or disenfranchise individuals based on their cognitive, physical or emotional state and perceived potential cannot be inclusive.

The concept of an 'inclusive' education system as outlined above is not necessarily the same as that of 'inclusion'. The nature of what constitutes an inclusive education system became a prominent topic of discussion among education reformers in Britain in the latter half of the twentieth century, with the debate raging as to the most effective way to ensure that all children, regardless of their individual needs, have access to an education system that fully meets those needs. What we now refer to as inclusion is better described as 'integration', in the sense that children who might previously have been educated in a special education setting should instead have the opportunity to receive their education in a mainstream school wherever it is possible. Thus, children of all abilities are educated together, and all the services required by children with SEN are provided in one place. Many in favour of full inclusion expound the benefits for all children. For example, they claim that inclusion encourages tolerance of difference (Boyles and Contadino, 1997). However, the path to inclusion has been a winding one and, even today, the debate continues. Nearly forty years after the Warnock Report strongly encouraged inclusion in British schools, Mary Warnock called the process of inclusion 'a disastrous legacy' and stated that inclusion may not be an ideal that is best for schools (Sigman and Warnock, 2005).

Being aware of the pivotal events that specifically guided and propelled the move towards inclusion in British education is helpful. Table 10.1 charts many of the influential events.

A history of education timeline with interactive links to some of the documents in Table 10.1 can be found at www.educationengland.org.uk/history/timeline.html. This website is a personal website maintained by Derek Gillard, who has an interest in archiving educational documents and other relevant information. Various papers and acts are also at the National Archives website (www.nationalarchives.gov.uk), the Parliamentary Archives (www.parliament.uk/archives) or at www.legislation.gov.uk. You will find the United Nations documents via their home page at www.un.org.

The dilemma of inclusion

Proponents of full inclusion argue that all children benefit when those with SEN are educated full-time within a mainstream classroom. Others hold the view that, for some children with SEN, the opportunity to learn alongside other students with similar educational needs would result in greater benefits. The case study in Box 10.1 highlights the dilemma of inclusion.

The decision to move Prajit was painful and complex and did not appear, on the surface, to be inclusive. However, in his case, successful inclusive practice meant opportunities to use large soft-play equipment, to take time out and use Lego, and to engage in role-play games with children of a similar age. For his primary school peers

TABLE 10.1 Historical influences on inclusion in schools

DATE	EVENT	IMPACT ON EDUCATIONAL LAW/PRACTICE
1944	Butler Education Act	Reorganisation of secondary education for equality of opportunity. More free places at grammar schools. 11-plus exam to determine allocation.
1948	Universal Declaration of Human Rights	The right to free elementary education for all children (Article 26).
1970	Education (Handicapped Children) Act	Transferred responsibility for education of severely handicapped children from health authorities to LEAs. Hospital schools were now led by qualified teachers.
1978	Warnock Report (UK)	Recommends the right for all children with special needs to be educated in mainstream schools.
1981	Education Act (UK)	New labels 'learning difficulties' and 'special educational needs'. Establishes the right for mainstream education.
1989	UN Convention on the Rights of the Child	Children are not to be discriminated against when receiving education.
1990	UNESCO World Declaration on Education for All	A basic education for all satisfying essential learning needs.
1993	UN Standard Rules on the Equalisation of Opportunities for Persons with Disabilities	Equal rights of all children, youths and adults with disabilities to education in integrated school settings.
1994	Salamanca Statement and Framework for Action on Special Needs Education	Asks all governments to adopt the principle of inclusive education, enrolling all children in mainstream schools, unless there are compelling reasons for doing otherwise.
1995	Disability Discrimination Act (UK)	Ensures that schools' policies are anti-discriminatory.
1998	Education Reform Act (UK)	Children have a right of 'equal' access to a broad curriculum.
2001	The Special Education Needs and Disability Act (UK)	Gives all children the right to a mainstream education 'where possible'.
2001 (revised in 2008)	SEN Code of Practice (UK)	Makes the rights of the child central, enabling pupils with SEN to reach their full potential, to be included fully in their school communities and make a successful transition to adulthood.
2006	UN Convention on Rights of People with Disabilities	Absence of discrimination; equality of opportunity; inclusion in education at all levels, particularly primary education; and educational opportunities throughout life aimed at facilitating the full development of their human potential, sense of dignity and self-worth.

BOX 10.1 Case study 1: Prajit

Prajit is a lively and caring twelve-year-old boy. He struggles with English. His family speaks Tamil at home. Following an early childhood accident, Prajit has moderate learning difficulties (MLD). He has gross motor difficulties and obsessive tendencies, making some activities almost impossible in group situations. He does not socialise well with children his own age and works consistently below national expectations. Prajit has always been in mainstream classes and has been in his current class of nine to ten year olds for four years. The gap between Prajit's social, emotional, intellectual and physical attributes and capabilities and those of his peers has widened over the years. Due to Prajit's developmental delays, all work is differentiated, and an increasing amount is unrelated to that of his peers. Owing to disruptive tendencies, Prajit has been removed from the classroom with increasing frequency. The school provided regular individual support for Prajit. The school believed that the caring environment and strong friendships played an important role in Prajit's development. In consultation with his parents and the LEA, a decision was made for Prajit to attend a local secondary school for pupils with MLD.

it meant uninterrupted, well-paced lessons. The school lost a valued and loved pupil. Some staff members considered the move to be brave, forward-thinking and necessary, while others asked whether it was the right decision.

Many, when asked to consider inclusion, would find their thoughts turning to the needs of the pupil with SEN. They will consider how they are cared for and how they access the curriculum, school buildings and experiences of school life. However, as Prajit's story illustrates, inclusion affects all children, learning to be aware of other pupils' difficulties, perhaps receiving a little less help than previously, or experiencing an enlarged and diversified peer group.

Some children with severe learning difficulties (SLD) may still attend settings that cater solely for children with similar needs, providing care that would be practically or logistically impossible or inappropriate within a mainstream setting, for example care that requires the use of hoists, pools, delicate medical equipment or specially designed changing facilities. Many units of this kind are attached to, or share grounds with, a mainstream school.

The process of deciding what setting will be best for a child is managed by the local authority. The process may be lengthy and can include numerous professionals, including the school SENCO, class teacher and head teacher (if the child is already in a school), social workers, speech and language therapists, educational psychologists and, in some cases, doctors, but in the vast majority of cases the final decision is in the hands of the parents. Although this honours the crucial role parents play, there are cases where the parents do not give consent for their child to change setting, or insist on a change that other professionals feel may be detrimental. In these cases great skill and care is required of educational practitioners in communicating complex educational matters to parents without appearing patronising or giving the impression that 'we know best'. It is helpful to presume that the parents know their children better than you do. In most cases, this is true.

Let us now look at how inclusion can be implemented effectively. The next section will explore some of the common difficulties that children in mainstream settings face, giving information about the conditions along with practical ideas and approaches to enable teachers and support staff to ensure that the curriculum is made as accessible as possible.

Categorising and separating difficulties, disorders and needs is complex and sometimes unhelpful. The key to addressing children's needs is not found when we know which box(es) they fit. Success is more readily found when educators *know* children and their unique make-up, appreciating their individual situation – their mix of experiences, strengths, weaknesses, needs and aspirations. In addition, teaching teams must understand a breadth of difficulties, their identification and their effects on learning and life. Most importantly, they must be aware of how they can improve a child's educational experience.

Learning difficulties

Moderate learning difficulties

Children with MLD form the largest group of children with SEN in mainstream schools. The term MLD usually refers to a child whose difficulties affect most or all of their educational experience, not just one area of the curriculum. Many require high levels of support because of an educational delay of up to three years. This creates greater demand to differentiate curriculum content, making a strong case for a specialist setting. Many suffer from lower levels of self-esteem and motivation. Like Prajit, they can often be accommodated within a mainstream classroom during the early years of their education; indeed, MLD can remain hidden until a child's capabilities are accurately assessed. Often, as they progress through school, the gap between their abilities and those of their peers grows wider.

Children with MLD can struggle to integrate successfully into mainstream secondary school after being reliant on the infrastructure and routines of a traditional primary setting. The challenges of navigating the complexities of secondary school buildings and timetables is often too much to cope with.

Severe learning difficulties

Pupils with SLD have significant cognitive impairments, sometimes coexisting with physical, sensory, social and/or emotional difficulties. They have difficulty accessing the school curriculum, and in learning and applying skills, and usually require full-time support. Their educational achievement is likely to remain at the P-levels of the National Curriculum in all areas. The levels currently consist of statements of ability that increase in very small increments from P1 to P8. P-levels are subject-specific after P3 and aid in assessing progress and setting manageable targets.

Many children with SLD have accompanying physical or medical needs, some using wheelchairs or walking aids, and may need adaptive technology such as speech synthesis. Consequently, most are educated in specially designed settings with access to specialist equipment and staff with relevant, high-level training, including physiotherapists or speech and language therapists. Such settings may have on-site pools, sensory stimulation rooms, changing and showering facilities, hoists, ramps and handrails, specialist outdoor play equipment and sensory trails. Housing these resources and facilities in one place makes financial and logistical sense.

Access difficulties

Mobility

Children with mobility impairment integrate into mainstream more easily than children with MLD or SLD. Their difficulties restrict place and position, not learning. Children who use wheelchairs, callipers, crutches and other walking aids are usually well catered for within mainstream schools. All schools have an accessibility plan, detailing improvements that make buildings more accessible. It will also outline how the school will:

- improve the physical environment;
- make improvements in the provision of information;
- increase access to the curriculum.

Because of these mandatory documents, all schools will have received funding to make changes where necessary, such as the addition of lifts and ramps.

Despite this, there are still areas of the school experience that children with mobility impairment could struggle to access, such as physical education (PE), swimming sessions, elements of outdoor activities and school trips. It is important to consider how much social bonding is heavily linked with physical play. Many schools use buddy systems to ensure that children with mobility impairment are not isolated at times when mobile children are engaged in inaccessible play such as tagging games and informal team sports.

Visual impairment

The term visual impairment (VI) includes a range of difficulties from short sightedness to blindness. Most children with VI join mainstream school quite readily with few adjustments. Their conditions may require them to have regular eye examinations and they may have glasses or contact lenses. Occasionally, they may complain of discomfort, headaches or sore eyes, usually temporary eyestrain. For children with monocular vision or more acute VI, such as tunnel vision, squints, myopia or profound degrees of low vision, care must be taken to ensure access to the curriculum through positioning in lessons, and by providing resources such as magnifiers and electronic text readers. Box 10.2 provides a case study about Daniel, who has severe myopia.

BOX 10.2 Case study 2: Daniel

Ten-year-old Daniel has severe myopia. Although he can see objects clearly within a few feet of him, the majority of his vision is heavily blurred. Although Daniel can read fluently, he must hold a text within centimetres of his eyes. Daniel's condition causes frequent headaches and eyestrain. On occasions this has led to sickness. Daniel is currently on the schools SEN register for monitoring and support. He has support from outside agencies, provided by the local authority's Visual Impairment Team. Daniel wears prescription glasses, helping his eyes to focus better. Although these help enormously, they are two years old and are less effective now due to recent deterioration in his sight. Daniel pushes one side of his glasses closer to his left eye when reading and this has caused marks and sores to appear on his face. Daniel struggles to see and recognise facial expressions, so does not notice subtle social cues from his peers or adults. On one lovely day his teacher took the class into the school grounds to read the class novel. The sun's glare was too bright for Daniel to see the page. Daniel listened instead. Daniel was also unable to participate when his class learnt to play the ukulele. He could not see the strings clearly enough. He opted to stay in the lessons, rather than do other work, apart from his friends.

To ensure that Daniel can access school life more effectively, Daniel's teacher provides an enlarged paper copy of all presentations to the class. All texts and worksheets are enlarged by converting an A4 sheet to A3. Daniel's teaching team do not stand in front of windows when addressing him. The silhouetted shape makes face recognition more difficult. Daniel's teacher has to use black on the white board, making some activities such as highlighting more difficult for the other students. He must be close enough to the board but not facing a window, or sideways to a projected image. Despite his disability he can create intricate and accurately detailed miniature drawings, as his focus causes him to be very close to his page. Daniel is looking forward to taking GCSE Art.

As Daniel's story illustrates, VI mainly affects the ways in which children access images, texts and information from a variety of sources. Some strategies to consider are:

- dark pens and clear writing on white backgrounds;
- natural lighting is usually best;
- large print, Braille and magnification aids for texts;
- assistive technology, e.g. personal reading machines or talking calculators;
- high-contrast colours in displays;
- clear labels and signs;
- non-glare lamination or none at all;
- clear walkways;
- textured strips along walls of different rooms and walkways.

Hearing impairment

Children with hearing impairment (HI) have a range of difficulties, from tinnitus, perforated eardrums and frequent ear infections to profound and total deafness. Deafness is classified as mild, moderate, moderately severe or severe and profound, and is either unilateral – single-sided deafness (SSD), or bilateral – affecting both sides.

Box 10.3 provides a case study about Ben, and illustrates difficulties that can occur in identifying and supporting HI in children.

Background noise is similar to a hearing person attempting to localise where speech is coming from while standing by a waterfall. As Ben's story illustrates, deafness can often be overlooked and many deaf children can initially be misdiagnosed with language difficulties, attention deficit hyperactivity disorder (ADHD) or behavioural difficulties.

For lip-reading children with HI it is important to have well-lit rooms, allowing facial expressions and mouths to be clear. Similarly, beards and moustaches can occasionally make lip-reading more difficult. Many people automatically raise the volume of their voice, or speak very slowly. Speaking clearly, ensuring that you have eye contact, is much more effective. A hearing loop or loop system is helpful and teaching teams may need to wear a small microphone to amplify voices. Acoustic tiling or carpeting absorbs unwanted classroom noise.

Dyspraxia

Dyspraxia or developmental coordination disorder (DCD) affects children's ability to plan, and their skills of perception, language and thought. It is more common in boys

BOX 10.3 Case study 3: Ben

Seven-year-old Ben is the youngest child of a Chinese family who speak Mandarin. When Ben started school, he only spoke Mandarin. Ben was immediately given support for English as an additional language (EAL). Over time his teacher became concerned that Ben understood so little English and constantly looked puzzled. He had become disruptive in lessons, would not sit still for prolonged periods and was making very little progress across the whole curriculum. She recommended a hearing test. Ben had bilateral moderately severe deafness. It was thought likely that Ben's deafness was pre-lingual, that is, he was deaf before he began to acquire language. The school was able to redirect Ben's support. He had hearing aids and he sat in clear view of the teacher during whole-class lessons. Ben and the teaching team began to learn and use Makaton sign language, which helps to promote speech development. A major change was a reduction in noise levels – talking, music and controlling sound from other areas. Ben's hearing aids were more effective without background noise. He has made some improvement in his work since using them, but still struggles with them because they cause discomfort and amplify unwanted loud noises.

and characterised most notably by a child's difficulties with gross and fine movement. There are a great many characteristics associated with dyspraxia, and knowing some of them can help in identifying children who may have the condition. They are:

■ fidgeting, tapping fingers and feet and swinging legs;

■ inability to sit still;

■ no sense of danger or consequences;

■ eating with fingers rather than with a knife and fork;

■ problems with listening and comprehension;

■ general clumsiness, constantly bumping into objects and falling over;

■ difficulties in PE lessons;

■ poor handwriting;

■ poorly developed drawing skills – pictures may appear child-like;

■ flapping of hands when running or excited;

■ inability to tie shoelaces;

■ difficulties in remembering instructions;

■ being emotionally sensitive;

■ difficulties in building and maintaining relationships with other children.

Dyspraxic children may benefit from engaging in role-play activities with the teaching team and other children to aid social development. The use of social stories to explain classroom rules can promote understanding of consequences, sequencing and development of routines. Multi-sensory toys and equipment help to develop writing and mark-making skills. Fluorescent lighting and 'busy' or fluttering ceiling displays should be avoided, as should disturbing pupils in mid-task.

Communication difficulties

Speech, language and communication needs (SLCN) are often the result of damage to the brain, either before or after birth. They are also caused by memory disorders, attention disorders, perception problems or trauma. Some common language impairments are dysarthia (a motor speech disorder) and apraxia (an inability to string sounds together). Aphasia can mean both partial and total language impairment. A child with aphasia may be able to write and not speak, speak and not write, do neither, or suffer from a wide variety of language comprehension and production deficiencies, such as being able to sing but not speak. In most cases, a speech and language therapist will devise interventions. Teaching teams must never finish off sentences for children; patience is important. Children with SLCN can develop behavioural, emotional and social difficulties (BESD), possibly suffering also from educational difficulties. Successful approaches can include the use of assistive technology, flashcard systems, social stories and sign language.

Another communication difficulty is seen in children who are learning English as an additional language (EAL). Such children are often classified as having SEN to enable them to receive the necessary support in school. EAL development is discussed fully by Roshan Ahmed in Chapter 8.

Perception and processing difficulties

Irlen syndrome

Although Irlen syndrome is likely to affect reading and accessing visual content, it is a problem of perception rather than an optical problem. Irlen syndrome can cause visual anomalies when reading, including swirling text, exaggerated white spaces, merging words and letters and a very restricted area of clear focus. Children with Irlen syndrome expend a lot of energy when reading and writing, as the brain compensates and interprets what they are seeing. They are often unable to concentrate on writing and listening simultaneously, making verbal instructions and dictation impractical. Strategies to be considered when planning work for children with Irlen syndrome are:

- seating them in natural light where possible;
- clear, brief and accessible instructions;
- providing a written version of instructions;
- with the child's agreement, providing a scribe when desirable;
- clear, uncluttered visual presentations.

Sometimes a specific coloured plastic overlay or tinted glasses of a specific colour significantly reduce the effects of Irlen syndrome.

In recent years, there has been a surge in interactive, *ultra-stimulating*, ICT-based resources for use within the classroom. While these have made some learning more relevant, accessible and enjoyable for many, such resources are often inaccessible to children with Irlen syndrome, dyslexia and some types of visual impairment because of the high glare, colours and patterns.

Dyslexia

The National Institute of Neurological Disorders and Stroke (NINDS, 2010) defines dyslexia as a brain-based learning disability that impairs a person's ability to read regardless of intellectual capacity. The disorder manifests itself in different ways, but common characteristics are difficulties with spelling, phonological processing (the manipulation of sounds) and/or rapid visual-verbal responding (responding verbally to a visual stimulus).

Numerous systems, resources and approaches diagnose and support children with dyslexia. Testing is managed by the school's SENCO, but is usually implemented by teaching teams. The results inform individual education plans (IEPs). A consistent routine is helpful, with daily, weekly and termly timetables displayed in the classroom for reference. The use of a precursive/cursive script helps dyslexic children in their spelling and in developing a legible writing style. Dyslexic children often have difficulties reading low-contrast or dull colours, especially on presentations. Red or pink text is a particular problem. Blue text on a yellow background provides the highest degree of contrast for easier reading. Some children benefit from using a coloured overlay through which the text appears clearer.

It is common to limit support for dyslexic children to literacy, but dyslexia can affect children's mathematical acquisition, causing difficulty with the language of mathematics, sequencing, orientation and memory, rather than with the mathematics itself (DFES, 2001).

Dyscalculia

Children with dyscalculia struggle with the basic principles that form the foundations of mathematical learning. One key indicator is a prolonged confusion between maths symbols and their related operations. Dyscalculia can occur as the result of some types of brain injury. Similar, and potentially related, to dyslexia and developmental dyspraxia, dyscalculia occurs in people of all intellectual capacities. Sufferers often, but not always, have difficulties with time, measurement and spatial reasoning. They cannot memorise number facts readily and tend to learn calculation strategies in a mechanical way rather than through understanding. They will have little confidence in their methods (DfES, 2001).

Other potential difficulties are:

- inability to calculate price totals and change;
- difficulty in telling analogue time and with remembering dates and appointments;
- confusing left and right;
- inability to estimate distance, length or other measurements;
- difficulty in remembering formulae, times tables or mathematical concepts.

Despite having additional support, many dyscalculic children do not improve their mathematical abilities as they progress through school, although they may discover compensatory ways of recalling facts and systems.

Genetic disorders

Down's syndrome

Down's syndrome (DS), also known as Down syndrome, is a genetic, chromosomal disorder that causes low intellectual capacity, developmental delay, physical abnormalities and limitations such as poor muscle tone and an increased susceptibility to congenital heart defects, recurrent ear infections, obstructive sleep apnoea and thyroid problems, among others. Children with DS tend to be enthusiastic, outgoing and affectionate. However, their unguarded nature and simplified perception of social situations can cause them to be led into inappropriate behaviour by other children. Using emotional literacy resources and role-play can be successful in helping those with DS to express and develop their emotions and empathise with those of others. Due to the syndrome's tendency to cause illness, some schooling may be lost to short stays in hospital. For many children with DS, the focus in secondary education will be on life skills and many go on to live independent, self-supporting lives.

Foetal alcohol spectrum disorder

Foetal alcohol spectrum disorder (FASD), sometimes referred to as foetal alcohol syndrome (FAS), is a condition affecting children whose mother used alcohol during pregnancy. FASD describes a range of effects that may include physical, mental, behavioural and/or learning disabilities with potential lifelong implications. Many children with FASD are adopted or fostered. Strong home–school relationships are essential.

FASD can be misinterpreted as ADHD, and children with FASD can often become stigmatised as 'naughty' due to their difficulty in reading social cues in others.

FASD is often accompanied by other behavioural difficulties. While sanctions and reward systems may be successful in modifying the behaviour for a short period, they do not provide long-term solutions. More research is needed into effects of FASD and approaches to combat them.

Autistic spectrum disorder, including Asperger's syndrome

Autistic spectrum disorder (ASD) refers to any disorder ranging from mild Asperger's syndrome to severe autism. All children with ASD share three specific impairments, irrespective of their position on the scale, which can manifest with varying severity. They have an impaired ability to:

- communicate effectively verbally or non-verbally;
- understand social behaviour;
- be flexible in their thoughts and behaviours, leading to limited, obsessive or repetitive tendencies.

Children with ASD can sometimes have developmental delay. Many children with ASD perform as well and sometimes better than other children in academic work. Occasionally, children will develop outstanding ability in one or more subject. Obsessive tendencies often lead to behavioural issues. An unexpected change in routine can result in stress and anxiety. Lack of ability to communicate through speech compounds the difficulties. ASD can lead to a child's perception of sensory information as heightened and distorted, which causes inability to enter certain rooms, face in a certain direction, use items and so on. For example, one child insisted on his chair facing west at all times. He was able to tell when his chair had been moved, causing considerable disruption at lunchtimes and lessons in different classrooms. He also developed an obsession with the colour red. After a few weeks in a new class, his teacher found all the red pens, pencils and crayons behind a bookcase, put there 'to keep them safe'.

After a period, it is usually possible to determine what triggers obsessive, repetitive or disruptive behaviour and to plan interventions. Many children with ASD are literal thinkers, so they may struggle to grasp abstract or complex concepts such as distance or historical time.

Working with children with ASD can often feel like a negotiation. The settings and tasks are fine-tuned to fit in with what they feel able to do. They are not always disruptive or reluctant to complete work. The powerful feelings and urges they perceive make complete sense to them. Therefore, teaching teams should not attempt to force a child with ASD to comply unless their safety or that of others is at risk.

Learning difficulties or disorders

Behavioural, emotional and social difficulties

Behavioural, emotional and social difficulties (BESD) is an umbrella term covering numerous conditions and behaviours. A child identified with BESD may also be diagnosed with other conditions.

Emotional and behavioural difficulties (EBD) refers to children with short-term emotional problems or long-term psychological difficulties. They may display a wide range of challenging and disruptive behaviours, including emotional immaturity, withdrawal, tantrums and physical and/or verbal aggression. This, compounded by that fact that different agencies often use different terminology, makes achieving a complete definition very difficult. Some mainstream schools have EBD units attached where children attend for a short time before reintegration. Others may spend their entire school life within a special EBD unit. Strategies to combat EBD are the use of rewards and sanctions, a clear and consistent routine and giving the child responsibility and encouragement to improve self-esteem.

Attention deficit hyperactivity disorder

Also referred to as attention deficit disorder (ADD), ADHD is a medical diagnosis made by a doctor. Children with ADHD often appear distracted, fidgety and impatient. The condition causes children to display behaviour that distracts them and others during lesson times. Classroom management plays an important role in helping to avoid inappropriate behaviour, which often has a clear trigger point. These triggers will be different for each child, although some common triggers can include:

- sitting with a particular learner or group;
- not understanding or having access to clear instructions;
- moving around to collect resources and stationary;
- sharing resources;
- a noisy environment;
- not having support for a difficult task.

Positive behaviours can be modelled and copied. Children with ADHD benefit from systems that allow a degree of autonomy, for example developing a behaviour code, which the children use to appraise themselves. Children with ADHD are often able to recognise and avoid trigger points with support and encouragement.

Exceptional achievement

Gifted and talented children

It is common for chapters and books about SEN and inclusion to focus on disorders, syndromes and disadvantages. It is equally important to ensure that children who are very able are given opportunities to reach *their* potential also. Those children referred to as gifted and talented can often be inadvertently disenfranchised and consequently demotivated by an education that lacks challenge, encouragement and recognition of their abilities. While there is nothing wrong with such children assisting others and completing unchallenging extension activities, long-term reliance on 'holding work' can quickly cause a gifted child to stop applying their talents. Such children can benefit from an IEP. Setting appropriate and challenging targets can provide great stimulation, as well as providing a record of progress. Teaching teams need to provide appropriately challenging work and to seek to be inventive and creative in encouraging and occupying gifted and talented children when they have completed their regular work. It is helpful to remember that completing six worksheets of addition does not really provide much more in educational terms than completing three. Be prepared to vary tasks and suggest real-life application where possible.

Conclusion

It is useful at this point to reflect on the question 'How inclusive is your practice or practice that you have observed?' Reflect on a familiar educational setting, for example your secondary school experience, your workplace or your university degree course. Consider your own experience and your knowledge of difficulties that some learners have. You might consider how your past or current experiences reflect some of the case studies and examples in this chapter, which aims to provide a broad overview of the issues rather than a definitive answer to resolving all difficulties.

This chapter summaries some key elements of the challenges faced by learners at all levels. It highlights the variability of those challenges and the fact that, by using compensatory strategies and suitable resources, and through quality relationships with teaching teams, many learners can overcome the challenges and learn to the best of their capability. I hope readers will use the resources provided as a starting point for further development of deeper understanding of these issues.

Discussion starters

1   Consider these definitions of full and partial inclusion. What are the advantages and disadvantages of each?
    Full inclusion: The complete integration of pupils with SEN into the general education classroom. The pupil receives all special services in the same general education classroom as all other students.
    Partial inclusion: Pupils with SEN are educated in regular classes for part of the school day, receiving additional help. Specialised sessions occur outside the regular classroom, requiring special equipment or intensive instruction.
2   Read a school's policy for SEN. Is it fit for purpose?

Reflecting on practice

1   Below is a selection of real statements made by practitioners supporting children with SEN. Discuss your thoughts about these statements and consider how you respond in situations where you work with others who have disabilities.
    (a) I have felt in the past that I didn't know how best to assist a child with SEN.
    (b) I value all of the children in my setting equally.
    (c) I don't think this (difficulty) is a real problem.
    (d) I had that when I was at school, and I managed fine.
    (e) Sometimes support is a waste of time.
    (f) I don't think this child will ever make any progress.
2   Read one of the case studies presented in the chapter – Prajit, Ben or Daniel. List the questions you have about the case and consider how you might find the answers. Consider the outcomes and the alternatives you might recommend.

Useful resources

Websites

www.csie.org.uk: the Centre for Studies on Inclusive Education – information on social inclusion and the Index for Inclusion can be found on this site.

www.direct.gov.uk: Directgov contains information about public services in Britain – search for special educational needs.

www.downs-syndrome.org.uk: the Down's Syndrome Association.

www.dyslexiaaction.org.uk: Dyslexia Action, a charity that aims to support dyslexics.

www.dyspraxiafoundation.org.uk: the Dyspraxia Foundation.

www.fasaware.co.uk: Foetal Alcohol Syndrome Aware UK.

www.irlenuk.com: Irlen UK, a commercial site with some useful information.

Journals

British Journal of Special Education, published by Wiley-Blackwell.
Dyslexia: An International Journal of Research and Practice, published by Wiley.
International Journal of Inclusive Education, published by Routledge.
Learning Disabilities Research and Practice, published by Wiley-Blackwell.

References

Boyles, N. and Contadino, B. (1997) *The Learning Differences Sourcebook*, Los Angeles, CA: NTC/Contemporary Publishing Group.
Department for Education and Skills (DfES) (2001) *The National Numeracy Strategy: Guidance to support pupils with dyslexia and dyscalculia*, London: DfES.
National Institute of Neurological Disorders and Stroke (NINDS) (2010) *NINDS Dyslexia Information Page*. Available online at www.ninds.nih.gov/disorders/dyslexia/dyslexia.htm (accessed 12 February 2011).
Sigman, R. and Warnock, M. (2005) *Special Educational Needs: A new look*, London: Philosophy of Education Society of Great Britain.

11

Assessing Learning: Informing Practice

Christine Bold

My values and beliefs

In the early 1980s, when I began teaching in a primary school, I realised that the best types of assessment were formative, enabling learning and informing teaching practice. I made judgements about individual children's capabilities and in my teaching I aimed to help children move forward in their thinking. I valued the opportunity that formative assessment gave me to change and extend my practice to ensure that children made progress. I learnt that summative assessment processes had little impact on learning. It is my belief that the current system of national testing has a negative impact on learning and teaching processes at key points in a child's educational history. Assessment should be a positive experience, enabling self-knowledge and growth rather than a process of labelling, categorising and the creation of a culture of failure. All too often the negative aspects of assessment processes override the recognition of the positive achievements of young people in our education system.

Introduction: Assessment for Learning

In reviewing my original 2004 chapter, I have retained many of the original features related to the principles of assessment, in particular formative assessment, since they have changed little in the past twenty-five years. In the original chapter I made cursory reference to 'Assessment for Learning' proposed in 1999 by the Assessment Reform Group (ARG) and promoted by the Qualifications and Curriculum Authority (QCA, 2001). Instead, I focused mainly on Mitchell and Koshy's (1993) text, used by many Initial Teacher Training programmes to explore assessment practices. My reasoning for this was that Assessment for Learning (AfL), as proposed by the ARG, was not, at that time, embedded in school practice. The documentation available at the time of publication was not very helpful in terms of supporting practice. Later, the DfES (2006) produced materials to guide senior leaders in schools and to encourage AfL as part of the National Strategies. All schools were to implement AfL by September 2009.

In the first edition, I included reference to historical national developments in the English education system from 1979 onwards, with the aim of ensuring that students new to the education system understood that recent initiatives in schools built on a long-term process of school development and government intervention. My purpose in 2004 was to focus on the concepts and practices of assessment rather than the constantly changing government agendas that appeared to do little in terms of changing the actual practice in classrooms. My aim then was to ensure that all students who were working in schools as teaching assistants, or on school experience as initial teacher trainees, or as part of another education-based degree such as Education Studies, understood that assessment, learning and teaching were interrelated concepts. In particular, I wished to emphasise the fact that tests are not the only form of assessment and that the outcomes of tests may only provide a brief snapshot of learning and progress.

My purpose in updating the chapter remains the same. However, since 2004 schools have begun to engage in AfL, essentially formative assessment, and in 'Assessing Pupil Progress' (APP), which is more summative in nature but also adds to the formative process. The Department for Children, Schools and Families (DCSF, 2008b, 2009) and the QCA promoted and guided these recently established initiatives until recent changes in British government. Schools are currently familiar with this terminology and with engaging in these activities, so it is now essential to explore some of the issues arising from these developments, despite the fact that they may not continue in their present form. In May 2010, the recently formed Department for Education (DfE) stated that they would not be following recommendations about changes to the curriculum based on Jim Rose's *Independent Review of the Primary Curriculum: Final report*, commonly referred to as the Rose Review and published by the DCSF in April 2009 (2010, www.education.gov.uk/curriculum). They will expect schools to retain the current curriculum until 2011/12 and use it flexibly, by which time they will have decided on their own approach to the curriculum and by implication its associated assessment.

The interest in improving the process of formative assessment in schools has increased over time, yet the English educational system still has a regime of externally marked national assessments, used for several purposes beyond that of measuring the attainments of children. In particular, the use of these externally derived assessment outcomes for judging the competency of schools and teachers may negate the potential to create a positive and rewarding formative assessment system aimed at developing learners and enabling them to fulfil their potential. Hall *et al.* (2004) identified that the Standard Assessment Tasks (SATs) appeared to impoverish pedagogical practice and, in particular, the inclusionary practices in the two primary schools they studied. Anyone who has been involved in observing schools, through visits to students or as a parent, will have noticed that many Year 6 (ages 10–11) classes often spend their time practising tests. Once the tests are over, the curriculum is much richer to make up for the tedium before the test. This chapter includes some consideration of the issues arising from the different uses of assessment and in the implementation of AfL and APP in schools, while acknowledging that the new government may change the emphasis on the use of AfL and materials for APP that the Rose Review supported as positive developments towards improving learning.

In this chapter, an assumption is made that both teachers and teaching assistants become involved in assessing children at all levels, and that, in general, the teacher and teaching assistant work in partnership to make holistic judgements about a child's capability. However, it is recognised that significant differences in practice exist in schools and one cannot assume that any school or college in any educational sector will work in exactly the same way. It may be that the teacher and teaching assistant rarely have the opportunity to contribute jointly to the assessment of a child for a range of different reasons. The term *teaching team* will be used, in order to avoid constant reference to *the teacher or teaching assistant*. The use of *teaching team* also emphasises the need for working in partnership to achieve consistency, while at the same time recognising that such partnerships will take many different forms in different educational settings. For example, in many primary schools a teaching team may have the opportunity to develop a close partnership in which they can establish common beliefs and values about assessment, while in many secondary schools the teaching assistants may work with many different teachers with whom they will have differing relationships. Teaching assistants now have a range of different roles in schools, including keeping assessment records and analysing assessment results, which this chapter cannot include fully. Instead, it will focus on the issues of assessment in relation to learning, progression and classroom practice.

The impact of beliefs and values on assessment processes

AfL is about using evidence to make judgements against a set of criteria about whether children have achieved a learning objective. It relies on the ability to make professional judgements using pedagogical and subject knowledge. The values and beliefs underpinning the philosophical stance of the assessor inform the process. Let us examine two possible approaches to assessing a child's performance in relation to the following objective, *Carry out long multiplication of a two-digit by two-digit integer*, typical of the expectations for an English school pupil aged ten or eleven. A teaching team who believes that performance of the calculation in a particular way to achieve a correct answer every time is an indication of achievement might have the expectation that the children use the most compact method as shown in Box 11.1.

In such a situation, the teaching team might assess children producing alternative methods as not having achieved the objective, even when the answer is correct. Such a teaching team might also have focused on teaching the method by 'rote' rather than through understanding. Teaching by rote means teaching children how to perform calculations without understanding why the methods work. Such a teaching team

BOX 11.1 The compact method for long multiplication

$$74 \times 36 \qquad \qquad \begin{array}{r} 74 \\ \times \quad 36 \\ \hline 2220 \\ 444 \\ \hline 2664 \end{array}$$

might value mathematical teaching and learning processes that appear to produce quick and effective improvements in test results for many children in the class.

In comparison, when a teaching team believes that understanding the *processes* of long multiplication is more important than the *product*, they may assess the child differently through questioning and discussion about different methods and connections with other aspects of mathematics. Such a teaching team might accept a range of informal methods of calculation, for example the 'grid' method in Box 11.2, and might even accept the occasional incorrect answer when a child has applied the correct processes and can identify and correct errors with understanding.

In using the grid method, the child has shown the ability to approximate the answer and to use knowledge of number structure in order to calculate effectively. A teaching team valuing the teaching of such methods might argue that understanding how to do this method demonstrates ability with two-digit numbers beyond that of a child who can learn the compact method by 'rote'.

These two cases illustrate two extremes of thought. Most teaching teams' values and beliefs lie somewhere along a continuum between the two, and are quite naturally affected by parental, school and government pressures to ensure that children succeed in national assessment tests. The two cases also highlight the close and influential connection between the assessment process and teaching.

An overview of assessment processes

Table 11.1 summarises the different purposes of assessment. In doing so it creates a partition between them that is not entirely representative of reality. However, there is a very good reason to explore the different purposes of assessment and understand them, otherwise people assume they are all automatically linked. In addition, it is important to note that the same types of assessment processes, for example probing questions, examining children's products, may be used as both formative and summative assessment evidence as the APP process aims to provide. Thus APP is included as both formative and summative, although I believe it is mainly a summative assessment process, since the daily process of formative assessment will already have

BOX 11.2 The grid method for long multiplication

74 × 36
An approximate answer 70 × 40 = 2800

×	70	4
30	2100	120
6	420	24

(child calculates the answer mentally)
e.g. 2100 + 400 + 100 + 40 + 24 = 2664
74 × 36 = 2664

TABLE 11.1 A brief overview of the assessment processes

TYPE	PURPOSE	WHEN	HOW	RECORDS
Formative – a judgement about a child's performance against a specific objective based on evidence gathered	To identify progress and inform future planning	All year round	Observation Probing questions Discussion Children's responses to classroom activities Children's self-assessment Peer assessment	Planning sheets Class teacher assessment sheets Teaching assistant feedback forms Comments on children's products Children's products APP record sheets
Summative – a summary judgement or end result of the child's attainments over a period	To identify a level of attainment at a specific moment in time	At appropriate points for reviewing learning, e.g. end of topic Half-termly End of term End of year	Assessment tasks and tests Aggregation of teacher assessment records or APP records	Class test results sheets APP record sheets
Diagnostic – identification of the specific aspect of understanding a concept that is causing a child difficulty	To identify the reason for a particular child's difficulty	At any appropriate point in the child's learning	Analysis of children's test responses Individual activity and discussions with the child	Teacher notes Child's responses to learning activities or assessment tasks Annotated work – recording discussions with children Individual test error-analysis sheets
Evaluative – an objective judgement of the effectiveness of teaching based on evidence of attainment in identified aspects of the curriculum	To identify whether the curriculum is being taught effectively	All year round (internal) End of year (internal and external evaluation of performance)	Observation Children's products Comparative analysis of test results	Teacher notes Teaching assistant records School self-evaluation report Ofsted report Class error-analysis sheets Parents' responses to children's written reports

taken place before the periodic review. However, the review of progress should lead to setting new medium-term targets for each child.

Teaching teams in schools are mainly concerned with individual children's learning needs. They need to develop formative assessment skills to inform their planning and diagnostic skills to help individual children overcome specific barriers to their learning. Although summative processes can also inform learning, particularly in relation to setting medium-term targets, it is the formative and diagnostic processes that inform everyday work within the school through short-term targets. Later in the chapter there is some discussion of the varying terminology used in schools to label learners, based on their assessed capabilities and consideration of the implications for learning.

The nature of formative assessment

Formative assessment is the process by which teaching teams use their knowledge of individual children and their responses to classroom activities to inform future planning. It is essential to the daily and weekly cycle of planning for learning as described by Mitchell and Koshy (1993). Mitchell and Koshy emphasise the dynamic nature of the formative assessment process and warn people not to confuse this with the formal recording and assessment processes required by central government agencies. Formative assessments are often informal in the sense that they might occur at any point in the day when working with children, and they rely on knowledge of the objectives that the children are aiming to attain. This is why both children and adults in the classroom need to have knowledge of the objectives. Children cannot attain if they do not know the nature of the objectives in language that is accessible to them.

Formative assessment occurs when the teaching team identifies a mismatch between the expectations of the activity and the child's level of attainment and then intervenes during the learning process (Brooks, 2002). The supporting adult modifies the activity to suit the child's current level of attainment and moves their skills, knowledge and understanding forward from this point. Good formative assessment processes are at the heart of inclusive practice, providing 'feedback', and 'feeding forwards' to ensure progress. Theoretically, through formative assessment and effective planning processes we should be able to ensure that all children reach their full learning potential. Brooks (2002) cites a survey of research on formative assessment that identifies clear learning gains in schools where formative assessment practices were improved. The challenge for adults who support learning is to discover children's capabilities and to move their learning forward in a way that suits their particular learning needs.

Mitchell and Koshy (1993) describe in detail the processes that support effective assessment for effective learning. They emphasise the need for assessment activities to be contextually relevant to the children and not separate from the curriculum. However, they do acknowledge that a teacher might assess either through their everyday activities with the children, or through activities designed to determine attainment of a specific objective. In 2001, the National Numeracy Strategy materials designed to support end-of-term assessments (DfES, 2001) seemed to follow this philosophy by encouraging teachers to use classroom activities in order to determine the specific achievements of a specific group of children. More recently, Assessment for Learning (DCSF, 2008b) and Personalised Learning (DCSF, 2008a) guidance materials seem to follow this philosophy – encouraging teachers to use everyday classroom activities and outcomes in order to determine the progress of individuals or a specific group of children.

The emphasis in the 2001 National Strategy materials was on the use of dialogue and probing questions to determine children's levels of understanding. Special assessment activities provided an opportunity for teachers to fine-tune their formative assessments that should be happening every day. The current APP guidance follows similar principles but, instead of providing half-term assessment activities, suggests reviewing the pupils' work and records over a period to come to a judgement about progress and to set targets. Thus, APP has moved away from using special assessment activities towards a more holistic review of progress. The danger in this approach is that teaching teams will not probe children's understanding deeply enough because there is an over-reliance on assessment of products rather than processes.

There is therefore a strong link between assessment processes and personalised learning. The intention of personalised learning approaches is to ensure that every child makes progress (DCSF, 2008a) and this does not mean a return to individualised learning in which children just plough through learning materials at their own pace, which was common in the 1970s. Such an approach in the past led to some children progressing through materials with little real understanding, and others, who might have made faster progress, just plodding along without ever being stretched to reach their potential. Instead, personalised learning responds to the pupil voice, setting appropriate targets and supporting children in monitoring and assessing their own progress. It relies on quality formative assessment processes linked to effective planning for learning, that is, quality teaching. Targets should be curriculum-specific, not level-specific, that is, children need to know what content of learning they need to achieve, not just which level they are aiming for. In fact, suggesting to children that they could be *a level 5 if they tried harder*, as sometimes happens, means very little in educational terms. In fact, it can be detrimental to progress since the child does not know exactly what to try harder at! Unfortunately, teachers do make such statements to children, and it is sometimes school policy to do so.

Recently a seven-year-old child came home to tell his mother, '*My teacher says I ought to be a level 2b in everything, but at the moment I am only a level 1c in English, a level 2a in Maths, a level 2b in Science and a level 4 in PE!*' This child did not know exactly what all this meant in relation to specific curriculum learning. The child interpreted it as, '*I'm no good at reading and writing. I don't like writing. And I'm not as good as my friend at maths, but I'm best in the class at PE!*' It led to children in the class, and their parents, trying to determine the comparative position of the children in the class. The point I am trying to make is that such *levelling*, without addressing the specific curriculum targets, is usually unhelpful in relation to making progress. What the child and his or her parents needed to know was the exact areas of the curriculum to work on and exactly what might help to make improvements in some areas. Luckily, in this instance, the information was forthcoming through parental discussion with the teacher. The child became more aware of exactly what was required and began to work on it.

Unfortunately, some teaching teams still lack confidence and skill in daily formative assessment through working with the children. Instead, they rely heavily on children's products that do not necessarily provide a realistic view of a child's attainments. Products are summative in nature. They tell us that a child 'can do' often in a supported situation, but do not often inform us of the understandings a child has, nor whether the child can apply their knowledge and understanding to another contextual situation. Assessing learning in a formative way, which identifies immediate and specific *next steps*, requires detailed knowledge and understanding of progressive steps through the subject curriculum, and the interrelationship between different aspects of the curriculum. It requires knowledge of children and their learning preferences and, above all, it requires a certain level of confidence in one's ability to make judgements and take action on them.

Issues for schools

The introduction of several national initiatives to improve the quality of teacher assessment in schools since the publication of the TGAT (Task Group on Assessment and Testing) report in 1987 has had little impact on practice until the most recent requirement to implement AfL and its associated APP. Despite much training and provision of supporting materials in some classrooms, primary and secondary, teacher assessment still consists of a series of tests and homeworks, from which teachers collate results and report a summative judgement to parents at the end of the year. Some schools will justify their approach by stating that the children all have to learn how to cope with tests and claim that it is the only way to judge a child's attainment without support. In other schools a more holistic approach is followed, with children being provided with rich, varied and open-ended activities through which their real understanding of concepts will show. Unfortunately, schools are so overwhelmed with external demands on their time that they cannot always implement effectively the more useful and focused assessment practices. Gardner *et al.* (2008) note that, despite many benefits to schools and their pupils in working to develop their formative assessment skills and processes, the AfL and APP initiatives may fail due to workload issues or because teachers cannot be convinced of their worth to encourage them to change.

Despite the fact that effective teachers constantly make judgements about their pupils' work, the maintenance of records can become onerous and consequently they carry less meaning than the continuous daily feedback from the teaching team to the child. The APP is intended to provide a structured, manageable and meaningful approach to assessment that replaces all previous teacher assessment records. Its aim is to be formative in nature while at the same time recording a summative snapshot of a child's progress over a period. However, my recent experience in working with teachers engaging in AfL and APP has demonstrated that the reality may be far from the intention, resulting in little real promotion of learning and instead providing a vehicle by which a school proves its worth in increasing the number of pupils achieving particular levels. Gardner *et al.* (2008) provide a set of principles of assessment practice by which an educational setting may be judged. These principles focus on the positive attributes of assessment for promoting and sustaining learning through student engagement. They also include reference to the fact that assessments of learning outcomes are approximations that cannot be totally free from error. This is an important feature, especially when considering the public perception of assessment results and their impact on national policy.

Involving children

When considering the formative assessment of design and technology in primary schools, I put forward the idea that children should be fully involved in the whole process of planning for their progression (Bold, 1999). Through identifying and setting appropriate targets for children to achieve, the teacher can enter into a cyclical dialogue with the child, resulting in the child identifying the next steps for making progress alongside the teacher. This approach works particularly well in practical subjects, when discussion about the development of a product inevitably results in consideration of how to improve both the process and the outcome. It also works at General Certificate of Secondary Education (GCSE) level, when children are encouraged to review their progress through a practical assessment through discussion with their teachers. Such an approach has been in place for years in early years settings, where young children play and adults intervene with questions to develop the children's thinking.

Formative assessment and encouraging children to consider their own development begin as soon as children enter a learning situation with a more capable person promoting development. The processes are sometimes evident when children play alone. The following event illustrates my point:

> When my daughter was two years old she walked downstairs with a teapot full of water when it began to spill. She said, '*Oh, it's coming out*' and promptly went back upstairs, I thought she had gone to fill the teapot again, but instead she emptied some out. She walked down the stairs and said, '*That's better.*'

My daughter's self-directed 'target' was to walk downstairs without spilling water. She recognised she was not attaining her target and so she adjusted the level of water to ensure that she did attain it. Young children do have insights into their own capabilities and the attainment of relevant goals. Of even more significance is the fact that my daughter seemed to lose the ability to make judgements about her own learning once she began school. At school, she waited for others to tell her of her capabilities, or, more often than not, her failings. School reporting processes seemed to encourage her to focus on the negative aspects of her learning rather than her positive achievements. 'A' Level (ages 17–18) and university experiences have rekindled her focus on positive self-management of learning.

From my observations of children progressing through the education system over a number of years, it seems that identifying and reporting levels of attainment from tests serves to widen the gap between those who are deemed successful in their education (e.g. those who pass more than five A–C GCSEs) and those who are not. Including children in identifying their own strengths and weaknesses, setting realistic and attainable targets and concentrating on self-improvement appear to have a more positive impact in encouraging all children to succeed. It is good to note that the AfL process aims to ensure that children know how they are doing and how to improve and achieve their targets (DCSF, 2008b). My main concern with some of the recent documentation, in particular that on personalised learning, is the emphasis on setting *ambitious* targets with the intention of motivating children to have high expectations. One danger is that the targets are too ambitious, especially if set by the teacher without involving the child. Children are often good judges of their own potential to achieve something within a certain period and adults who work with them should not underestimate their judgement. Too great a challenge and the motivation to succeed soon turns into feelings of failure and inability to keep up with one's peers. Another danger is that the targets are expressed in terms of *levels* rather than curriculum learning and, as indicated previously, this has little meaning in a learning environment.

Effective teaching and formative assessment processes ought to alleviate any such dangers and ensure the targets are appropriately grounded in what the child is already able to do. Unfortunately, the target-driven nature of the evaluative processes by which schools are externally judged for their performance tends to push schools down a slippery slope to using *level* targets in an effort to boost their local and national ratings on the published league tables.

The importance of marking and feedback

Weeden *et al.* provide some useful principles for marking and feedback:

- Marking should be linked to clear learning objectives.
- Assessments should be 'fit for purpose' and have appropriate mark schemes.
- Marking should help identify pupil misconceptions.
- Marking should be focused and prioritised.
- Marking needs to be planned for and should be integral to teaching and learning.
- Marking and feedback should take place quickly so that pupils remember the context.
- Recording may need to take a variety of forms that are manageable but informative.

(2002: 101)

Younger children will record less of their lesson outcomes on paper but they can collaborate with an adult to create short records of their significant achievements, as suggested by Clarke (1998). In this way, children can become involved in a dialogue with the teaching team in order to improve their learning, while at the same time providing a record of their formative development.

Intervention and differentiation

Set against the advice to use formative assessment to improve learning are the national testing arrangements requiring the teaching of a specific curriculum and, over the past twelve years, a series of 'intervention' strategies for children who are 'falling behind'.

There are certainly conflicting philosophies at work within the different government agencies that impose curriculum change on schools. Primary schools are under pressure to increase the numbers of pupils exceeding the *average* levels set for each key stage, that is, for more children to achieve level 5 at Key Stage 2. This pressure seems strange since it has already been recognised that there was little worth in the Key Stage 3 (age 14) national tests, which added nothing of value to the Key Stage 3 curriculum and resulted in most children achieving a level 5 or 6. Achieving level 5 at Key Stage 2 is not the same as achieving level 5 at Key Stage 3, because there is a far greater breadth to the curriculum assessed in the first three years of secondary school. Secondary schools also constantly strive to increase the numbers of pupils achieving grades A★–C at Key Stage 4. In such a climate, teachers have difficulty justifying their own judgements about success, and the nature of attainments for children. There is pressure to teach a curriculum that is inappropriate for some pupils because the national tests will have some content at a higher level. For example, Key Stage 2 teachers feel obliged to teach the content of English and Mathematics to level 5 to all ten to eleven year olds, although the majority of children will attain level 4 and some might attain level 3 or below. Level 5 curriculum content is inappropriate for many children and achieving a level 5 at Key Stage 2 is a dubious success. Achieving a secure level 4 at age ten to eleven is a suitable grounding for secondary school education.

Differentiating the curriculum because of assessments raises another issue, the 'self-fulfilling prophecy' (Wragg, 2001), with regard to assessment and targeting for future performance. If we tell children they are identified as being capable of a 'D' or a 'C' in their GCSE examinations, they might not achieve as well as they could because they reinterpret the *label* negatively as 'being unable to gain an A or B'. As soon as we attach levels or grades to an assessment result, the interpretation often rests on the lack of achievement rather than the positive achievements. Teaching teams must identify the place of formative assessment for individual pupil learning within a system geared to evaluative outcomes for schools that are related to status and funding. Fortunately, there is now a move towards much more reported teacher assessment, rather than the provision of externally designed tests, but this move is heavily reliant on all teachers having the necessary skills to assess children accurately.

My own view, based on my classroom and advisory experience, is that formative assessment should inform the taught curriculum and aid differentiation, but at the same time teaching teams should not limit a child's opportunities to learn by providing a curriculum that does not enable them to move forward in their learning. Unfortunately, this often happened in the past. Children identified and labelled as needing a differentiated curriculum did not always receive a rich range of experiences. All children should have realistic and achievable targets to aim for across the curriculum. There is therefore logic in the argument for the inclusion of all children in some whole-class teaching and for them not to be always removed from class into a small-group situation. Children learn from each other. If we separate some children and give them a very different curriculum, they are missing a learning opportunity. There is also logic in the argument that all children deserve the attention of the most qualified person in the room, the teacher, working in partnership with the teaching assistant for the benefit of all. Partnership is important with each professional offering the qualities that they bring to the teaching and assessment of each child, together, as a team, not as separate units within the same classroom walls.

Assessing children who are learning English as an additional language

It seems appropriate to include in this section some thoughts about children for whom English is not their first language. There is evidence in our education system that the assessment criteria are the same for EAL learners at different stages of acquiring English and monolingual, monocultural learners. For example, the DfES (2005) suggests that EAL pupils have to have attained a certain competence to engage in the curriculum. As Roshan Ahmed discusses in Chapter 8, long-term specialised EAL support extending up to nine years is necessary before a child's level of English is on a par with monolingual peers. Thus, bilingual learners, who are still developing competency and confidence with the English language, will clearly be at a disadvantage during assessments in all subjects. Because of this, they sometimes find themselves labelled as having special educational needs (SEN) when their capability in a subject is high if assessed in their first language, alongside English. I do not have room to explore the challenges faced by bilingual children in detail, but wish to raise the concern and urge readers to examine practice in assessing bilingual pupils for potential disadvantage.

The impact of summative assessments

National tests as a summative assessment of children's attainment can have a negative impact on the quality and value of formative assessment. A summative assessment is one that summarises the achievements over a period, and this might be by teacher assessment over the year, including half-term assessment activities against key objectives by APP processes or an annual test across several levels and objectives. A test provides a snapshot of how a child performed on a particular day. By contrast, formative assessment is a qualitative, objective judgement over a period. It culminates annually in a summative 'best-fit' assessment against a set of criteria. In England, the majority of people tend to judge children's yearly achievements by the reported levels of attainment based on national test results. These summative results should have equal weighting with the teacher's reported assessment levels for the same subjects, but the reality is that, where test results exist, they often take precedence. Assessing children to allocate a level to their attainment is a summative judgement that often labels children very early in their school career as being 'high ability' or 'low ability'. These labels seem to be prevalent in many schools, despite the fact that Ofsted uses the terms 'higher attainers' and 'lower attainers'. You may question the difference between them. They do mean something very different.

In fact, the labelling begins on entry to school with an assessment designed to provide a means of measuring 'value-added' in relation to evaluating school performance. In order to measure 'value-added', Lindsay and Deforges (1998) suggest that such assessment needs to be valid and reliable so that schools can determine the impact on a child's original capabilities over a period. They also discuss a range of issues in relation to such measures as part of determining school effectiveness, and in using them to determine children's educational difficulties. It is useful to identify children having difficulties early in their education, but unfortunately it can lead to labelling and self-fulfilling prophecies where children only perform to the level expected of them throughout their school career. We must also remember that the criteria we use in our summative judgements of children's attainments, and the labels we attach to them, are currently age-related, not child-related. They do not take into account that different people learn at different rates and in different ways.

Do the labels matter?

My own belief is that the labels we use to identify different groups of children based on our assessment processes do matter because they hold different meanings. Let us consider 'ability'. Everyone is born with the ability to learn. We might be able to determine such innate ability by an intelligence test, but growing acknowledgement of the idea of multiple intelligences, outlined by Pat Hughes in Chapter 3, and knowledge that we can alter our intelligence test scores with practice, make this approach to determining 'ability' very unreliable. Tests and examinations in school do not assess our ability. They determine our level of attainment at a specific point in time. The label 'low ability' or 'high ability' implies that the child cannot alter that position. The reality is that many adults previously labelled as incapable of academic success are now gaining higher education degrees, thus dispelling the myth that 'ability' is the main factor in determining success. Attainment is a much more tangible concept in assessment. We can measure attainment against a set of clear objectives. We can identify a child as having attained a set of criteria, or not.

The TGAT (1988) recommended the use of the term 'attainment' before the introduction of the National Curriculum in 1989, and Ofsted favours 'attainment' as a measurable item. The TGAT supplementary report identifies the difficulty of defining 'ability', although the group admitted to inadvertently using the word 'ability' in some sections of their original recommendations. More recently, the principles of the ARG (2002) refer to 'all learners', thus making no distinction between different groups of learners at all.

Sometimes people talk about 'underachievers' in relation to children whom they perceive as not reaching their full potential. The main dispute with labelling children in this way is that none of us knows the exact potential that a particular child has. The nature of a person's achievement depends on a variety of characteristics, as identified by Gagné (1994, cited in Eyre, 1997), who provided a complex model of the interrelationships between personal traits, the environment and developmental processes. Eyre (1997: 7) presents a simplified model and suggests that there are three interrelated factors influencing success: (1) innate ability, (2) opportunity and support, and (3) motivation and hard work. She also indicates that the balance between these is different for different children and so there is no clear recipe for success. Many high achievers in adult life did not show outstanding talent in their early schooling, so labelling children as 'high achievers', 'low achievers' or 'underachievers' really does not mean very much.

Attainment is clearly about the assessment process of making judgements or testing according to a set of clear criteria. If labels are necessary, then it is better to use 'higher attainers' and 'lower attainers' as this reflects the level of attainment and does not make judgements about innate ability or attempt to predict potential success in later life with regard to achievement. Recent assessment guidance materials avoid such labels altogether.

A summative statement

The focus of adults working with children in the teaching and learning situation on a day-to-day basis is that of making formative judgements in order to help a child make progress. However, we must also acknowledge that the summative results from national tests can also be informative. For example, if many children in a class or a whole school perform badly on the same or similar questions, the teacher must consider the effectiveness of their teaching. The mistakes children make on national tests are analysed by various agencies who produce annual reports on the types of questions causing children difficulty. Although these reports are informative and teachers might act on them, there is a sense of them having little real impact on learning, because in the next test a 'new' type of question tests something a little different that most children have difficulty with and the whole cycle repeats itself. Thus, the value of the national diagnosis is limited. Formative assessments by the teaching team are therefore the most likely way to improve learning. Linked with in-depth diagnosis of problem areas, such formative assessments have the potential to raise achievement, thus fulfilling the government's agenda more effectively than the 'cramming' that occurs before national tests. More importantly, helping children to raise their level of achievement and, along with that, their self-esteem can only improve society in general, as these children become adults who value positive achievements in preference to negative levelling and labels.

Discussion starters

1   What is your experience of formative assessment?
2   What are your views on the reporting of national test and examination results in relation to their value as summative judgements of children's attainment levels?
3   What are your observations of the impact of national tests and examinations on the formative assessment processes in school?

Reflecting on practice

1   While working with a group of children, or peers, make observations of their responses to the activity. How do these observations help you determine their level of understanding. Is there any other information you need and how might you acquire it?
2   When you look at school assessment data, is there any noticeable gender difference in attainment levels? If so, what do you think might cause this and what might be done to alter the situation?

Useful resources

www.assessment-reform-group.org: the Assessment Reform Group.

www.nfer.ac.uk: the National Foundation for Educational Research provides access to online research reports and publications about assessment-related issues, including issues such as designing a new assessment system.

www.ofsted.gov.uk: for reports, publications and data on school performance.

www.tlrp.org: the Teaching and Learning Research Programme.

References

Assessment Reform Group (ARG) (1999) *Assessment for Learning: Beyond the black box*, Cambridge: University of Cambridge, Faculty of Education.

Assessment Reform Group (ARG) (2002) *Assessment for Learning – 10 Principles: Research-based principles to guide classroom practice*. Available online at www.assessment-reform-group.org/publications.html (accessed 12 February 2011).

Bold, C. (1999) *Progression in Primary Design and Technology*, London: David Fulton.

Brooks, V. (2002) *Assessment in Secondary Schools: The new teacher's guide to monitoring, assessment, recording, reporting and accountability*, Buckingham: Open University Press.

Clarke, S. (1998) *Targeting Assessment in the Primary Classroom: Strategies for planning, assessment, pupil feedback and target setting*, London: Hodder & Stoughton.

Department for Children, Schools and Families (DCSF) (2008a) *Personalised Learning: A practical guide*, Nottingham: DCSF.

Department for Children, Schools and Families (DCSF) (2008b) *The Assessment for Learning Strategy*, Nottingham: DCSF.

Department for Children, Schools and Families (DCSF) (2009) *Getting to Grips with Assessing Pupil Progress*, Nottingham: DCSF.

Department for Education and Skills (DfES) (2001) *The National Numeracy Strategy: Using assess and review lessons*, London: DfES.

Department for Education and Skills (DfES) (2006) *Assessment for Learning: Guidance for senior leaders*, London: DfES.

Eyre, D. (1997) *Able Children in Ordinary Schools*, London: David Fulton/The National Association for Able Children in Education.

Gardner, J., Harlen, W., Hayward, L. and Stobart, G. (2008) *Changing Assessment Practice: Process, principles and standards*, London: Assessment Reform Group.

Hall, K., Collins, J., Benjamin, S., Nind, M. and Sheehy, K. (2004) 'SATurated models of pupildom: assessment and inclusion/exclusion', *British Educational Research Journal*, 30(6): 801–17.

Lindsay, G. and Deforges, M. (1998) *Baseline Assessment: Practice, problems and possibilities*, London: David Fulton.

Mitchell, C. and Koshy, V. (1993) *Effective Teacher Assessment: Looking at children's learning in the primary classroom*, London: Hodder & Stoughton.

Qualifications and Curriculum Authority (QCA) (2001) *Using Assessment to Raise Achievement in Mathematics: Key Stages 1, 2 and 3*, London: QCA.

Rose, J. (2009) *Independent Review of the Primary Curriculum: Final report*, London: DCSF.

Task Group on Assessment and Testing (TGAT) (1988) *National Curriculum – Task Group on Assessment and Testing: Three supplementary reports*, London: DES and Welsh Office.

Weeden, P., Winter, J. and Broadfoot, P. (2002) *Assessment: What's in it for schools?*, London: RoutledgeFalmer.

Wragg, E.C. (2001) *Assessment and Learning in the Secondary School*, London: RoutledgeFalmer.

12

Study Support: Opening Minds with Out-of-Hours and Out-of-School Learning

Joe Gazdula

My background, values and beliefs

I am a Senior Lecturer and Head of Education and Society at a university in Liverpool. My strong commitment to the principles of study support developed while creating placements for undergraduate students with primary schoolchildren. After seeing children benefit from a few hours a week of well-led, but essentially self-directed, learning outside their normal classroom situation, I became committed to using study support projects to help children become motivated and enthusiastic about learning in a way that helped their attainment and attitude in formal classes. Since I started in 2005, I have helped to organise and set up hundreds of study support clubs in schools and then, as wider appropriate settings became available, through schemes such as Playing For Success at Everton and Liverpool football clubs, Jaguar's Partnership for Learning, and at a number of community, museum and library settings across the northwest of England. More recently, I have been involved in developing a series of sustainable themed primary school study clubs run as school businesses. I am particularly interested in the effects on pupils' self-esteem of learning in study clubs in wider settings than schools.

Introduction

This chapter outlines the changing nature of study support and considers how new policy initiatives have widened the scope of study support and out-of-hours school clubs to include in-school hours and out-of-school study support. It considers recent policy initiatives, and examines how to use them to develop innovative, quality study support experiences for all those involved in organising, running and participating in them, and shows how developments in children's services can create opportunities to engage positively in children's education. Using experience gained while creating study support placements for undergraduate education students, the chapter outlines the broadest possible approach to creating exciting study support experiences. Our journey takes us from after-school clubs to Everton Football Club's 'Extra Time' Study Support Centre and on to the development of one of Liverpool's largest and most sustainable projects – the Liverpool primary schools young entrepreneurs' project, 'Dragon's Den'.

The content of this chapter uses my own experiences with undergraduate placements and undergraduate student reflections during and after running study support activities. It includes:

- defining study support;

- the benefit of study support activities to children;

- the development and organisation of study support opportunities – *Every Child Matters After School Clubs* and '*Extra Time' at Everton Football Club*;

- marketing and developing projects to generate funding – '*Dragon's Den*';

- funding study support;

- how to manage projects and create usable support systems;

- monitoring your project and using feedback.

This information will provide important knowledge to readers wishing to partake in out-of-hours learning.

Defining study support

The original and best definition of the term 'study support' originates from the document *Extending Opportunity: A national framework for study support*:

> Study support is learning activity outside normal lessons which young people take part in voluntarily. Study support is, accordingly, an inclusive term, embracing many activities – with many different names and guises. Its purpose is to improve young people's motivation, build their self-esteem and help them become effective learners. Above all it aims to raise achievement.
>
> (DfES, 1999: 1)

This definition encompasses many of the key aspirations of study support. Cunliffe (2004) recognised the broadest possible range of activities as qualifying under the term 'study support' and outlined three criteria. For children, the activity needs to be voluntary and outside compulsory school hours, and needs to have an impact on attendance, attitude, achievement or aspirations. Many activities are acceptable as study support, yet the measurement of the success is strongly linked to school-focused criteria. Cunliffe also argues that the terms 'study support' and 'out-of-hours school learning' are synonymous and interchangeable, suggesting they are one and the same thing. However, this may not now be the case, as recent experience suggests that 'in-school hours' but 'out-of-school learning' also qualifies as study support.

The DfES (1999) also conceived the emergence of a new type of setting important in supporting school-age education. These were 'Extra Time' study support centres started under the 'Playing for Success' initiative in 1997. This allowed study support to take place off school premises and within school hours. These centres were given impetus under the government's *Excellence and Enjoyment: A strategy for primary schools* (DfES, 2003). Research by Sharp *et al.* (2005, 2007) showed that these centres were having a positive effect on pupil attainment and behaviour, which carried over into school. Three pilot centres were set up in the grounds of major football clubs in 1997 and, by 2009, had expanded to over 162 centres in various settings, mainly football clubs or other popular sports venues. These settings are recognised as valuable to educators and, in 2008, the Training and Development Agency for Schools (TDA) included out-of-school education in their teachers' standards. The TDA recognised that children were gaining valuable learning experiences in alternative settings, and that these should be acceptable places for prospective teachers to gain experience.

Study support therefore covers a wide range of learning support activities in school hours, out-of-school hours and on or off school premises, and includes all study support initiatives centred around supporting pupils with learning in any context, subject or skill. For the purposes of this chapter, the term 'study support' will be used as an all-encompassing term wherever and whenever groups of pupils are educated beyond their formal national curriculum in school.

Study support and educational placements

Undergraduates have been able to broaden their knowledge and understanding of education with the development of out-of-hours and out-of-school educational placements involving children and young people. Because placements are integral to modules, they are usually thirteen weeks or less. Students are required to reflect on their experience for assessment, and tend to have a less subjective view of the club than someone employed in the club would. A large body of qualitative information now exists to inform this chapter and research projects. Placements in education are necessary and desirable. The placements are of value for the undergraduates, but most important are the benefits to the children and the setting. Children gain in a number of ways from interacting with the wider population during study support activities. They:

- gain skills . . . reading, numeracy etc.;
- have an intergenerational experience;
- have regular contact with active citizens;
- have regular contact with positive role models;
- develop long standing supportive friendships with the volunteers.

(Murphy, 2010: 5)

The benefit of study support activities to children

Various documents highlight the impact of study support on pupils. McBeath *et al.* (2001), in a significant study of over 8,000 school pupils, reported that participating pupils had shown 'significant and substantial' (p. 7) improvements in General

Certificate of Secondary Education (GCSE) performance in Mathematics and English and overall achieved 1 A–C pass more than students of equal ability who were non-participants of study support activities. Mathematics and Science attainment improved by a third where students participated. GCSE attainment was most affected by specific, drop-in, revision clubs, however all pupil participants were affected positively and no gender differences were reported. Participation at study support sessions also helped general attitudes towards school and attendance. McBeath *et al.* argue that the voluntary nature of pupil and staff participation is responsible for this as it creates a 'set of relationships and climate which encourage learning' (2001: 9) and encourages pupils to become self-regulated learners.

Further reports of the positive effects on children of study support activities are reflected in evaluations by Cummings *et al.* (2005) and Sharp *et al.* (2005, 2007). The general improvements in attainment have been attributed to the voluntary nature of the clubs, creating an ethos that causes students to become independent learners. Some observers (e.g. Elliott *et al.*, 2004) have argued that the study support has a wider impact on learning, not just improving pupils' recorded knowledge, attitude and attendance, but influencing teaching methods in mainstream schooling. Elliott *et al.* report that:

- Strategies for teaching and learning, developed in study support settings, frequently transfer directly to compulsory education settings.

- Study support settings provide a risk-free context for teachers to experiment with innovative techniques and to refine practice before adoption in the mainstream classroom.

(2004: 3)

This suggests that study support has an impact on mainstream teaching practice and appears to show that study support is now regarded as an important aspect of mainstream education. The Department for Children, Schools and Families (DCSF, 2003) publishes a useful free summary of the impact of study support called *The Essential Guide to the Impact of Study Support*. This is recommended reading.

The development and organisation of study support opportunities

Every Child Matters After School Clubs

In 2005, I approached Liverpool Children's Services for any projects in which under-graduates could become involved. Box 12.1 outlines a case study of eighty-three undergraduates placed in one project and contains lessons for readers considering how to develop study support activities.

This type of project had a number of implications for the development of study support clubs. The recognition by local authorities that schools could not provide all the practical requirements for pupils recommended by the Every Child Matters guidance meant that schools were looking outside the school workforce for support as they worked to extend their schools. In a far-sighted move, Liverpool Children's Services thought that students, with the guidance of a trained mentor, would fill a

BOX 12.1 Case study 1: Development of placements in school

I began the search for alternative placements to widen the opportunities available to undergraduate students on Education Studies and similar degrees. After a few fruitless months during which small-scale placements were secured at large cost in terms of time spent developing them, I decided to reassess my approach and felt sustainable placements would only come with large-scale placements. This needed some sort of methodology to engage large groups of providers under one banner. I decided to research current policy initiatives and found schools in Liverpool were being set targets to extend the school day until 6.00 pm under the Every Child Matters initiative. After talking with local School Improvement Partners (SIPs), I approached Liverpool Local Authority Children's Services with a proposal. I would offer Education students (not Initial Teacher Training) to deliver a series of after-school clubs across Liverpool in line with Every Child Matters themes – twenty-three in all – if they would pay the travel expenses. All students had current Criminal Records Bureau (CRB) clearance from the university as a cover organisation and students would choose the actual topic areas in negotiation in school.

This proved attractive to Children's Services because it meant they would get a large number of schools involved in the initiative without great cost. However, this would need close monitoring and this was done by agreeing that a member of teaching staff should be present as well as a university-employed member of staff working as the group mentor. Mentors observed and advised the groups running the clubs but did not get involved. This ensured a high-quality product but was a little more costly to maintain than I envisaged. However, I had found eighty-three student placements through one provider.

skills gap and would begin to train people who might wish to work in the many supporting vocations beginning to appear in schools and related educational institutions. Additionally, the students may themselves decide that employment in these areas would be attractive.

Box 12.2 provides a checklist to guide people when investigating the development of an out-of-school club or project.

The understanding of current policy and its relationship with after-school study support was critical in the success of these clubs and we learnt some important lessons. Some students found it difficult to attend due to commitments at university, for example lectures at the same time as the clubs, or work commitments. This caused reorganisation of some clubs, but the number of clubs we had meant opportunities for change. Schools were often flexible and would move clubs to lunchtime or even breakfast time if that was better all round. The organisation of Saturday clubs was a pleasant surprise as was their popularity with pupils and the schools. The key idea to gain from this is that establishing a workable timetable is essential in any project, as is ensuring cover for absentees should someone fall ill.

BOX 12.2 Checklist for developing out-of-hours school projects

---

1 Read current national policy and guidance documents

Policy advice and support is widely available via the Department for Education (DfE) website (www.education.gov.uk), which currently has links to previous departments such as the DCSF. Search for Study Support and Extended Schools.

2 Make contact with the right people before approaching schools

Schools are sometimes under pressure, through SIPS for example, to deliver certain outcomes. They often have difficulty staffing out-of-hours sessions. Get to know which schools need help and what the likely themes are.

3 Get to know current initiatives, including what is happening in free schools

Local and national initiatives often guide schools and it will help greatly if you have read recent documents. They will be pleased if you are offering something that is relevant to a current initiative.

4 Approach the school with a plan for the content and target age group

This does not need to be very detailed and you might need to be flexible, but it will help if you look organised and appear professional. It provides a starting point for further discussion.

5 Try it and time it!

Work through your sessions and have an idea of the days/weeks the club will run. The timetable will be one of the first questions you will need to clarify with the school.

6 Have your costs/price in mind

You will find you incur expenses in running a study support project, even if this is only travel expenses. Most schools have had some form of extended schools provision since 2005 and, from 2010, budgets were devolved to individual schools (and they will probably want to know what you cost!).

'Extra Time' at Everton Football Club

In 2006, I began a long-standing relationship with Everton Football Club's Study Support Centre, which is outlined in Box 12.3 as a case study. It contains useful lessons when organising study support activities.

The organisation and development of the Study Support Centre at Everton Football Club took study support activities to a new level for the students. Study support clubs in school have a broad remit; they do not need to be curriculum bound. At Everton, the remit was much more specific and more closely tied to the curriculum, yet the setting gave huge scope for creative development. For literacy, one group of pupils wrote up an interview with a player in a match programme, and for ICT they made a video about working in the ticket office. There were also many more planning requirements generally, including how to get small numbers of students and pupils

BOX 12.3 Case study 2: 'Extra Time' – study support at a Premiership football club

The manager of Everton Football Club's newly opened Study Support Centre approached me for advice on how to include Education students in developing the centre into a modern study centre under the guidelines produced under the 'Extra Time' initiative. The club had a wonderfully equipped ICT facility in the ground's main stand and it wished to develop into a study support centre for enhancing numeracy, literacy and ICT for local primary schoolchildren. This would be my first experience of out-of-school but 'in-school hours' study support. Primary schoolchildren would attend the centre for two hours a week in blocks of eight to ten weeks. The Centre Manager was a qualified teacher with a support assistant but no other teaching or support staff.

This became a more complex project to organise than the Every Child Matters After School Clubs. We agreed to use specific curriculum-linked learning challenges developed by the students for the pupils. After explaining this to the students, we negotiated a series of steps. They would design and produce materials, write session plans, deliver lessons and create resource packs. After the placements finished, these would be available at the centre with guidance notes for further use. In addition, the students would run the sessions they developed after an initial induction period. The students' module assessments would be adjusted and linked to the production of materials and reflective learning. This would allow the centre to gain the maximum amount of materials and support for a full academic term, while students gained academic credits. Other considerations included risk analysis, travel arrangements, registration and tracking of students. The centre agreed to pay travel costs at a public transport rate and let the students have working access to the centre to prepare materials and lessons.

Because of the size and complexity of the tasks involved in the project (rather than the number of pupils), we had a number of 'blue sky' meetings in the form of mind-mapping with the centre. We would place thirty-six students in groups of three or four from the BA Education Studies Supporting Schools module (and one student from the TDA-supported BA Qualified Teacher Status (QTS) course, who asked specifically to join a group for personal interest). Each group would take responsibility for developing their own block of eight to ten sessions for a group of primary pupils in a specific year in a specific National Curriculum subject such as literacy. Support systems for the placement students while at Everton would come from the Centre Manager and Support Assistant and from the module tutor at the university acting as a consultant.

This preplanning helped the students to develop wide portfolios of materials and skills, which meant that the Study Support Centre delivered a full series of sessions throughout the term. A number of students volunteered to continue working at the centre into the summer term. In summer 2006, I accepted the local authority's Partnership in Excellence Award on behalf of the students.

there in rotation. This project created a new level of operational requirements for the successful running of clubs, including managing rotas, checking attendance, organising buses, informing parents and liaising with teachers (who were required to attend but not to take part). The critical aspects for the success of this project were:

- the development of a close relationship with the setting provider early in the process, which allowed for openness and expression;
- predetermined outcomes negotiated in advance with all parties;
- involvement of all parties from the beginning;
- flexibility of expectations from all parties;
- a sufficient lead time to allow all partners involved to negotiate and adjust the 'model' of study support;
- identification and access to appropriate resources early in the project.

The delivery of teaching to a curriculum with set learning outcomes is a big step from delivering general interest clubs where few specified outcomes are required. Children can often find their own outcomes from activities. In homework clubs, pupils generally have an idea of the curriculum, and can often be reasonably prepared with little guidance. However, with this setting, so new and different from school, there were many worries about the possible number and level of distractions. This did not appear to affect the children as much as the students running the club. Box 12.4 provides an extract from a reflective assessment by an undergraduate student running the club on placement.

Marketing and developing projects to generate funding

'Dragon's Den'

Marketing yourself as an individual or as part of a group can be one of the most important and demanding aspects of getting involved in study support with children. The idea of marketing themselves and their ideas, as a product or service, is a difficult concept for many educationalists to understand, yet also one of the most important.

BOX 12.4 Undergraduate helper (age 19), Everton Football Club Study Support Centre

The children were brilliant. When the first team players visited us, they just talked to the players like they knew them. When they interviewed them, they just fell into the role of interviewer, like it was Match of the Day. I thought they might rush over and mob them (the players). It was just brilliant the way they all behaved. This happened every week for eight weeks. They just came in, sat down and got on with the tasks we'd set them. I enjoyed it as much as the kids and I think the players did too!

You must consider a number of key questions before you approach an educational provider. These include:

- Why should the school or other setting trust you with their children?
- What are you going to do that adds to the education or wider experiences of the children?
- How will you convince them that your ideas are valid and that you can deliver?
- Are others offering the same service as you?

In 2010, the recently decommissioned DCSF Standards website suggested various types of clubs, for example:

- breakfast clubs – which may include a mix of activities and food;
- homework clubs – calm, informal places to do homework;
- subject-based activities – such as language or science clubs;
- opportunities to pursue particular interests – such as chess, ICT or art and design;
- creative activities – music, DJ workshops, street dance, steel bands and drama;
- physical education and sports;
- learning about learning – advice on how to study/revise, and thinking skills.

Various guidance, research and review documents are found on the Department of Education website (www.education.gov.uk) by searching for Study Support.

In 2008, Liverpool Children's Services asked me to develop a project for an initial series of thirteen interrelated after-hours study support clubs with the theme 'Economic Well-being'. Again, being aware of and ready to use the formative policy developments on enterprise education helped to start this project up. Box 12.5 provides a case study of the 'Dragon's Den' project.

The 'Dragon's Den' project took my approach to setting up study support activities from a partnership-centred solution to a much more commercial one. After my initial exploratory discussions with the SIP, I actually followed a market-led approach. The set-up and running of the clubs was much more involved and regulated than previous attempts, and I felt some funding would be important to help the students with resources, which the local authority duly provided. While marketing can seem an alien concept in education, this need not be the case. Kotler describes marketing as a 'social process by which individuals and groups obtain what they need and want through creating and exchanging products and value with others' (1991: 4). Most educational processes involve complex social interaction, so it is perhaps the identification and promotion of what constitutes value that is important here.

In the 'Dragon's Den' project, value can be seen in a number of ways:

- the number of school clubs involved;
- the school club business outputs, e.g. revenue, products, innovations;

BOX 12.5 Case study 3: The 'Dragon's Den' Enterprise Advisers Project

By 2008, we had a reputation for developing and delivering large, successful educational projects. On investigating current out-of-hours policy for Liverpool Children's Services with their SIP, I discovered that Economic Well-being was targeted and they wanted to run a primary schools' young enterprise project with after-school clubs. The local authority had approached the BBC for permission to use the 'Dragon's Den' title from the popular television show of the same name and wished to run a business entrepreneurs' competition between schools, based around businesses run as after-schools clubs in thirteen Liverpool primary schools. On approaching Liverpool Children's Services, I found they had a need for support not just with running after-school clubs but also with training support staff in most of the schools. I therefore devised a short training plan for school staff and modified the students' university Education Studies Enterprise Education module.

I approached Liverpool Children's Services with a proposal containing an outline delivery plan and gave detailed numbers of the schoolchildren and schools we could involve. The Enterprise Education module would provide the pedagogy for running the clubs, as well as providing staff as students went on placement. There was a charge for staff training and this would provide the finances to support students with materials and resources. A judging day would be held at St George's Hall in Liverpool city centre during the school day, where pupils would set up business stalls. The schools would be judged on their predetermined outcomes, such as innovative products, revenue and business approach, by key entrepreneurial figures from the northwest of England.

Students subsequently worked in groups with a primary school delivering after-school learning clubs programmed to run for eight to twelve weeks. In practice, most ran longer than this, as students, teaching assistants and teachers became very involved with their school's club. Here, ideas for products or services were being developed. These had to be realistic and involved a wide range of ideas, including musical CDs, safety films, visibility clothing, healthy eating dinner mats with recipes, recycled products, games and tourist items (2008 was Liverpool's City of Culture year). Being mindful of safety concerns, each school identified the initial target audience, which generally included parents and relatives. As the project progressed, some of the clubs attracted commercial sponsorship (with a major record company enquiring about a music CD and a games manufacturer about a game called Schoolopoly). Two schools even got free adverts on local radio.

- the improvements in esteem for the schools and individuals;
- the skills developed by the placement students;
- the targets achieved by the local authority;
- the cost value of not having to employ someone to run the school clubs;
- the intra-generational employment skills left in a community;
- the sustainability of the club once students had left.

These were the key marketing ideas I used in my proposal to run the enterprise schools clubs during my meeting with Liverpool Children's Services. The following list is a reminder of some things to consider when marketing your school club idea:

■ Have you checked current local educational initiatives?

■ How is your club different from clubs currently running in the school or area?

■ Is another provider offering a club similar to yours?

■ Does the school offer out-of-hours, out-of-school study support?

■ Will my idea attract interest?

■ Does my proposal/promotional material look professional?

■ Have you sounded out your idea?

Funding study support

Funding your club can be difficult and the 2009 recession resulted in cuts for all of the public sector suggesting a tough funding climate for some time. Up to the general election in 2010 some, if not all, funding for school clubs was usually held by local authorities and other organisations concerned with out-of-hours study support. However, since the 2010 election there has been a move to devolve these budgets to schools. This makes the issue of how to fund an after-school club more uncertain, but it has advantages and disadvantages for people wishing to set up clubs.

The advantages include a reduction in the number of types of agencies likely to be involved. Schools will put on study support activities to benefit children in the school directly, so a good place to start would be the head teacher or Study Support Coordinator. They will have a good idea of local needs and may be able to advise you on the type of clubs that would interest their pupils. However, this does have the disadvantage that school clubs could be exclusive to a school and you might get only a few chances to repeat the club programme. You may also find teaching teams within a school or commercial, semi-commercial and third sector organisation already doing something similar to you. Table 12.1 contains a list of sources where you may look for funding to support you. Because of the establishment of the new Department for Education, some current government websites have not been included.

Books such as *The Schools Funding Guide* by Nicola Eastwood, Anne Mountfield and Louise Walker Price, published in 2001, are a relatively cheap but worthwhile resource. The new edition is due in 2011. The Directory of Social Change website (www.dsc.org.uk/Home) offers many different publications to advise on fundraising.

A key issue in many areas is sustainability of study support when initial funding ends. Some schools will be successful in charging pupils for attendance, but schools in less affluent areas often find pupils are unable to pay for the continuation of clubs. Suggestions in your initial discussions on a continuation strategy might prove important. With the 'Dragon's Den' clubs, some schools were able to find support from local organisations in the form of sponsorship, while others found the revenue from their business operation was sufficient to fund further sessions.

TABLE 12.1 Possible funding sources for study support activities

BODY	SOURCE
Government funding	www.governmentfunding.org.uk
Charitable trusts	www.acf.org.uk
The Directory of Social Change	www.dsc.org.uk
Grants for Schools	www.grants4schools.info
Big Lottery	www.biglotteryfund.org.uk
CIB (Charities Information Bureau)	www.cibfunding.org.uk
The Extended Schools Support Service (TESSS) from ContinYou	www.continyou.org.uk
Funderfinder	www.funderfinder.org.uk
Playlines	www.playlines.org.uk
Fit4Funding – The Charities Information Bureau	www.fit4funding.org.uk
Regional government offices	For the northwest, www.go-nw.gov.uk
Awards for All	www.awardsforall.org.uk

How to manage projects and create usable support systems

The 'Dragon's Den' project was the first time undergraduate students had run clubs in schools without a member of teaching staff on school premises. Liverpool Children's Services had asked if the staff trained in our training sessions could take part in the study support clubs. This seemed appropriate and we included a session in the training so they could, if necessary, take up the role of school club mentor. We also felt the income generated from the training and the school clubs should be used to support the after-school clubs. This would allow them to continue beyond the project date if required. There are many considerations involved in managing a successful school club, which can range from issues about content to general organisation, behavioural aspects and health and safety issues.

A common worry among new club organisers is whether you have the skills to run sessions or topics of your choice. Some topics will have special qualification requirements too, so make sure your idea does not require any specific training to allow you to run the club. Generally, stay with the topic areas you are comfortable with, especially for your first clubs. However, do not be afraid to try and innovate. At Everton Football Club, students were particularly concerned that they did not have the ICT skills necessary to teach nine-year-old children. In the 'Dragon's Den' clubs, students were worried that they did not have the business skills to produce business-related sessions or activities for children as young as six. Once the clubs started, however, the lack of specific subject skills was not considered an issue. More critical was the knowledge of how to deal with children, manage difficult or unforeseen situations, having someone to talk things through with, and producing sufficient materials within a given timescale. Feedback from these clubs gave some important requirements for running a school club. Club organisers should:

- have an affinity with the participating children;
- always have a formal session plan;
- plan a series of sessions for coherence;
- try to work with staff or other club workers as a team;
- have a mentor – this may be someone in the school or outside;
- work 'with' the children rather than teach them;
- encourage participation and freedom around the topic;
- ensure sessions are interactive and participatory for children;
- ensure that the delivery team has a designated leader;
- ensure that everyone has clear rules and regulations.

While study support sessions should be enjoyable, they need good leadership and having club rules will be necessary. These are best issued in writing at the beginning of the session to all the people involved; this includes liaison people at the school, parents and children. Children do not like study support experiences where they are inhibited by unruly participants or bad behaviour. Box 12.6 provides an extract from feedback written up by an after-school club attendee, John, aged nine, highlighting the positive and negative attributes of the club experience.

In addition to developing policies to manage the running of the club, you will also need to be aware of the importance of:

- developing a health and safety policy;
- performing risk assessments;

BOX 12.6 Feedback from an after-school club attendee

Culture Club

We were told at the start by Amanda (the Club Leader) that we had to enjoy the sessions on culture she had prepared just for us, but I liked her because she said we had to tell her our ideas about how we saw culture from different countries. We got a list of exciting countries together and things we were going to do. One week we made buildings from papier mâché – I made a tower from Paris. I didn't like the dressing up idea – I did like dressing up as an Arabian swordsman. Amanda was very good and made people behave when they wanted to do other things and messed about. She explained people would have to leave the group if they didn't behave and she would have to tell the head teacher and their Mum. Zoe (Club Assistant) helped our group every week and we bought her a present. We were sad when the club finished.

■ having the appropriate insurance;

■ meeting food standards, if appropriate;

■ developing a child protection policy;

■ ensuring security of premises.

Safe Keeping: A good practice guide to health and safety in study support (DfES, 2002) is an excellent, if lengthy, guide to the requirements of running a study support club and is recommended reading covering the above requirements. Generally, clubs running on school premises will have some of the regulations already established, but other settings may not. Child protection regulations will apply to all school clubs and there are usually local authority and national regulations with which to comply. While these are outside the scope of this chapter, you will need to be familiar with these and ensure your club adheres to them. Ofsted, the government's school inspection body, might inspect the provision you make and will ask you to produce documentation showing individual pupils' learning. Local authority Extended Schools Services are able to give up-to-date advice on these and other statutory regulations.

Monitoring projects and using feedback

All of our school clubs were heavily monitored and assessed. This has ensured a high-quality experience for pupils and students. Monitoring has taken a number of forms and levels of intensity and students are encouraged to complete a personal reflection on the session plan and do group evaluations. In addition, schools get feedback from pupils. A particularly effective tool we found for monitoring pupils' progress was the use of a simple tick sheet showing happy or unhappy smileys, with questions about enjoyment, learning outcomes, pace of the session, etc. A simple example of this type of feedback is shown in Figure 12.1.

Children's Services in Liverpool also received feedback through the schools and clubs by observing sessions. There are many methods of monitoring, including:

■ pupil information, e.g. they might tell you they do not like a session;

■ people involved in the club, e.g. a co-student or worker;

■ parents;

■ teaching staff;

■ other school staff;

■ external monitors.

How did you feel about interviewing footballers?

FIGURE 12.1 Using smileys to get feedback from study support activities

Regular feedback on your club sessions is important. As a general rule, all sessions have a simple smiley sheet filled in by the pupils; this ensures that all possible efforts can be made to identify poor sessions that the pupils do not like.

Recording feedback is also important as it:

- informs you of the children's experience;
- enables you to intervene if things are going wrong;
- tells you what is working and what is not;
- gives you a record of children's learning;
- helps monitor staff development;
- creates evidence for inspections;
- allows you to alter the style or format;
- creates a portfolio to market future clubs.

Students valued the use of mentors in monitoring the groups. Mentors were non-delivery members of the groups who advised the groups during the delivery of the sessions but did not take part. Mentors gave feedback on the club in a formal but non-threatening way, immediately after the club in preparation for the next session.

Giving feedback is as important as collecting it. In all cases, students received regular feedback from sessions with children. Feedback can be categorised into three types:

- *Developmental feedback.* This is where students were advised by club mentors or observers about individual or group performance (good or bad and how it might be improved).
- *Intervention feedback.* This is when something goes wrong and needs dealing with urgently.
- *Supportive feedback.* This is to help a new member of staff or give confidence.

Maintaining records is an important aspect of managing a study support activity and you would be well advised to keep a database of the information you collect. This will help you with your Ofsted inspection and it is a legal requirement to keep information safe as you will need to comply with the requirements of the Data Protection Act. This can be complex, but the Information Commissioner's Office (www.ico.gov.uk) has good guides to help you. The DfE might make changes to the requirements for recording and reporting information for study support initiatives, for example they have already decided that local authorities do not have to collect data about extended services.

Conclusion

This chapter summarises the key aspects of study support provision across a range of settings and builds from the experience and opportunities created from running school clubs as an active observer in a reflective manner. The general reflections from a large number of students (>300) involved in a large number of diverse study support situations (>100) has allowed this to be an informed chapter that captures the essence of study support. The reported improvements in attitude and attainment of the pupils involved have been confirmed regularly in assessed work by undergraduate students engaging with pupils in a qualitative way, which large formal surveys regularly achieve. This should prove informative to students of contemporary education, individuals and groups wishing to run after-school clubs, and inform the wider interested community of the genuine and lasting benefits of voluntary study support to schoolchildren.

Discussion starters

1   Why are study support centres in non-school settings expanding so quickly?
2   What effects does 'in-school hours' but 'out-of-school' study support have on the school itself?

Reflecting on practice

From your own experience of study support as a participant, observer or organiser, consider:

1   Why is the principle of volunteering for study support so important to the improvements in attainment and attitude reported for children who have attended study support activities?
2   What lessons may be learnt from study support initiatives that are transferable into mainstream schooling?

Useful resources

Websites

www.continyou.org.uk/studysupport: ContinYou.
www.education.gov.uk/publications: here you can search for *Safe Keeping: A good practice guide for health and safety in study support*.
www.legislation.gov.uk/ukpga/2004/31/contents: the Children Act 2004.
www.playingforsuccessonline.org.uk/Pages/default.aspx: Playing for Success is a partnership between the DfE, local authorities and a broad range of sports.

Book

Rex Hall Associates/DCSF (2010) *A Handbook for Playing for Success (PfS) Centres*, London: Rex Hall Associates/DCSF.

References

Cummings, C., Dyson, A. and Todd, L. (2005) *Evaluation of the Full Service Extended Schools Project: End of the first year report*, London: DfES.

Cunliffe, M. (2004) 'Study support – opening minds with out of hours learning', in Bold, C. (ed.) *Supporting Learning and Teaching* (1st edn), London: David Fulton.

Department for Children, Schools and Families (DCSF) (2003) *The Essential Guide to the Impact of Study Support*, Nottingham: DCSF.

Department for Education and Skills (DfES) (1999) *Extending Opportunity: A national framework for study support*, Nottingham: DfES.

Department for Education and Skills (DfES) (2002) *Safe Keeping: A good practice guide to health and safety in study support*, Nottingham: DfES.

Department for Education and Skills (DfES) (2003*) Excellence and Enjoyment: A strategy for primary schools*, London: DfES.

Elliott, J., Harker, E. and Oglethorpe, B. (2004) *Lessons from Study Support for Compulsory Learning*, Sunderland: University of Sunderland/DfES.

Kotler, P. (1991) *Marketing Management: Analysis, planning, and control*, Englewood Cliffs, NJ: Prentice Hall International.

McBeath, J., Kirwan, T. and Myers, K. *et al.* (2001) *The Impact of Study Support: Research report RR273*, London: DfES.

Murphy, D. (2010) *Intergenerational Volunteering in Schools – A research project*. Available online at www.wrvs.org.uk/vita/resources_2.htm (accessed 12 February 2011).

Sharp, C., Blackmore, J., Kendall, L., Greene, K. and Keys, W. *et al.* (2005) *Playing for Success: An evaluation of the fourth year*, Nottingham: National Foundation for Educational Research, DfES Publication RR402.

Sharp, C., Chamberlain, T., Morrison, J. and Filmer-Sankey, C. (2007) *Playing for Success: An evaluation of its long term impact*, Nottingham: National Foundation for Educational Research, DfES Publication RR844.

13

Transforming Practice through Critical Reflection

Christine Bold

My beliefs about critical reflection

Critical reflection is at the core of professional development. Through critical reflection, education professionals have the opportunity to transform their practice, to change it for the benefit of the children and young people they teach. Engaging in action research projects, as individuals and in larger collaborative groups, supports professional development through rigorous evaluation and creative change. Teaching teams consisting of teachers and teaching assistants work most effectively when they collaborate to reflect upon and review their practice in a systematic way.

Introduction

First I will establish some meanings of key words and phrases: reflection, critical reflection, reflexivity and transformation. In the academic world students are expected to move from being reflective to being critically reflective as they progress through their degree courses. Often they do not know what the difference is and sometimes these terms are not easy to define without reference to a specific context. My focus initially in this chapter is on the individual capacity to reflect critically, but later gives consideration to team and whole-school development through action research. The chapter cannot include a comprehensive guide to research methods, but introduces some useful approaches and suggests some further reading.

Reflection

If we describe reflection as 'looking back at oneself', as when looking in a mirror, the definition is inadequate in relation to practice. Reflection on educational practice is much more than this, and looking back at oneself has to involve an evaluation of the impact of one's actions in a particular situation. It is very context-oriented. Reflection requires a comparison of current observations of practice with previous knowledge and understanding. It usually results in making a judgement based on that comparison.

In the first edition of this book, I expressed a belief that reflection occurs at three different levels. I described and explained the levels, as I understood them, based on my own experiences in my career. I also introduced other people's understandings of reflection or reflective experience that parallel processes engaged in by action researchers. For example, Dewey (1933, 1916, cited in Pollard, 1996: 4–5) wrote about reflective experience in an event as passing through these steps:

1   A perplexing and confusing event occurs.
2   A tentative interpretation of the event is made.
3   A careful analysis of the event defines the problem.
4   The original hypothesis is modified based on the analysis.
5   A plan of action is applied to the situation and evaluated.

Dewey's steps are very like the scientific inquiry process, or a problem-solving process. Dewey was suggesting that a reflective experience had to result in some action or response to the situation and a continued state of doubt about the responses made. Stages 3, 4 and 5 are crucial in identifying the experience as reflective and moving beyond trial and error to resolution of a problem. In applying this sequence to the classroom situation, reflection might result in a change in practice, potentially for the better. It implies that reflection on practice must necessarily involve practitioners in making judgements about effectiveness.

Dewey's description of the process seems rather rigid and time-consuming for the contemporary classroom situation, where adults working with children have to 'think on their feet' and continually face variants of previously understood events. Donald Schön (1983) describes the reflective practitioner as one who engages in 'reflection-in-action', reflecting on practice while events are unfolding and not just after the event. Schön pioneered the suggestion that professionals reflect in action and that this was a legitimate form of professional knowledge. Previously, research into any work-related practice was often more scientific, treating the professional as a technician rather than a thinking, active being. He therefore moved away from the idea of the professional as technical expert towards the idea of a professional as an interactive learner within the practice environment.

Schön (1983, 1984) also wrote about the importance of reflecting-on-action, looking back at an event afterwards and considering different responses to it and the potential for change. He highlighted the notion of the reflective conversation as central to enabling this reflection on practice, and thus essential to developing professional practice. He also identified the tensions that exist in a world where policy imposes itself on professional integrity and freedom. These tensions are very evident in the modern educational setting, where professionals are required to 'deliver' a given curriculum and have little apparent freedom to manage the learning situations they create for children and young people. As governments change, so do the expectations. This happens in every country, but in England teaching teams have felt the force of these changes very strongly over the last twenty years, as outlined by Alan Barrow in Chapter 2.

A third type of reflection from Schön is the idea of reflecting-for-action. This means thinking of the next steps to take, after reviewing practice. In general, reflection engages

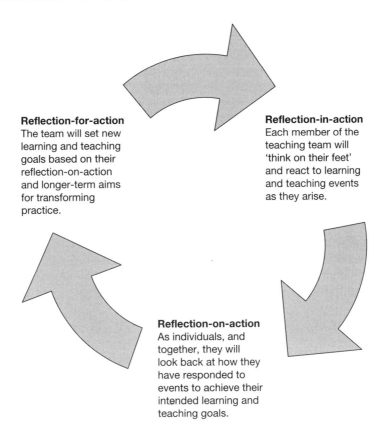

Reflection-for-action
The team will set new learning and teaching goals based on their reflection-on-action and longer-term aims for transforming practice.

Reflection-in-action
Each member of the teaching team will 'think on their feet' and react to learning and teaching events as they arise.

Reflection-on-action
As individuals, and together, they will look back at how they have responded to events to achieve their intended learning and teaching goals.

FIGURE 13.1 The reflective cycle

professionals in extended periods of thinking, looking for common features between previous and current actions to find solutions to problems, or to affirm current practice. Reflecting in, on and for practice can start at any point in a continuous cycle, as illustrated in Figure 13.1.

Teaching teams will recognise this as part of the planning and reviewing cycle that most of them engage in regularly. Not all teaching assistants are fully involved in this cycle, especially the planning stage. Sometimes their position does not require them to plan, for example those working at level 1, and there is a range of other reasons why teaching assistants are not always fully involved. However, the requirements of the role at any level expect all teaching assistants to work constructively within the team and therefore, in order to support learning effectively, they surely must develop skills of reflection and self-reflection on practice, and the ability to reflect on children's learning.

In the current educational climate, reflection-on-practice often results in a focus on children's levels of attainment and not necessarily on the quality of learning and teaching. In many people's minds, 'levels of attainment' and 'quality of learning and teaching' are synonymous, but I disagree with this, having had personal experience of children's results being inflated through revision practices that enabled success in the short term at the expense of secure conceptual learning. This is not the place to debate the nature of learning and its relationship to teaching, nor conceptions of quality, but to highlight that different interpretations exist that will have an impact on the type of reflective activity occurring in classrooms.

The reflective cycle I have described is a step beyond my original notion of 'classroom reflection' introduced in the first edition. I originally described classroom reflection as *reflection at a very personal level relating to satisfaction about one's own performance in a specific situation* and I related it to the 'feel good' factor. Typically, teaching teams will engage in this type of reflection on coming out of a lesson, feeling good, knowing that the children or young people responded well to it. This level of reflection probably occurs more in training, at the early stages of becoming a teacher or teaching assistant, rather than later. Most education professionals, especially teachers, should be engaging in the full reflective cycle in an effective manner by the time they qualify. Even so, it is possible to identify differences in the way different education professionals engage in reflection-on-practice. These differences relate to another concept, reflexivity, and to the ability to focus on self-reflection rather than reflection on others' actions. The concept of reflexivity relates well to the idea of critical reflection, which takes us beyond a response to the immediate professional situation to consideration of other people's perceptions of it and comparison with other similar situations.

Critical reflection

Engaging in critical reflection requires teaching teams to challenge their underlying beliefs, values and assumptions when they look back at events. To be critically reflective about practice they must question their actions and challenge previously accepted ways of working. In reflecting-on-practice critically, they should analyse and interpret the situation in a variety of ways, from differing points of view. In reflecting-for-practice critically, they should consider alternative ways of moving forward, weighing up the best approach to changing practice within their context.

Critical reflection is therefore at a different level than reflection and logically the development of the capacity to reflect critically should build on that of being able to reflect. Over the years, several people have tried to identify different levels of reflection. Rosenstein (2002) discussed some different models of reflection with reference to student practice learning, and each model expects students to develop theoretical understandings of practice in a systematic way, and to examine assumptions, consider alternatives and reconstruct ideas in relation to theory. Other models have similar features to the ten principles of reflective practice proposed by Ghaye and Ghaye (1998), which appear to encompass several levels as features of all critical reflective practice. It is an excellent list to guide reflective practice development. I have had much success using these principles with various teaching assistant groups, supporting their professional and academic development.

Ghaye and Ghaye (1998) suggest that reflective conversations are a central feature to the development of reflective practice. It is a social construction, involving others, not a solitary process. Thus, teaching teams should collaborate in their reflective cycle if they wish to become more critical. In their conversations, colleagues should interrogate experiences by asking questions and challenging each other's ideas, for example by asking a colleague whether they might have tried a different approach to teaching something. They should ask each other probing and challenging questions, such as 'What if you hadn't shouted, would he have responded differently?' I particularly like Ghaye and Ghaye's inclusion of the 'reflective turn', also an idea from Schön. It is a point at which an experience makes you see something with new understanding, for example recognising that school uniform does not eliminate social difference. According to Ghaye and Ghaye, being critically reflective means that we should be able to account for ourselves and justify why we are doing things. I agree with them, especially in relation to teaching approaches and the school curriculum, part legislated and part guided by government agencies, leading to some teaching teams falling into the trap of saying 'This is the way we have been told to do it.' Being professional requires teaching teams to question what they believe they are being told to do and to apply their knowledge and understanding of teaching, learning and the curriculum to teach in the best interests of their learners.

Ghaye and Ghaye (1998) suggest that education professionals need to understand their whole workplace environment, to know their place within the organisation and how the learning in their classroom fits with learning in others. Being critically reflective requires teaching teams to view situations problematically, to be aware of potential difficulties, to know that people will have different points of view and that everything will not necessarily happen as we plan. It is a process of knowledge creation, where teaching teams will learn something new, develop theory from practice and integrate new theory into practice. The relationship between theory and practice is important since, too often, there is a theory–practice divide between those who describe themselves as practitioners and those who are described as academics. Educational theory ought to emerge from educational practice. Education practitioners ought to be able to use educational and other theories to inform their practice. The interrelationship between the two is essential for critical reflection on practice.

Reflexivity

Reflexivity is described by different people in different ways for different contexts. According to Siraj-Blatchford and Siraj-Blatchford (1999), making judgements about observations based upon our previous understandings is a reflexive process. We 'refer back' and compare our new experiences with the previous ones, trying to accommodate these experiences within our current understanding. Each person who observes the same incident might see exactly the same thing, but will interpret the event differently according to their previous understanding. Each individual involved in the situation ought to recognise that others will interpret the situation differently and should be able to represent the differing views in constructing a holistic account to present to others. Reflexivity therefore requires an awareness of the dynamics between people.

I believe that being reflexive involves the attributes required for critical reflection. For example, Gergen and Gergen's (1991) description of reflexivity as elaborating a problem through experience and interacting with others is very similar to some of the principles outlined by Ghaye and Ghaye (1998). I agree with their idea that reflexivity requires self-awareness and it seems similar to Mason's (1994) notion of 'researching from the inside'. Reflexivity is about knowing oneself and knowing about the world in many different ways. It is also about creating reactions in others, stimulating them to have new thoughts. The descriptions of critical reflection and reflexivity have many parallels.

A reflexive person is open to creating new knowledge and understanding based on previous ideas. Such a person will refer back to previous experience and accommodate it, while at the same time acknowledging that there are other views about situations. A reflexive person can also see themselves from other people's perspectives and take account of these multiple viewpoints. I agree with Somekh (2006) that the process of action research requires reflexivity. The next section intoduces action research as a process by which teaching teams can transform their practice.

Action research

Action research requires a systematic and rigorous process through accepted and appropriate research methods. It is excellent professional development leading to deeper consideration of the events that teaching teams may sometimes take for granted in their everyday existence. Various models of action research exist. Many of them are cyclical, in a similar way to the reflective cycle in Figure 13.1. For example, Stringer (1999) proposed a model that is expressed in straighforward terms for professionals to follow. I have put his process into Figure 13.2 to show how it has the same cyclical quality.

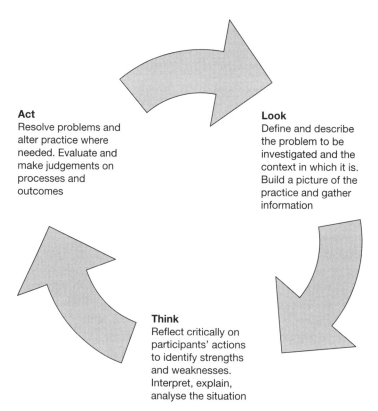

Act
Resolve problems and alter practice where needed. Evaluate and make judgements on processes and outcomes

Look
Define and describe the problem to be investigated and the context in which it is. Build a picture of the practice and gather information

Think
Reflect critically on participants' actions to identify strengths and weaknesses. Interpret, explain, analyse the situation

FIGURE 13.2 An action research cycle. Based on Stringer (1999)

In various texts you will find references to models that are more complex than this one, showing action research as a spiral, for example. How you perceive the process depends on how you intend to apply it. For many teaching teams the action research project will consist of one full cycle of research designed to fit in with the cycle of reflecting in, on and for practice. For others it may involve more cycles in an iterative approach to transforming a particular aspect of their work, in a similar way that Kurt Lewin (1946) described it. His description focused on the idea of a spiralling step of circles of planning, acting and gathering facts about the result of the action. His initial thoughts about the process and purpose of action research have provided a solid foundation for many variations on the same theme. Over the past few years the action research community has sought to gain wider acceptance of it as a rigorous methodological approach to researching professional practice, not just in education but across the health and social care professions too.

Somekh (2006) describes action research as a methodology and she outlines some very useful principles to guide action researchers. She, too, writes about the need for cycles of integrated research and action, while emphasising the need for flexibility in any model adopted. Flexibility is important since teaching teams will sometimes find that they have to adapt their approach to researching their practice as the project develops. Somekh also encourages collaborative partnerships in action research. As discussed before, working with others enhances the ability to become critically reflective on practice. Most important is Somekh's principle that action research involves the development of unique knowledge and understanding of the situation, which is something already identified as an outcome of critical reflection on practice – creating theory from practice. Action research supports the development of critical reflection and reflexivity since it requires their application.

Some texts describe action research as a problem-solving process in which teaching teams will identify a problem and seek to resolve it by changing their practice. It does not have to be about problem solving; it can start from a more appreciative stance, having a vision about how the good practice that already exists can transform into even better practice. Somekh (2006) and Whitehead and McNiff (2006) emphasise the values that people bring to their action research and that it is framed by political, ideological and social contexts. Action research does not lead to the abandonment of theory, and teaching teams who engage in action research must engage with existing knowledge and academic ideas from relevant sources. It is an opportunity for powerful learning in a relevant professional context involving a high level of reflexivity. Action researchers must be self-aware, and sensitive to their impact on a particular situation in the context.

Action research methods

An action research methodology can include any relevant research method, more often qualitative methods than quantitative. The most important factor in designing an action research project is to ensure that the method is fit for purpose. Some methods are particularly useful to teaching teams in educational settings because they can fit into their regular practices and routines. In the next few sections, I will briefly explain the following different methods of data collection and analysis with reference to the practicalities of researching in the workplace: the reflective diary, interviews and questionnaires, observation, documents and lesson outcomes. In addition, I will focus on the use of oral and written narrative within these methods, because I believe that narrative approaches are suited to many action research projects that teaching teams may engage in.

Narrative inquiry by teachers has been encouraged by Clandinin and Connelly (1991, 2000), who focus on the idea of teaching professionals studying a phenomenon that is of interest to them, in order to find out more about it and reformulate their ideas. In their view, the narrative inquirer begins with experience and works from that rather than an academic stance. Action research also starts from experience, when teaching teams identify an area of interest that they would like to explore, or possibly a problem that they would like to resolve. However, at some point it is essential to develop a theoretical framework around that experience, drawing on other viewpoints from previous research literature.

Before engaging in action research, teaching teams must give consideration to the ethical issues involved in researching their own practices, especially since those practices involve others and, in particular, the children and young people in their care.

Sometimes, education professionals assume that the safeguarding measures that they have in their settings already cover them for the research situation. However, these do not cover the specifics of the research situation, nor identify and consider the benefits or potential harm arising from the research. The British Educational Research Association (BERA) produced a set of excellent guidelines in 2004, available from their website. They urge educational researchers to respect people, and the knowledge they gain from the research. It is important to use guidelines such as these before the project starts so that it begins within an ethical framework. Ethics is more than asking permission of parents or participants for their involvment. It requires teaching teams to accept their responsibilities towards all participants, including themselves, and responsibilities to the sponsors of their research, often their organisation but sometimes an external funding group. Teaching teams will not necessarily perceive themselves as researchers, but when engaging in action research they have dual roles and therefore also have a responsibility to engage in their research in such a way that acts responsibly towards the community of education researchers.

In addition to gaining access to the research context and seeking informed consent from participants, Campbell and Groundwater-Smith (2007) identify the following issues for teaching teams to address when engaging in action research. They advise them to acknowledge their own position in the research. I believe this is one of the most important elements, acknowledging the assumptions, beliefs and values that each one in the team brings to the research and considering how they may affect its progress and outcomes. Campbell and Groundwater-Smith also suggest that researchers pay attention to the storage of data and the reporting of outcomes. These are very important considerations. The storage of data in a situation where many different people might have access to it can be a problem in educational settings. I will discuss some data storage issues as they arise. Research reports might be part of an academic programme as an assignment, but teaching teams also might report findings to colleagues, to governors or to other educational researchers at a conference. All reporting requires the application of ethical principles.

The reflective diary

The reflective diary is not simply a log of events or a set of observations, but is a place in which a person may reflect-on-action. It is a place for critical exploration of one's practice, or the practice of others. Each member of the teaching team might keep a diary during the project. Participants in the research, such as children, might also keep diaries or daily logs of their thoughts about particular events, depending on the nature and purpose of the research. The reflective diary is a valid source of evidence. It is a place where a researcher may place observations, and express personal thoughts and emotions, and it allows for deeper critical reflection through repeated rethinking and comparison with relevant literature about similar events. Keeping a reflective diary can be time-consuming, but it is possible to replace other record-keeping procedures with the reflective diary for the short period of research activity. If it is part of a daily routine, allowing time for individual reflection-on-practice, it is most effective as a research and a professional development tool. The diary may be handwritten or in electronic form. It can include drawings and creative forms of writing. It might also include the use of photographs and audio or video recordings.

Teaching teams must take care not to leave a handwritten diary lying around, or an electronic file in a place for others to see. Electronic files can have security passwords and other hard copy materials can be securely locked away.

Interviews and questionnaires

There are three broad categories of interview: structured, semi-structured and unstructured. A structured interview is rather like an oral questionnaire, having a set number of questions that each participant must answer. Often, in educational research, neither the written questionnaire nor the structured interview is relevant because they allow no flexibility or deviation from the questions to allow the researcher to delve more deeply into an issue. However, where large numbers of responses are required to gain an overview of a particular phenomenon within a setting, the written questionnaire can provide this, and can be easily set up in a secure electronic form for participants such as children and other teachers to access.

Before setting up a questionnaire, give some consideration to the nature of the information you are seeking. Most electronic programmes such as SurveyMonkey (www.surveymonkey.com) provide a range of different types of questions ranging from multiple choice to short answer. When surveying a large number of people in action research about a whole organisation, it is possible to quantify some of the data. If a programme such as SurveyMonkey is used, the individual data security is built into the set-up. This data might inform the qualitative direction of the action in the research; for example, a questionnaire can help to identify colleagues or children with whom you would like to conduct an interview in more depth.

Most often, in small action research projects involving only a few participants, for example a teaching team and one class of children, semi-structured interviews with individuals or groups are most effective in finding out more about the events under scrutiny. A semi-structured interview usually consists of a small number of questions that invite participants to speak freely about particular events, sometimes encouraging them to tell stories of their experiences. The advantage of the semi-structured interview is that the interviewer may ask additional questions, to clarify points or draw specific information from the interviewee(s). It allows new insights to emerge that a structured interview may not allow to surface. The challenge for the interviewer is knowing when and how to ask the additional questions in a way that does not seem to lead the interviewee(s) into a desired response. Focus group activities tend to fall somewhere between structured and unstructured situations. It is usual to start the group discussing the phenomenon you wish to study, but the group may gain a life of its own, discussing many issues that might not be relevant. It takes great skill for the interviewer to maintain the focus, while at the same time allowing the group to share their own ideas, without leading them towards a particular outcome.

Unstructured interviews have no set agenda, and can include specific meetings in which the informal conversation is intentional, or can involve situations where an ad hoc conversation occurs that has some relevance to the phenomenon. For example, a parent may tell the teaching team something, or some children might have an informal chat with one of the team while on the playground. Any interview situation can lead to the telling of stories, and teaching teams might choose to deliberately elicit stories from others because, for many participants, storytelling is the best way for them to share information about their lived experiences.

Many researchers choose to audio or video record interviews so that they have a record of the data, thus allowing them to return to it for later analysis. However, it is possible to interview and make notes. If you are mainly interested in participants' stories, another alternative is to ask participants to write their own story, or to keep a video diary or blog. For some this may be preferable to the interview situation.

Observation

Teaching teams will constantly observe their learners as part of their reflection-in-practice, but in action research the nature of the observation should be more systematic and focused. Various methodology texts will explain different approaches to observation but, for action research projects, the most useful are participant observation or non-participant observation. In most projects, the focus is on what people do and say, rather than on time spent on or off task, for example. You might read methodology texts that suggest ways to make 'objective' observations and suggest that you should eliminate 'subjective' influences. In the main, most action research is necessarily subjective. It is about people, their ways of working, and their responses to others in specific situations. Observation of people, by people, is essentially a subjective activity.

Participant observation occurs when teaching teams go about their everyday practice and make a note of specific events that occur and the responses of people in the situation. We might call these critical events. Mason (1994) suggested that teachers need to develop the art of 'noticing', having an awareness of moments of change, for example when a child suddenly appears to understand something. Sometimes, if a teaching team wishes to explore a specific style of teaching, they might set up opportunities for participant observation to occur. Members of the teaching team might note observations immediately after a lesson, or another useful strategy is to use sticky notes with comments on. These might relate to children's responses to learning, something that the teams can share with children by putting them on the child's book or desk. Alternatively, the sticky notes might relate to the team's own performance and be collated in a more secure way.

Non-participant observation is also very useful, especially if teams regularly work together and can afford each other time to sit and observe practice. Sometimes people feel like an Ofsted inspector when they do such observations, and a good way to make it more appealing and less judgemental, and to gain a strong understanding of someone's viewpoint, is to write a story observation – the story of the lesson. In this way, through narratives of each other's lessons, teaching teams can become more aware of the ways that others perceive their ways of working. Non-participant observation thus allows each member of the team to step back and observe without the distraction of being involved.

Video recording is an excellent way of capturing lessons for everyone in a teaching team or even the learners to observe. Video records cannot replace the actual lesson, but they provide an opportunity for critical reflection-on-action, and identification of issues and actions related to the phenomenon under study, and support a truly collaborative approach to analysis.

Documents and lesson outcomes

Teaching teams will have access to a range of documents in their educational settings that may provide useful and relevant evidence to inform their research into practice. These might include lesson plans and evaluations, records of assessment outcomes and their analyses, and items such as Ofsted reports. Lesson outcomes, in the form of learners' products, also provide evidence for some projects, especially when teaching teams are researching the impact of learning and teaching initiatives.

Analysing data

Of course, identifying the practice issues and the phenomena of interest to the teaching team and collecting data are only part of the project. Analysis of data usually begins as the action research progresses, often in an iterative approach to changing practice. Analysing data is usually the aspect of research that causes the greatest challenge. It is at this point that the teaching team will bring together some different pieces of data, some of which will not necessarily link with other data very well. For example, they might have asked six children for their learning stories about a particular lesson or set of lessons. Each story will be different and will not necessarily have common features. The teaching team might interpret their actions in different ways and sometimes appear to have conflicting views. These contradictions and challenges are important and support the development of critical reflection-on-practice. These are the events that teaching teams need to discuss, posing questions of one another and problematising the situations.

I believe that analysis should begin from the teaching team's perspective. They should consider how the data they are gathering fit with their previous knowledge, understandings and experiences. This will deepen their professional learning experience. Another useful way to deepen professional learning is to engage in, or even develop, an online community – a forum where critical reflection can be enhanced through written dialogue with others in similar professional or research roles. However, they should also seek to relate these context-bound data and initial analysis to the broader research context and the findings of other educational researchers' ideas about the same or similar phenomena.

Evaluating and goal-setting

The final stage of the action research involves making judgements and drawing conclusions about the analysis of the data and its implications for practice. The teaching teams will therefore evaluate their findings and consider different possibilities for altering practice before setting new goals for change. These new goals are the signal for the cyclical process to begin again. Although I have described this as the final stage, it might be the first stage in a project – an evaluation of practice might lead to the development of an action research project. The cyclical nature means that the process can begin at any point. In reality, the cycle is rarely so clear, since there may be times when the research phase moves backwards and forwards between two parts of the cycle, for example data collection and analysis, before culminating in a concluding phase.

Using the action research cycle

In Figure 13.3 I have attempted to show how a teaching team might outline a project in brief, using the action research cycle illustrated in Figure 13.2. It translates Stringer's (1999) steps of 'Think' as Analysis and 'Act' as Evaluate and Set new challenges.

Using the cyclical diagram can help teaching teams to begin to formulate their ideas about how to investigate a phenomenon they are interested in, or resolve a professional problem in a systematic and rigorous way.

Transforming practice as professional development

My aim in this chapter was to emphasise the links between critical reflection and transformation of professional practice. Professional development is evidenced through transformation, changes in thinking about, and acting in professional situations. Action research, as a means of researching professional issues, dilemmas and interests, provides an opportunity to reflect critically on practice, often in collaboration with others. This chapter has identified the potential for transformation of practice through engaging in a cycle of reflection in, on and for practice, and for deeper professional learning, engaging in a cycle of action research.

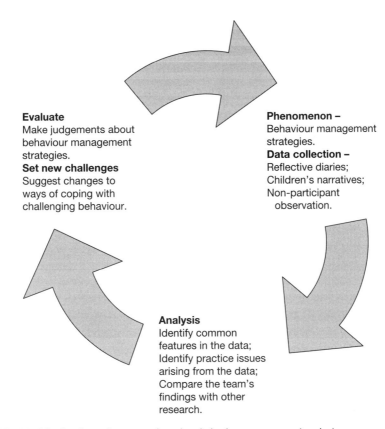

Evaluate
Make judgements about
behaviour management
strategies.
Set new challenges
Suggest changes to
ways of coping with
challenging behaviour.

Phenomenon –
Behaviour management
strategies.
Data collection –
Reflective diaries;
Children's narratives;
Non-participant
  observation.

Analysis
Identify common
features in the data;
Identify practice issues
arising from the data;
Compare the team's
findings with other
research.

FIGURE 13.3 Adapting the action research cycle – behaviour management project

Discussion starters

1 Observe practice in an educational setting. How might you identify reflecting-in-action, reflecting-on-action and reflecting-for-action?
2 How does the act of reflection manifest itself in writing?

Reflecting on practice

1 Looking back:
   (a) Write a paragraph about a time when you engaged in changing something in your personal or professional life.
   (b) How did your beliefs change?
   (c) How did your thoughts about yourself change?
   (d) How did relationships with others change?
2 Use Figure 13.3 as a starting point to develop ideas for a small action research project. Feel free to adapt the model to suit your project.

Useful resources

Websites

www.actionresearch.net: ActionResearch.Net, a site maintained by Jack Whitehead.
www.actionresearch.net/otherpages.shtml: links to home pages of others interested in action research.
www.bera.ac.uk: the British Educational Research Association.

Books and journals

Bold, C. (2011) *Using Narrative in Research*, London: Sage.
Stroobants, H., Chambers, P. and Clarke, B. (eds) (2007) *Reflective Journeys: A fieldbook for facilitating life-long learning in vocational education and training*, Rome: Leonardo da Vinci REFLECT project.
Reflective Practice – International and Multidisciplinary Perspectives – journal.
Educational Action Research – an international journal.

References

British Educational Research Association (BERA) (2004) *Revised Ethical Guidelines for Educational Research*, Macclesfield: BERA.
Campbell, A. and Groundwater-Smith, S. (eds) (2007) *An Ethical Approach to Practitioner Research: Dealing with issues and dilemmas in action research*, London: Routledge.
Clandinin, D.J. and Connelly, F.M. (1991) 'Narrative and story in practice and research', in Schön, D.A. (ed.) *The Reflective Turn: Case studies in and on educational practice*, New York: Teachers' College Press.
Clandinin, D.J. and Connelly, F.M. (2000) *Narrative Inquiry: Experience and story in qualitative research*, San Francisco, CA: Jossey-Bass.
Gergen, K. and Gergen, M. (1991) 'Toward reflexive methodologies', in Steier, F. (ed.) *Reflexivity and Research*, London: Sage, pp. 76–95.
Ghaye, A. and Ghaye, K. (1998) *Teaching and Learning Through Critical Reflective Practice*, London: David Fulton.
Lewin, K. (1946) 'Action research and minority problems', *Journal of Social Issues*, 2(4): 34–46.
Mason, J. (1994) *Researching from the Inside in Mathematical Education: Locating an I-You relationship*, Milton Keynes: Open University, Centre for Mathematics Education.
Pollard, A. (ed.) (1996) *Readings for Reflective Teaching in the Primary School*, London: Cassell.
Rosenstein, B. (2002) 'The sorcerer's apprentice and the reflective practitioner', *Reflective Practice*, 3(3): 255–61.
Schön, D. (1983) *The Reflective Practitioner: How professionals think in action*, Aldershot: Basic Books.
Schön, D. (1984) *Educating the Reflective Practitioner*, San Francisco, CA: Jossey-Bass.
Siraj-Blatchford, I. and Siraj-Blatchford, J. (1999) 'Reflexivity, social justice and educational research', in Scott, D. (ed.) *Values and Educational Research*, London: Institute of Education, University of London, pp. 93–110.
Somekh, B. (2006) *Action Research: A methodology for change and development*, Maidenhead: Open University Press.
Stringer, E.T. (1999) *Action Research: A handbook for practitioners*, London: Sage.
Whitehead, J. and McNiff, J. (2006) *Action Research: Living theory*, London: Sage.

Index

Page numbers in bold type indicate main pages of interest for that topic.

www.routledge.com/education

ICT for Teaching Assistants
Second edition

John Galloway and Hilary Norton

The role of ICT in enhancing both teaching and learning in classrooms continues to develop, no more so than when in the hands of effective practitioners. This easy-to-use book outlines the many ways in which ICT can be used, both as a subject and as a tool to support learning across the curriculum.

Now fully updated to take into account innovations in ICT and the revised National Occupational Standards, *ICT for Teaching Assistants* looks at the impact of these changes and includes:

- practical examples of how ICT can be used, including web-based tools such as 'blogs' and 'wikis';
- guidance on working competently and safely on the internet;
- suggestions for activities with ideas for how these can be used in a variety of contexts;
- advice on gathering evidence to help build assessment plans;
- information on health and safety and legal requirements.

With links throughout to the National Occupational Standards for Teaching Assistants at Levels 2 and 3, this accessible book is essential for teaching assistants who wish to develop their confidence in ICT.

Published June 2011
192pp.
Hardback: 978-0-415-58306-0
Paperback: 978-0-415-58307-7
eBook: 978-0-203-81585-4

For more information and to order a copy visit
www.routledge.com/9780415583077

Available from all good bookshops